Stop Sleeping Through Your Dreams

Stop Sleeping

Through

Your Dreams

CHARLES McPHEE

A Guide to Awakening

Consciousness During

Dream Sleep

HENRY HOLT AND COMPANY
NEW YORK

Henry Holt and Company, Inc.
Publishers since 1866
115 West 18th Street
New York, New York 10011

Henry Holt™ is a registered
trademark of Henry Holt and Company, Inc.

Library of Congress Cataloging-in-Publication Data
McPhee, Charles.
    Stop sleeping through your dreams: a guide to awakening consciousness during
dream sleep / Charles McPhee. —1st ed.
        p.   cm.
    Includes bibliographical references and index.
    1. Lucid dreams.   2. Dreams.   3. Consciousness.   I. Title.
    BF1099.L82M37   1995   95-22519
    154.6'3—dc20   CIP

ISBN 0-8050-2500-6

Henry Holt books are available for special promotions and
premiums. For details contact: Director, Special Markets.

First Edition—1995

Designed by Katy Riegel

Printed in the United States of America
All first editions are printed on acid-free paper. ∞

10 9 8 7 6 5 4 3 2 1

Excerpt from *Views from the Real World* by G. I. Gurdjieff,
copyright © 1973 by Triangle Editions, Inc.
Used by permission of Dutton Signet,
a division of Penguin Books USA Inc.

To Bill Niemann

Acknowledgments

I wish to thank the people who contributed, in one way or another, to this book. I owe my thanks first to Harriett Wasserman, who thought enough of the manuscript to take it on, and second to the people at Henry Holt and Company, who nursed it through its various manifestations. At Holt I am especially indebted to Allen Peacock, and to Sandra Dhols, Carole Berglie, and Carrie Smith, for their editing work on my behalf.

I spent five years of my life "living at night" while I wrote this book. It was a fantastic odyssey. For this opportunity, I owe my thanks first to Dr. Wallace "Wally" Mendelson, at the National Institutes of Health in Bethesda, Maryland, who hired me at the NIH sleep lab when I was fresh out of college. In my introduction to the world of sleep research, Dr. Mendelson led me through an extraordinary series of studies concerning drugs, REM sleep deprivation, chronic sleep deprivation, brain temperature, and stimulus arousal. Drs. Thomas Wehr, Norman Rosenthal, and David Sack, with their excellent research on manic–depressive illness, contributed to this rich learning environment. In Los Angeles, I wish to thank Dr. Philip Westbrook, whose expertise in the practice of sleep disorders medicine sharpened my clinical skills immeasurably and whose professionalism I always admired. I am also indebted to Dr. Allan Rechtschaffen, in Chicago, whose ability to integrate sleep, dreaming, and consciousness research into the larger questions of everyday living is rare in academic worlds, and vitally needed.

Along the road, hundreds of people played supportive roles: Katherine McGlothlin, nestled in the mountains of Malibu, California, encouraged my dreams and turned me on to the lifestyle of Radiant Health. I have never looked back, at least not for long. Also in Malibu I wish to thank Russell McGlothlin, Kevin Michael Reily, Steve, Gilson, Tiger, Kent, Jerry, Sally, Myrna Rae, the infamous Greggus the Menace, a.k.a. Gregory Pollan, Katherine Sibley Cahill, the divine Miss Leila Cabo, and John Howard and Paintings On The Beach. In Albuquerque, I wish to thank T.J., Martha, and Phoenix Baldez. Also in the land of wide open spaces: Pam Weese and Holly Ledbetter from Farmington, and Marco "the dark" Sella: Wandering in the Land of Entrapment. In Denver at the foot of the Rockies I owe my thanks to: Scotti Lix, mad poet, Richard "Dick" Laleman, sovereign of the Bat House, and Johnny "The King" Howe—Never lose your horses, Johnny. In New Jersey I wish to thank David Lopresti, who introduced me to a rich stream of writings on human consciousness, and I wish to thank Michelle and Cecille Mockers, for their steadfast support of the creative life. To Marvin Bressler at Princeton University: Without your early support, my dreams may never have come true.

There are so many others. The Denison and Niemann families. The Thomson and Elliott families. Landon Bandfield and John Penovich. Luggage and the House on Melvern Street. Gary and T. A. Beer (legends in your own time). John Heckert, Alex Kroll (I owe ya one), Bruce Judge, Roderick Bates Benjamin Barr. John and Kirsten Buckner. James Norris and Rick Busch. Steve and Laurie Rosen. Tom McGrail, Clifton Swiggett, Justin Gause, Timothy Rourke Slivka. Donatella

Trotti and Richard Sullivan. Kate Randall and Patricia Jean Kazmaier. And Robert Bergner—the *divine* Mr. Robert Bergner. I thank you all.

And I thank my family—my large, ever-growing family—for their constant love in my life. Blood is the sweetest wine of all.

Contents

1. Human Sleep   1
2. Dream Sleep   15
3. Consciousness During Dream Sleep   30
4. The Body of Time   42
5. Why We "Sleep" Through Our Dreams   46
6. Consciousness in the Dream Lab   62
7. Myths and Truths About Dreams   71
8. Techniques for Awakening Consciousness
   in the Dreamscape   91
9. The Language of Dreams   132
10. Duality and Unity   158
11. Searching for Consciousness   202
12. Mental Health   227
    Index   249

Stop Sleeping

Through Your

Dreams

I

Human Sleep

Where do time and experience, those familiar stepping stones by which we log our lives, vanish to in the night? What happens to our minds and bodies in sleep? What happens to our consciousness—our self-awareness—during the night? And, not least of all, what are we to make of those curiosities of sleep, our dreams, which seem so real when we experience them but which retreat so precipitously from the newly awakened mind?

The great mystery of sleep in our lives is that we can know so little about it. To put our familiarity with sleep into perspective, consider that we spend roughly a third of our lives sleeping—about eight hours' sleep in every twenty-four-hour period. Sleep's familiarity, however, paradoxically seems to blind us to its comprehensiveness. Many of us will be surprised, for example, to reflect that we spend as much time asleep each week as we do at our jobs. Similarly, when we view sleep in cumulative perspective, the lengths of time we log unconscious rapidly grow striking. Adult humans sleep between three and four months a year, while children and adolescents devote close to half of their young years to sleep. Over the course of a lifetime, by the time we have reached seventy years of age, each of us will have spent well over *twenty years* asleep. And, curiously, five of these years will be spent dreaming.

Sleep surely is a cornerstone of human experience. Given this, one would think that sleep long ago would have become a natural candidate for investigation by the human sciences. But only to a certain extent has this been true. The myriad mysteries of sleep—in particular the existential no-man's-land that sleep represents—long have intrigued humankind. Nevertheless, we still are only in our infancy in our quest to unravel sleep's riddles.

Certainly an essential enigma of sleep revolves around the observation that, as a rule, we lose our ability for consciousness during sleep. *Consciousness*, as the term is used in this book, refers to our ability to experience our experience of sensation as it is occurring.[1] Because we lose this ability during sleep, we become unable to experience our sleep *as it occurs*. This loss of consciousness, in turn, is what creates the "existential no-man's-land" of sleep referred to above. Without consciousness, we are never able to experience our sleep in the present tense. While we awaken from sleep able to sense how rested we feel, and while we frequently possess a waking memory for dreams experienced during the night, notice that in either case we are still forced to look back on our experience of sleep. Indeed, we quickly find that we must always look back on any period of unconsciousness.

Coupled with this loss of consciousness, however, is a factor that has served only to compound the mysteries of human sleep. Memory for *un*consciously experienced sensation, that is, the events of sleep, is fabulously poor. Put more simply, sleep, for most of us, typically appears as little more than a blank entry in our memory books, albeit a familiar blank. This failure to remember the events of sleep explains to a large degree

---

[1]The reason for this convoluted definition of consciousness will become apparent as we explore the nature of dream experience more closely in chapter three.

humankind's historical ignorance of sleep and
cause we are deprived of consciousness duri
cause our memory for unconsciously experi
so poor, subjectively we are left with the i
much occurs in sleep.

The great exception to this generally absent memory for
sleep is, of course, our recollection of dreams, which on occasion
is quite good. This exception acknowledged, the reader nevertheless is encouraged to note that even our memory for dreams
is elusive at best. When we consider that we spend approximately
one hundred minutes a night dreaming, and that we just as easily
can awaken from sleep not recalling dreaming as recalling it,
then we can see how impaired our memory for sleep truly is.

The failure of memory for the events of sleep does not
mean that nothing occurs during sleep. Rather, it means simply
that our memory for those events that *do* occur is not very
good. Distinguishing between the actual and the recalled experiences of sleep is critical to understanding the nature of sleep.
Yet as we shall see, this distinction is rarely made. To the contrary, humankind's awareness and comprehension of the processes of sleep has been characterized by a *failure* to make this
distinction. Historically the tendency has been to equate our
memory for sleep with the actual events of sleep. As a result, all
too often we have arrived at the conclusion that sleep is an
empty or absent period of time sandwiched between periods of
great activity, such as when we are awake. The truth, however,
could not be more the opposite.

CHISELING AWAY AT THE MYSTERIES
OF HUMAN SLEEP

In 1953, in a small physiology lab at the University of Chicago,
two young research scientists were studying attention lapses in

hildren. During their investigations, Eugene Aserinsky, the primary researcher, noticed that attention lapses were often accompanied by eye closures, which he speculated might be significant. To document these eye closures over time, he used a fairly new machine in clinical research settings, the electroencephalograph, or EEG. The EEG would record the children's eye movements. Almost as an afterthought, Aserinsky decided to record the children's brain activity as well, to see if there were any unusual developments accompanying the lapses.

EEG machines, developed in the 1930s, had been used for several decades to make rough recordings of brain activity. But, curiously, prior to Aserinsky's effort, no one had ever used an EEG to make a diligent study of the activity of the human brain in sleep. This had not been Aserinsky's intention either, but when several of the children fell asleep during their attention lapses, Aserinsky suddenly found himself with a great number of EEG tracings of human sleep. When he reviewed the tracings, he noticed that a few of the children's brain waveforms looked significantly different from the others. He brought the peculiar waveforms to the attention of his coinvestigator, Nathaniel Kleitmann. Kleitmann suggested that the EEG might have recorded some of the children's dreams. Intrigued with the prospect of locating periods of dreaming during sleep, the two investigators began recording the sleep of a wide variety of subjects, including adults, who could report on their mental activity when awakened. During the experiments, Aserinsky and Kleitmann would awaken their subjects whenever they saw the unusual waveform on the EEG. When asked to report on their sleep, the overwhelming majority—85 percent—reported that they had been dreaming just before being awakened. The two researchers were right! Thus in 1953, Eugene Aserinsky and Nathaniel Kleitmann discovered that dream activity in the human mind could be detected through the use of an electroencephalograph. With this discovery, the field of sleep research began to grow in earnest.

Prior to the application of the EEG to sleep studies, scientists had presumed that the physiology of sleep more or less congruently paralleled the physiology of waking hours. That is, it was believed that body processes during sleep were essentially the same during wakefulness, only slower or, in some cases, suspended. The absence of consciousness during sleep was routinely attributed to a lack of stimuli—for example, usually we sleep in dark, quiet rooms—and it was presumed that rest came with generalized relaxation of the mind and body. But because it was able to record the subtleties of sleep, the EEG gave the world a new instrument through which to peer into the physiology of the body during sleep. In the forty years since Aserinsky and Kleitmann's discovery, science has moved from viewing sleep as a passive and quiet event in the body to uncovering its dynamic and highly regulated nature.

THE INTRODUCTION OF THE EEG
TO THE STUDY OF HUMAN SLEEP

When we fall asleep at night, two specific physiological events occur in our bodies. The first event occurs after we lie down, close our eyes, and allow ourselves to relax. At some point during this relaxation process, we lose consciousness; that is, we lose our ability to monitor our experience of thoughts and other sensations as they are occurring. Coincident with this loss of consciousness, our bodies also begin to spiral into a unique physiological state.

Through the use of electrodes attached to a person's head, an EEG is able to measure the activity of neurons in the brain.

EEGs are very sensitive electronic instruments that are able to monitor the low-voltage fluctuations in the energy potentials of large groups of neurons in our brains (voltages of neurons are measured in millionths of a volt). On an EEG, fluctuations in neural activity are recorded onto a piece of moving graph paper, which allows for changes in brain activity that occur over the course of a night to be observed and compared against one another.

An EEG typically uses small, cup-shaped electrodes, about the size of a button on a dress shirt. The electrodes are filled with electrical conductant and then glued onto the scalp (there is no need to cut a subject's hair). From this site of contact with a person's head, the electrode is now sensitive enough to detect electrochemical neural activity in the brain, all the way through the bony structure of the skull!

Once the electrodes are attached, the rest of an EEG is comparatively simple. A thin wire, so lightweight it won't disturb a patient during sleep, leads from the electrode to an amplifier. The signal—that is, the variance in electrical activity that the electrode senses, when referenced against a stable signal—is amplified tremendously, cleaned with filters to remove undesirable waveforms and electrical noise, and then traced by means of an oscillograph onto a chart of moving graph paper. When researchers speak of brain waves in the human mind, all they are referring to are the variations, up and down in amplitude, in the aggregate activity of large groups of neurons as viewed over time.

While a single electrode can measure the aggregate activity of only tens of thousands of neurons at a time (out of the *twenty-plus billion* neurons speculated to comprise the brain), it has been demonstrated that from a "single-locus" recording—that is, from a solitary electrode placed centrally above either hemisphere of the brain—one can infer generally about neural activity in the brain as a whole. For example, for the purposes of sleep monitoring, one electrode placed centrally above either hemisphere of the brain typically is sufficient to enable one to accurately gauge a subject's stage and type of sleep, although in clinical practice four electrodes commonly are used. Remarkably, through the use of this relatively simple arrangement, the activity of large groups of neurons in the brain can be monitored.

The tracings produced by an EEG are recorded on very long sheets of graph paper. This is because sleep records, naturally, run all night. Once a patient's sleep cycles have been charted, the record is gathered and then scored against standard sleep patterns and cycles. Thus, if you were to go to a sleep lab to have your sleep read, the doctors the next morning would look at the record and compare your sleep patterns to what is considered normal or healthy sleep. Good sleep generally is characterized by the following factors: not too long to fall asleep, not too many awakenings during the night, and all sleep stages, including dreaming, in the right place and for the right lengths of time.

THE ARCHITECTURE OF HUMAN SLEEP

Studies using the EEG have revealed that brain activity during sleep fluctuates between two basic types of action: *synchronized* activity, when our neurons fire together; and *desynchronized* activity, when they do not. Let's look first at desynchronized activity.

When recorded on a graph, desynchronized sleep appears to have no rhyme or reason; the signals generated by the neurons look random. But this type of sleep is also when dreams are known to occur.

Now, you might be saying to yourself, "So that's why my dreams are so jumbled. My neurons are desynchronized." It's possible, but think about this: What type of activity characterizes your brain right now, when you are awake, reading this? Are your neurons firing in synchrony, or are they generating random, desynchronized activity?

Oddly enough, when we are awake, our neurons show *de*synchronized activity.

So now you might figure, "This is why I haven't been able to get anything *done* all week. My neurons are firing randomly." The fact that our brains are characterized by desynchronized activity both when we are awake and when we are dreaming is counterintuitive at first. That is, it would seem logical that when we are awake, when our brains are up and "humming," so to speak, our neurons would display synchronized activity. After all, during wakefulness, much of what we experience certainly falls into the category of being "synchronous." In other words, when we are awake, we know many things simultaneously. The sensory information we receive from our different senses is organized into a coherent and unified "sense environment." We see, hear, smell, feel, touch, and taste all in one synchronously organized sensory environment. But the paradox of desynchronized neural activity defining both waking and dreaming activity is explained by the observation that the synchronicity of waking experience, and even of dream experience, does not necessarily translate to the cellular level of neural behavior.

When an EEG monitors neural activity, all it is able to detect—from the particular setup that an EEG utilizes—is the gross aggregate of neural behavior. The desynchronized activity that appears on the EEG chart does not really mean that the neural activity is uncoordinated or that it is random. It means simply that the neurons being measured are firing at different times and that the signals being created by these firings tend to cancel each other out. It may be helpful to think of desynchronized activity as a state in which neurons are actively communicating with each other—relaying sensory information among each other and among different areas of the brain. If we can envision desynchronized neural activity as an indication that all parts of the brain are "up" and actively communicating with each other, then we can see this highly active state as being necessary to support the synchronized experience of waking activity. Consciousness (to use the term in its most colloquial sense, that of indicating wakefulness) requires that all of our sensory ability be active and integrated, all at once, into a unified sense environment.

Synchronized activity, on the other hand, occurs *only during sleep*. During synchronized sleep, the neurons in our brains all begin to fire more or less in concert with each other.

As researchers continued to explore the nature of sleep, they also observed that over time, neurons exhibit varying *degrees* of synchronous firings. That is, at certain points during the night, it seemed that almost all of the neurons in the brain were firing at the same time. At other times it was evident that the firings, while still synchronized, were not as synchronized. Thus it was discovered that the brain moves gently into this deeply synchronous state, and then, after reaching its rhythmic crescendo, just as gently withdraws. Today almost all of us are familiar with the idea of sleep stages; it is these gradations of synchronous activity to which these stages of sleep refer. Four distinct types of synchronized activity were identified early on, the commonly referred to "four stages of sleep." Stage 1 sleep, at the upper end of the spectrum, indicates light synchronous activity and, accordingly, is a light stage of sleep. Stage 1 sleep is visible just after a person loses consciousness for the night. Stage 4 sleep, the most heavily synchronized stage, indicates very deep sleep.

Researchers also found that sleep was orderly, that there is a

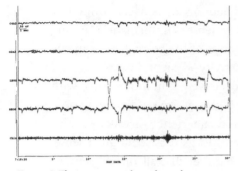

FIGURE 1. The fast activity of the awake mind.

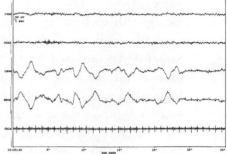

FIGURE 2. The transition to sleep: Stage 1. Note the relaxation of the EEG and muscle tone.

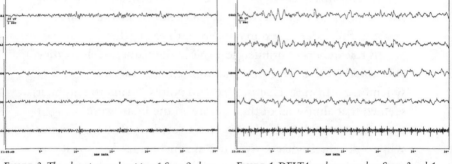

FIGURE 3. The advancing synchronicity of Stage 2 sleep.

FIGURE 4. DELTA or slow-wave sleep, Stages 3 and 4. This is very deep sleep.

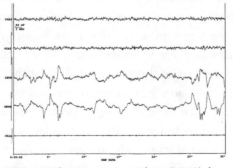

FIGURE 5. The fast eye movement of dream (R.E.M.) sleep. Note the relaxed muscle tone.

pattern to the stages of sleep that repeats in regular ninety-minute cycles.[2] When we first fall asleep, we enter into stage 1, normally a very brief transition to the subsequent stages of sleep. Stage 1 is significant in that it indicates that a sleeper is beginning to lose consciousness, or the ability to be aware of his or her experience. Occasionally in stage 1 sleep we experience what is called *hypnagogic* imagery—light mental visions of stars, lines, colors, geometric patterns, visual impressions—which we can watch as we drift off to sleep. Sometimes we awaken with a start from this imagery, as it has gotten more vivid, to the point where we are engaged in what might be called a light dream. This is not to be confused with dream sleep, however, as there are many important differences.

After a few minutes of this vaguely synchronous activity, our brain enters stage 2 sleep. The EEG begins to indicate greater synchrony in the neuron firings, and in sleep labs around the world, where sleep is continually monitored, measured, charted, evaluated, and pondered over, it is standard procedure not to count a subject's "sleep onset time" until he or she reaches this stage. This is because people often awaken briefly from stage 1, perhaps just to roll over, to adjust a pillow, or to find a more comfortable position before "going under" for good. Once stage 2 commences, however, one can be fairly confident that the course of a night's sleep has begun and will not be interrupted.

We stay in stage 2 sleep for about ten or twenty minutes,

[2]Sleep is incredibly regular among all people. All of us, unless we have some specific disorder that interferes with our sleep, sleep in ninety-minute cycles and move through the sleep stages alike. In fact, sleep's "architecture" is so precise in "normals" that it is believed that disorders of architecture—for example, misplaced sleep stages or the appearance of dream sleep too early in the night (both are frequently found in people who suffer from depression or schizophrenia)—actually contribute to these types of mental illness. This is why, when people are having problems with their sleep and/or their mental health, they frequently go to sleep labs to have their sleep charted. Depending on how their sleep pattern compares with the norm, various diagnoses and therapeutic treatments are indicated.

during which the brain's neurons are firing fairly synchronously. Then, if we are going to have any stage 3 or 4 sleep, we move into it at this time. Stages 3 and 4 are both considered deep sleep (from studies that measure the difficulty of awakening subjects from these stages), and these stages often are not found in persons who claim to have poor sleep, or insomnia, or who suffer from depression. Most of us, however, do have this sleep.

Combined, stages 3 and 4 last about forty to fifty minutes, during which time neuron activity is highly synchronized. Then, as the pendulum of synchronicity completes its downward arc, we begin to climb out of these deeper stages of sleep, back into lighter sleep again, stage 2. After about seventy-five or eighty minutes, our bodies begin to show signs of moving into yet another stage of sleep. So far all of our sleep has been characterized by synchronous activity. But now our bodies are preparing for a major shift in physiology. As if timed by a fine Swiss watch, our bodies suddenly propel us into dream sleep. The motor neurons in the back of our necks are inhibited from obeying commands for movement (which prevents us from physically acting out our dreams), our neurons display highly active, desynchronized activity, and our eyes begin to dart around beneath our eyelids, as if we are watching a movie or looking for something. Inside our minds, we have just emerged into the fantastic world of the dreamscape.

This pattern of sleep (stages 1, 2, 3, 4, and 3, 2, 1, dream sleep) repeats itself every ninety minutes. But as we sleep, the pattern also changes shape. With every cycle of sleep we complete, the amount of time we spend dreaming gradually increases, while the amount of time we spend in stages 3 and 4 gradually decreases.

For example, if we sleep uninterrupted for six hours, the EEG would show four ninety-minute cycles, with the amount of dream sleep progressively increasing. We might have eight minutes of dream sleep in the first cycle, fourteen minutes in the second, twenty-two in the third, and thirty in the fourth, for a total of seventy-four minutes of dream sleep in a six-hour period. If we sleep another cycle, the amount of dreaming sleep increases again, perhaps to thirty-six minutes. This additional cycle of sleep gives a total of 110 minutes—nearly two hours—of dreaming in a seven-and-a-half-hour period of sleep.

The ninety-minute sleep cycle is a peculiar human biorhythm; no one really knows *why* it is this length of time. Nevertheless, we adhere to its schedule religiously. And as we are more likely to awaken from light stages of sleep than from deep stages, and from dream sleep versus synchronized sleep, this ninety-minute cycle tends to determine our wake-up time.

Because dream sleep is the most unstable stage of sleep, due to all of the hallucinated activity that attends it, it is the time when we are most likely to spontaneously, or naturally, awaken. In fact, every morning, prior to our real or final awakening, we all awaken momentarily several times. Typically in a morning dream sleep period there are five or six of these tendencies toward waking. The dreamer may not even open his or her eyes, but on an EEG these "microawakenings" are readily apparent. This is why when we awaken in the morning, we frequently are able to recall having just been dreaming. Our dreaming literally wakes us up. Because of this propensity to awaken from dream sleep, and because dream sleep always comes at the end of a ninety-minute cycle, we tend to sleep in periods that are rough multiples of ninety minutes—most commonly four cycles, or 360 minutes (six hours), or five cycles, which is 450 minutes, or seven and a half hours. If you should awaken during the night and look at your clock, you will see that these ninety-minute cycles do indeed define our sleep periods; our awakenings from sleep are almost always in multiples of ninety minutes.

While there is a propensity for us to sleep in ninety-minute cycles, that is, to awaken at their completion and thus from dream sleep, there are many variables—alarm clocks, children, roommates, dogs, cats, street noises, needing to go to the bathroom—that cause us to awaken from all of the various stages of sleep. What has been demonstrated is that if we awaken from dream sleep, we most likely will recall having been dreaming, whereas if we awaken from any stage other than dream sleep, we most likely will *not* recall having been dreaming or, for that matter, having had any dreams during the night. Even when we do awaken directly from a dream, it can still be difficult to recall the dream in detail. Most dreams are lost by the time we get to the shower.

2

Dream Sleep

In the late 1890s, when Sigmund Freud was completing his soon-to-be-published masterwork *The Interpretation of Dreams* (1900), the nature of time in dreams was a popular topic of debate. Some enthusiasts held that despite the feeling that dreams seemed to go on for extended periods—perhaps as long as half an hour or even an entire night—in reality they were extremely brief occurrences. These people argued that dreams occurred in a "time warp"—that they were accelerated experiences that *appeared* to endure great lengths of time. Others, however, argued that talk about time warps was pure nonsense, that dreams clearly occurred in "real," or ordinary, time. They felt that there was continuity of time between waking and dreaming.

Freud, who was an avid consumer of local lore concerning dreams, found the debate compelling enough to include it in his *Interpretation of Dreams*. After considering the competing evidence, he concluded that in certain instances, there was some distortion of the experience of time in dreams. How else, he reasoned, could one explain those dreams that contained "a great amount of material compressed into the briefest moment of time"? In particular, popular anecdotes of the long and elaborate dreams of sleepers who had dozed off only for a moment offered the most convincing evidence.[3]

While Freud never took an unequivocal stand on the issue, his suspicion that dreams might be accelerated experiences became popular belief within the school of psychoanalysis. Dreams, in Freudian theory, were disguised events, as it were; thus it was logical to speculate that our sense of time in dreams might similarly be altered. Among psychoanalysts, then, it grew popular to think that during the course of a night's sleep, a person might experience five or six sudden "bursts of energy," or dreams, and that collectively these bursts might last only a few seconds. It also was possible, given the nature of Freudian psychodynamics, that a person might not dream at all.

These early estimates of the time we spend dreaming shared one common element: They were based on people's ability to *recall* their dream sleep. But recall for dreams, as we have suggested, is fraught with difficulty. Not until the use of the electroencephalograph in sleep research could anyone accurately determine the amount of time spent dreaming.

The discovery that we dream about one hundred minutes per night, every night, caught everyone off guard. It was the first big discovery made with the EEG, and it was a spectacular fact to learn, simply because no one—subjectively—could really believe it. One hundred minutes is as long as a feature film! And yet, as we know from personal experience, we often awaken from sleep without recalling any dreams. No one was more shocked by these figures than the Freudian psychoanalysts.

It is perhaps difficult now, especially for younger readers, to appreciate how dominant a force Freud was in the field of psychiatry in the 1950s. Suffice it to say that both Europe and

---

[3]We return to the subject of time in dreams in chapter eight.

the United States were steeped in Freudian theory. In fact, at the time of Aserinsky and Kleitmann's discovery, Freud was experiencing a resurgence of public interest, which many attribute to the aftermath of World War II. In 1953 the psycho-analytic school was dominant in the field of psychiatry, and more and more people were visiting psychoanalysts to undergo analysis.[4]

THE FREUDIAN VISION

Sigmund Freud argued with enormous success that people's normal, seemingly nonsensical dreams were actually full of meaning. He said that if we could understand the meanings hidden within our dreams, we would gain superior insight into the inner workings of our being. A person's fears and fantasies, deep angers and frustrations, secret vanities and powerful inner drives, and much more, Freud promised, were packaged in the curious dream. Yet one had to learn the language of dreams, or else the clues would fall upon deaf ears.

Because dreams are not consciously produced, they proved for Freud the existence of an "unconscious" mind within each of us. According to Freud, dreams were the battlefield where the conflicting urges of the id and the superego achieved psychic release and resolve. The battle was performed behind the curtain of a "censor"—some mechanism in the mind that made these conflicts palatable for the ego, or conscious self. Thus, the censoring mechanism was responsible for the mystery of dream meanings, and for their apparent nonsensicalness. In fact, as far as

---

[4]The popularity of dream interpretation and psychoanalysis in the 1950s is readily reflected in the films and literature of the day. Ingmar Bergman and Federico Fellini's films in particular included confused dream sequences for the "cultural intelligentsia" to decipher.

Freud was concerned, it was the job of the censor to make our dreams unintelligible to us. Through the use of dream symbols and disguised images, the censor transformed our true, unconscious desires into representations we would be unable to identify. If we could remember our dreams, however, before they were repressed yet again by the continuing operation of the censor in waking, we could, through a process called free association, trace back through the manifest content of the dream to its true source, or to the latent content. Once we were able to penetrate the manifest layer and arrive at the source of a dream, then we could glimpse into the unconscious forces that Freud said were at work within all of us. Dreams, then, were the window through which we could glimpse the subtle dynamics of the unconscious mind.

According to Freud, dreams were a release valve for the tensions that, in the course of living, build up between the id—that part of our psyche that houses the primitive, sexual, and savage drives within us—and the superego, which embodies the constraints civilization puts on these drives. Freud, without the benefit of modern science, posited that neurons stored energy. He also hypothesized that when enough tension accumulated as a result of unconscious conflict, these neurons would release this stored energy in the form of a dream. Dreams, therefore, were clues to the tensions felt by our unconscious mind.

Extending his model, Freud postulated that the amount of dreaming a person experienced would reflect the extent of his or her inner psychic turmoil. If the turmoil was great, if the desires of the id were frustrated by the restraint of the superego, then there would be restless nights of transformed dreams. If, on the other hand, a person was "psychologically fit"—having achieved a balance of power between the id and the superego—then it was entirely possible that he or she would dream not at all, or perhaps only once a month or so, as matters of concern came to bear.[5]

The psychodynamic model was thus a flexible model. Within its broad framework, many varieties of behavior could be accommodated. A person's sexual urges might be twisted any number of ways through confrontation with the superego, which invariably sought to contain those urges. Conversely, the model could also accommodate the lucidness of mental health: a stable, organized mind, untroubled by deep inner conflict and thus also untroubled by dreams.

But these new findings! Suddenly it was being demonstrated, at a small physiology lab in Chicago, that *all* people dream, and that they dream, on average, a hundred minutes every night, rain or shine. And it was further being demonstrated that periods of dreaming occurred at extremely regular intervals during the night. Indeed, dream sleep was so regular that researchers discovered that if they knew a person's "drop-off" time—the point at which a person loses consciousness and begins spiraling down into synchronized sleep—then they could predict within minutes when the subject's first dream period would be and how long each dream period would last. Given the absence of major interruptions during the night or the presence of an illness that would affect sleep composition,

---

[5]Within this conceptual framework there exists a subtle bias against remembering one's dreams or, further, even to admit to having dreamed. Since, according to the model, dreams are a symptom of psychological turmoil and frustrated urges, they can be viewed as manifestations of an unconscious full of conflicting base and primitive energies. If one admitted dreaming, it was an acknowledgment, to a certain extent, that one was experiencing psychological conflict. Thus, dreams may have been interesting psychologically, but they probably were more interesting in *other* people, to whom one could sit back and give advice. While readily admitting, and perpetually chronicling and analyzing, his own dreams, Freud frequently said that dreamless sleep was the best kind of sleep; indeed, he said it was the only good kind of sleep.

researchers found that they could do a pretty good job all night long of predicting the onset of dreams and their duration. And as research progressed, it was found that this regularity of dream sleep was universal—there were no people who did not dream and there were no people for whom the cycles did not exist.

From the Freudian perspective, the problem with these new findings was their stress on the universality of dreaming. Freudians had judged dreaming to be highly variable—that is, the amount of time a person spent dreaming was expected to correspond with his or her particular psychological need. A person who was depressed, for example, dreamed a lot, as the unconscious mind labored to release pent-up frustrations. Or if an unconscious tension existed, then the person would be prone to dream more than usual. Indeed, the occasion of dreaming was perceived to be an alert to the presence of unconscious conflict.

What was gradually being learned, however, was the extent of the difficulty people experience *remembering* dreams. The truth is that although we all spend a great deal of time dreaming every night, the overwhelming majority of dream experience is not recalled. Even more unsettling to the Freudians was another aspect of dreams suggested by the new findings, that dreams might be a reflection of some other, more basic function in the body. This suggestion was disturbing because it struck at the heart of Freud's psychodynamic theory. Nevertheless, it was clear, as sleep's "architecture" was replicated in experiment after experiment, that dream sleep was regulated by some sort of internal timer. And the constancy of dream sleep, the solid ninety to one hundred minutes per night, every night, regardless of the dreamer's psychological condition, not only refuted psychodynamic theory but strongly suggested another explanation. Could it be, scientists began to wonder, that dreams were only a *by-product* of some neurobiological function in the body? Could it be that there was no correlation whatsoever between one's dreams and one's psychological condition?

Blasphemy! Ludicrous psychiatric blasphemy! To propose this new vision of dreams would have brought on enormous public and professional ridicule. Freud was revered in the psychiatric community: He had illuminated the psychological correlation between dreams and unconscious activity. People believed Freud was right, and at stake were many careers, based in many elite institutions. And then there were the countless thousands of patients who had been through Freudian therapy and who felt they had been liberated from psychic disorders through psychoanalytic technique. Dream interpretation was one of the most powerful tools of psychoanalysis. These new findings represented a genuine dilemma for the Freudians.

The early findings were not in themselves strong enough to reverse the tide of opinion in Freud's favor. Instead many researchers, armed with EEGs, set out to demonstrate the validity of Freud's model. For example, if dreams were a "release valve" for psychic tensions, as Freud had hypothesized, then it made sense that depriving a person of his or her dream sleep would cause latent or otherwise manageable neuroses to come closer to the surface, particularly in subjects classified as "borderline" personalities (prone to instability). Accordingly, experiments were run whereby subjects were selectively deprived of dream sleep but allowed all other stages of sleep.

At first the results from these experiments were promising, and a few reports were published that supported Freud's thesis. But as time passed and the early studies were replicated, it became clear that much of the work that supported the Freudian thesis suffered from poor study design—in particular the employment of questionnaire givers who were not "blind" to the experiments. These workers, subtly or not, coaxed many "right" answers from the subjects and made many expected observations. It has since been found that while it is difficult to deprive persons of dream sleep for any length of time (the longest anyone has ever been deprived of dream sleep without the use of drugs is fourteen days), a lack of dream sleep does not cause psychotic symptoms. Rather, it only causes the body to try harder, once it is asleep, to achieve that stage. Dream-deprived subjects are grumpy and sleepy, but they are not psychotic or psychologically unstable.

While the observation was a setback for the Freudian school, there was another finding that challenged Freud's psychodynamic model even more substantially. Some subjects who were described as borderline patients, in whom the most visible psychotic reactions to dream deprivation were expected, actually reported feeling *better* following dream sleep deprivation. In fact, depriving depressed patients of dream sleep was found to produce a remission of the depression in 70 percent of the population. What's more, the result was instantaneous and robust; in some cases, symptoms actually disappeared. What a remarkable discovery! People who had been depressed for years came into labs and were selectively deprived of a night's dream sleep, with the expectation that they would feel much worse the next day, and perhaps be psychotic, with hallucinations breaking in on their waking thoughts. But instead the majority of them felt the best they had in years. To this day, depriving patients of dream sleep, through drugs that act to eliminate this phase from the sleep cycle, is the most widely used method for treatment of depression.

While this unexpected finding was an enormous clue to identifying the cause of depression, for the school of psychoanalysis it was another fact that didn't fit with the original wisdom. How could a depressed person suddenly feel better after being deprived of dreaming, and without any therapy? Depression, according to Freud, was a complex state of psychological confusion in which the object of a person's libido becomes unavailable to him and then is "projected" onto his own ego.[6] Simply put, the individual has confused the identities of the object of his libido and himself. Having lost the object of his sexual affection, he wishes to punish it, but because the object is now confused with his own identity, he begins to punish himself, thinking he is punishing the lost object. This, for Freud, explained depressed patients' merciless self-torment as well as their love-hate relationship with themselves. On the surface, the hate aspect is embodied by the self-torment while the love aspect is characterized by the narcissistic fixation depressives have on themselves as objects of torment. Subconsciously, depressives are still in love with the lost object, but they are punishing it for leaving.

Then the results of dream research came cascading in. Soon it was found that every warm-blooded creature in the world (except the echidna, or Australian spiny anteater) experiences dream sleep. For the Freudians—and this is almost unfair to Freud because of the technological limitations of his day—these findings raised some interesting questions:

- Are rhinoceroses relieving their Oedipal tensions?
- Are tigers sorting out those nagging conflicts between their ids and superegos?
- Did my cat have a tough day?

It certainly is ironic that the discovery of dream sleep would be the undoing of one of Freud's major theories. In the last forty

[6]Every attempt has been made to eliminate gender-biased language in this book. However, in the interest of general readability, some passages may use one gender pronoun consistently. This should in no way be taken to mean the exclusion of one sex or the other.

years, Freud's theory of the function of dreams has been proved unsupportable by the findings of research using the EEG.

MODERN PSYCHIATRY

The discovery of dream sleep in 1953 stands as a watershed marker between two very different approaches to understanding and treating mental illness. In no small way, Aserinsky and Kleitmann's discovery heralded the birth of the neurobiological sciences, and it challenged, in a liberating way, the dominance of the psychoanalytic approach to understanding mental illness.

What was gradually being witnessed within the psychiatric community was the discovery of the neurobiological underpinnings of many forms of mental illness. While awareness of the physical aspects of mental illness is just beginning to pervade the lay community, the "neurobiology of experience" has dominated the professional medical community for some time. The turning point came in the early 1970s, as the psychological research work of earlier years began to wash out. Medical literature from the 1960s is filled with reports of experiments that placed a strong emphasis on the role of dreams and consciousness in mental health. This research naturally reflected the prevailing culture, when the psychoanalytic school was still dominant and when consciousness was a highly investigated phenomenon and consciousness-altering drugs were widely used. Experiments performed in the seventies, eighties, and early nineties, by contrast, were nearly completely devoid of such references. The transition was dramatic. Today one is much more likely to come across a study titled "The role of 5-gamma hydroxyphelantomine in the re-uptake of dopaminergic ganal cells in the basal medulla" than some experiment involving the subjective state of a patient. The world of neurobiology has arrived.

That psychoanalysis is suffering growing pains is no secret. More and more, theorists must support their claims about mechanisms of the mind by demonstrating the underlying neurobiological substrates. A principle in psychology, coined by Freud himself, is *psychological isomorphism:* for every phenomenon of thought, for every mental experience, there must exist a neurologic corollary. Psychological isomorphism asserts itself as a first principle simply by claiming, logically enough, that the mind is not free of the biology that supports it. It is this important principle that dominates modern psychology. Ethereal and flighty as it is, thought does not float on the wind! Mental activity is rooted in the billions upon billions of neurons in the brain that support our experience of mind.

While Freud studied dreams extensively—and, arguably, better than anyone else to date—it is apparent in retrospect that many of the most striking characteristics of dreams remained hidden from him. Indeed, it is interesting that the difficulty we all experience with remembering our dreams never really struck Freud's fancy, other than that he believed it to be an extension of the censoring-repression mechanism. Freud never let his mind wander in any other direction as to what the implications of this observed tendency might be. As a result, he phenomenally underestimated the actual occurrence of dreaming. Historically this may prove to be one of Freud's costliest errors. It has, through association, caused a significant devaluation of much of his thought not necessarily related to psychodynamics.

Nearly four decades have transpired since the discovery of dream sleep, yet we still do not know exactly what function it performs for the mind. Theories abound, but no one knows for certain what dreaming achieves. If dream sleep were strictly a human phenomenon, then credence could be lent to theories that argue in favor of its psychological dynamics. But its near

universality in warm-blooded creatures suggests a more fundamental function.[7]

PARADOXICAL SLEEP

As studies involving dreaming sleep were begun in start-up sleep
labs around the world, dream sleep came to be known by many
different names: desynchronized sleep (D-sleep), rapid eye
movement (REM) sleep, active sleep, and paradoxical sleep. The
term *paradoxical* was applied to dreaming sleep because the signals produced on an EEG during that stage present a type of
paradox. An electroencephalogram, in its standard setup for
monitoring sleep, measures three variables: neural activity of the
brain, muscle tone of the body (a type of relaxation gauge), and
eye movement. As mentioned in chapter one, the waveform
produced by the excitation of neurons in the brain during
dreaming is virtually identical to that produced during wakefulness. Similarly, the eyes move about as if the dreamer is looking
at something or reading a book, except that the eyelids are
closed. But the channel that measures the body's muscle tone
shows that the dreamer is relaxed—indeed, far more relaxed
than is a resting awake person.

Despite the awakelike signals, it was evident from simple ob-

---

[7]A current interest in the field of sleep research is the possible role dream sleep may play
in thermoregulatory processes. Briefly, dreaming increases blood flow to the brain. The
brain, because it is so active during dreams (burning glucose), warms up and in turn
warms the blood that flows by it. As a result, those areas nearest the brain—many glands
of the neuroendocrine system are located directly beneath the brain hemispheres—are
warmed during dream sleep. There also are many temperature-sensitive processes in the
neuroendocrine system that occur at night. Thus dream sleep, when it occurs during the
night and for however long it endures, is suspected of influencing the secretions of these
glands. The timing of dream sleep is thus seen as crucial to the regulation of hormonal
balance. Hormonal imbalances (such as premenstrual syndrome) are known to affect
mood. In short, dream sleep is still believed to be crucial to mental health, but in a decidedly more neurobiologic fashion than was previously imagined.

servation that subjects were still asleep. In fact, as researchers soon learned from attempts to awaken subjects during this stage, people in dream sleep are *deeply* asleep—in some instances as deeply asleep as they are in stage 4 of synchronized sleep. And when awakened, 85 percent reported that they had just been dreaming. (As for the remaining 15 percent, it is likely that many of these people simply were unable to recall their dreams.) Thus a type of paradox was presented: During dream sleep, people were deeply asleep, but at the same time the eye movements and the neural activity of the brain were indistinguishable from those signals generated by an awake person. Only the body's muscle tone indicated a difference.

As mentioned earlier, it is conceivable that desynchronized neural activity in the brain is necessary to support an awake consciousness. This observation, coupled with the observation that desynchronized activity also characterizes neurons during dream sleep, raises an interesting question. From a subjective point of view, aren't we conscious in our dreams? Aren't we "awake" in them?

If we reflect on our own dream experiences, we find that while dreaming, we always *believe* we are awake. We describe our dreams as, "*I* was walking down this long and winding road, then *I* came to a bridge, which stretched out over an ocean, and then *I* saw a rainbow," or something like that. The point is that we almost always recount our dream experiences in the first person, and we also feel awake during our dreams. Accordingly, it seems possible that this "awakeness" during our dreams, though we are not fully awake, as we are when we are *really* awake, is responsible for the desynchronized waveform that appears on the graph.

To continue on this theme, it also may be possible that eye movements during dream sleep correspond with what we are looking at in our dreams. Are we watching a dream plane cross a dream sky, for example, and does this activity within the dream cause the eye movements seen on the graph? There are studies that support this idea, but ultimately the question is not that important. For instance, eye movements are also observed in newborns. What are they looking at? The eye activity may be just a reflexive reaction to general stimulation of the visual cortex.

The third major event that occurs during dream sleep involves the body's muscular system. With the onset of dream sleep, the main motor neurons of the body, located at the top of the spinal cord in the back of the neck, are inhibited. Called *muscular atonia*, this inhibition prevents us from physically acting out our dreams.

In a famous 1963 experiment involving cats, conducted by the French sleep researcher Michael Jouvet, the area responsible for inhibiting motor-neuron response, the pyramidal tract, was removed. Jouvet found that removal of the pyramidal tract allowed the body to receive commands for movement sent by the brain during dream sleep. When they went into dream sleep, the cats actually got up and began to act out their dreams. Most of the behavior was what one normally sees in cats—play fighting, pouncing and leaping, dodging things—but this time it was all with imagined playmates and objects!

If one thinks about it, it is apparent that the body must be inhibited during dream sleep, for in our dreams we are very active. Like the cats, we are fooled by our dreams, and we too send commands to our bodies to move in accordance with our perceived needs. However, it seems that from an evolutionary standpoint, to have sleeping people up and about and hallucinating might be dangerous. One might easily walk off a cliff or something. Similarly, acting out one's dreams greatly increases the chances of disturbing the sleep and ultimately threatens to interfere with the accomplishment of dream sleep.

Once the inhibition of the muscular system is achieved, the

experience of dreaming begins. The sensory cortex is massively stimulated from somewhere in the brain stem (current theories hold with the reticular formation), and this stimulation is the first part of the equation of how dreams are created. The sensory cortex produces the dream impressions of touch, smell, sight, taste, and sound. All of our senses are present in dream experience. The second part of the equation is that our consciousness awakens to these stimuli—gets up to answer them, as it were—and we experience a dream.

Here the paradox of dream sleep rears its head once again. We *do* exist in our dreams. Our "presence" in dreams is responsible for there being any retrospective experience of dreaming. But we have already observed that one of the defining features of sleep is the *absence* of consciousness. So which is it? Are we conscious during our dreams, or not? And if we are conscious in our dreams, then how is this consciousness different from an awake consciousness?

3

Consciousness During Dream Sleep

O, what a world of unseen visions and heard silences, this insubstantial coun-
try of the mind! What ineffable essences, these touchless rememberings and un-
showable reveries! And the privacy of it all! A secret theatre of speechless
monologue and prevenient counsel, an invisible mansion of all moods, musings,
and mysteries, an infinite resort of disappointments and discoveries. A whole
kingdom where each of us reigns reclusively alone, questioning what we will,
commanding what we can. A hidden hermitage where we may study out of a
troubled book what we have done and yet may do. An introcosm that is more
myself than anything I can find in a mirror. This consciousness that is myself
of selves, that is everything, and yet nothing at all—what is it?

—JULIAN JAYNES,
THE ORIGIN OF CONSCIOUSNESS IN
THE BREAKDOWN OF THE BICAMERAL MIND

TOWARD A DEFINITION OF *CONSCIOUSNESS*

Do we possess consciousness in our dreams?

If we wish to search for consciousness in our dreams, we
must know what we are looking for. What do we mean, specifically, when we use the word *consciousness*?

At first it seems obvious. "Why, it is this," we say, and point
to our head and the air around us. "It is this experience I'm hav-

ing now. It is me talking to you. It is us being here together, at this moment. And tomorrow I will remember this, and it will be part of my life. It is my living, my experience, my life."

If pressed further, what else could we say about consciousness? "Consciousness," we might respond, "is that state that characterizes us when we are awake. When we are asleep, we are not conscious; neither are we conscious when we can be said to be *un*conscious."

This definition is better, but can we be more specific? At this point perhaps we wax philosophic. Taking a broad look around us, we assert, "Consciousness is our awareness. It is our ability to be aware of ourselves. It is our awareness that we are living, that we are alive, and that we will die."

This definition is the best so far, but is it possible to identify consciousness empirically? While these definitions give us a feeling for the experience of consciousness, they are a bit vague for our purposes. For example, consider each of the above definitions in relation to dreaming. We are seeking to answer the question of whether or not we possess consciousness in our dreams. According to the first definition of consciousness, which centers on our ability to experience things, it seems safe to say that we do have consciousness in our dreams. After all, things happen to us in dreams. We have conversations with people, we walk and talk, we think, act, and feel, and we make decisions. We have experiences in our dreams. But is this what we mean by *consciousness*?

If we check our second definition of consciousness—consciousness is when we are awake—then it is obvious that we do not possess consciousness in our dreams. After all, we are asleep! But if we look closer at dream experience, it seems that while we definitely are asleep during our dreams, in another way we are also awake. In our dreams we act awake and believe we are awake.

Even the third definition of consciousness is problematic. Are we self-aware in our dreams? It seems we can make a good case either way. We enter the dreamscape acting and feeling like our familiar selves, and we respond to dream situations much as we would in waking life. On the other hand, we often don't possess much critical ability in dreams; some of the things we do in dreams are nonsensical and absurd. It seems like we are self-aware in some ways but lack self-awareness in others.

If we look in the Random House unabridged dictionary, we find *consciousness* defined as follows:

1. The state of being conscious; aware of one's own existence, sensations, thoughts, surroundings, etc. 2. The thoughts and feelings, collectively, of an individual or of an aggregate of people: *the moral consciousness of a nation.* 3. full activity of the mind and senses, as in waking life: *to regain consciousness after fainting.* 4. awareness of something for what it is; internal knowledge: *consciousness of wrongdoing.* 5. concern, interest, or acute awareness: *class consciousness.* 6. the mental activity of which a person is aware as contrasted with unconscious mental processes. 7. *Philos.* the mind or the mental faculties as characterized by thought, feelings, and volition.

It appears that we've already covered most of these definitions. That is, the dictionary says that consciousness is awareness of one's own existence, sensations, thoughts, and surroundings, and that it is a quality that we possess when we are awake. The sixth definition, which describes consciousness as "the mental activity of which a person is aware," also seems close to our description of consciousness as being our self-awareness. But all of these definitions leave something to be desired. It is important for our purposes that we distinguish consciousness even further from these other qualities and characteristics of thought.

Let us begin again. Do we possess consciousness in our dreams?

In its everyday usage, *consciousness* is broadly maintained to be an attribute of the mind that characterizes us when we are awake. When we are awake, we are said to possess consciousness, and when we are asleep, we generally are said to not possess consciousness. This traditional pairing of the meanings of the words *conscious* and *unconscious* with the words *awake* and *asleep* has caused the words, respectively, to become virtually synonymous.

Nevertheless, if a person gets hit on the head and is said to have lost consciousness, it is understood that this type of unconsciousness is different from that of sleep. For instance, we don't say that a person got hit by a log and was "knocked asleep." We say the person was hit by a log and "knocked unconscious." While superficially the two states may look similar, we easily distinguish between them.

There are many other usages of the word *consciousness*. As we saw in the Random House definitions, it is frequently used in political and sociological contexts, when we say that people "become conscious" of world events or external situations. In this context one frequently hears such turns of phrase as "He is not very politically conscious" or "He had a well-developed social consciousness." Similarly, one can be conscious of internal events, such as thoughts, feelings, and memories: "I was conscious of how much I had grown when I returned to my hometown that year."

When consciousness is linked to the idea of awareness, it most often is viewed as a quality of mind measurable on a continuum. One's consciousness is judged as being greater or lesser, dependent on a person's general level of awareness. Statements such as "He is very politically conscious" or "I don't think he was altogether conscious of his actions" imply levels and gradations of awareness.

If we investigate other uses of *consciousness*, we find that this concept of awareness is stretched far beyond what one might expect, often including behaviors normally associated only with automatic or reflex levels of responsiveness. For example, one occasionally hears the argument that pepole *do* possess consciousness during sleep. Not dream sleep, but rather good old, regular, synchronized sleep. Our definition of consciousness certainly is growing comprehensive. When we began our investigation, the one thing we probably thought we could be certain of is that people do not possess consciousness during sleep. It seemed a safe bet. People who argue for consciousness during sleep point to the responsive and purposive behaviors that regularly occur as we sleep.

For example, if we need to awaken at a certain hour, say to prepare for an important exam, interview, or business meeting, don't we often awaken only a moment or two before the alarm clock sounds? Of if the telephone is far from our bedroom and we normally sleep through phone calls in the morning, how is it that we awaken to its sound when we are expecting an important call?

Similarly, it is well documented that people awaken relatively quickly to the sound of their own name, but they can sleep through up to ninety decibels of white noise being played over loudspeakers next to their beds. Mothers likewise are especially sensitive to their newborn's cries, while they readily sleep through other types of noise. These and other examples point to the presence of some level of awareness and ability for purposive responsiveness while we are asleep. Be it conditioned or automatic, there is a great deal of evidence that suggests that while we are asleep, some part of us is still "awake"—keeping time, processing information, and making decisions.

If we define *consciousness* as the ability to respond or react at any level—a continuum-type conceptualization of conscious-

ness, where even automatic and reactive behaviors are included—then the answer to our question of whether or not we
possess consciousness during dreams must be yes. For in dreams,
not only are we responsive at basic levels, but we also regularly
perform complex behaviors: We respond purposively to all types
of sensory stimuli, and we perform higher mental functions such
as thinking, making decisions, and experiencing emotions.

Recall your own experience with dreams. Generally you are
involved in whatever is occurring in your dreams, and all the
while you believe you are awake. You navigate the dreamscape
with your familiar sense of self; you react and respond to situations much as you do in daily life. All of your familiar sensory
abilities are intact. You are present in your dreams; you see in
them, you feel in them, you perceive in them. You experience
emotions, have thoughts, and make decisions. You see, hear, feel,
smell, touch, and taste. You are inquisitive. You evaluate, analyze,
and investigate. You feel the earth beneath your feet, you scan
the horizon with your eyes, and you feel the wind blowing
against your cheek. Things happen to you in your dreams.

But before we proceed too far along in examining the simi-
larities between our dreams and our waking experience, it
would be prudent to remember that for all of the familiar aspects of our self that we carry into the dreamscape, some aspect
of our self is glaringly absent. The key evidence in support of
this statement is that while dreaming, we almost never notice
that we are dreaming. And, stated plainly, we *should* notice that
we are dreaming.

THE MISSING ELEMENT

During dreams, and in any dream sequence, there are literally
hundreds of clues that would tip off an awake consciousness that
one *had* to be dreaming. Violations of physical laws—abrupt,

impossible scene shifts and connections of events—are not the exceptional features of dream experience; rather, they characterize dream experience. People and objects metamorphose as we watch, and incongruities and absurdities are everywhere. Most dream scenarios do not correspond at all with our everyday, waking lives. Suddenly we are back at school, a mixture of high school and college, and we are writing a paper, making ink marks with our fingertips as we pull our hands down the page. In dreams, clues abound, but for some reason, we consistently fail to recognize the dreamscape. What has happened to our minds? What should be an immediate and facile reality-discrimination task is suddenly next to impossible. Something, something very comprehensive, is missing.

Now, let us return again to our question. We possess a lot in our dreams, but do we possess *consciousness*?

In our dreams, as we have seen, we are "awake" and able. We think, make decisions, and navigate our bodies around the dreamscape. We are cognitively oriented in a three-dimensional environment. We are able to perform highly complex behaviors. But do these abilities constitute consciousness? Can't any animal do these things? Don't all animals do these things?

It is popular wisdom that consciousness is the ability that distinguishes human beings from the rest of the animal kingdom, that humankind, with consciousness, is "like unto gods, knowing good and evil." It also is popularly told that consciousness is what liberates us from the hard-wired confines of genetic evolution. We are aware of ourselves, of our existence, of our potentiality and mortality. Consciousness heralds the birth of inner experience. It is the template for the "rich inner life." This is the birth of will, of experience, of the *I*—the individual sovereign self. Our criminal justice system is predicated on the assumption of consciousness—that human beings possess will and the ability to choose between different possibilities of behavior.

The advent of consciousness within a species lays claim to an entirely new category of existence. But for all of the great and noble benefits attributed to this super-phenomenon of the mind, we can still find it difficult to agree on *what it is*.

For those who have sought to understand it, consciousness has always proved a challenge. Philosophers, poets, artists, religionists—all have struggled with understanding consciousness, this greatest of all gifts. Even today, as the quest for artificial intelligence continues, the search for a precise understanding of human thought and consciousness eludes us. In the past, the conceptual difficulties of describing human consciousness encouraged thinkers to stray into religious and metaphysical domains for an explanation of thought and self-awareness. Is consciousness a property of the soul? Does consciousness float free of the neurobiologic substrate upon which some assume it must rest?

That these questions have been answered in the affirmative in the past attests to the difficulty great thinkers have had in understanding consciousness. To this day, consciousness remains loosely defined and only vaguely understood, even though it surely is the most distinctive characteristic human beings possess.

Perhaps it is difficult to identify the mechanics of consciousness precisely because it is so much of what we are. We are so close to our consciousness that it is difficult to gain perspective on it. It is the old story of being too close to the trees to see the forest. We are asking thought to describe itself, and this is more difficult than we might expect.

In an essay on lucid dreams written by the famous sleep researcher Dr. Allan Rechtschaffen, "The Single-Mindedness and Isolation of Dreams," notice how the word *consciousness* is used nonspecifically.

I have often been asked why we occasionally have lucid dreams. It is a peculiar question. The question should be

why are not all dreams lucid as is most of conscious experience. Yet the fact of occasional lucidity in dreams is
useful as a demonstration of what most dreams are not.
Only when we can see the possibility of the lucid dream
do we fully realize what a massively nonreflective state
dreaming *usually* is—what a truly distinctive psychological experience it is. In fact, I can think of no other single
state short of severe and chronic psychosis in which
there is such a persistent, massive, regular loss of reflec-
tiveness. Herein may lie the most distinctive psychological characteristic of dreaming. We can all have peculiar
thoughts and images dozens of times a day, and these
may symbolically reflect motivational forces of which
we are not aware. This is like dreaming. But it is only
during dreaming that most of us regularly lose so completely the road map of our own consciousness.[8]

Is consciousness the road map, or is consciousness the
thought that is being guided? Rechtschaffen continues:

Waking consciousness generally contains at least two
prevalent streams. One stream contains "voluntary"
mental productions, thoughts and images that "pop" into
our heads, and sense impressions. The other is a reflective or evaluative stream which seemingly monitors the
first and places it in some perspective. The reflective
stream seems to judge whether the thoughts or images
are integral to the mental task of the moment or irrelevant intrusions from a separate part of our minds—
whether the thoughts are deliberate, voluntary mental

[8]Allan Rechtschaffen, "The Single-Mindedness and Isolation of Dreams," *Sleep*, Vol. 1,
No. 1 (New York: Raven Press, 1978), 100.

productions, or spontaneous, uncontrolled thoughts—whether the images come to us from the external world or from within. In dreams, the reflective stream of consciousness is drastically attenuated.[9]

Rechtschaffen writes that the reflective stream of consciousness "monitors" and "places in some perspective" the other stream of consciousness, which he describes as being "voluntary" and says has a momentum of its own. In dreams it is the absence of this ability to monitor and place into some perspective the voluntary stream of thought that causes us to believe our dreams are real. As Rechtschaffen so astutely observes, without the ability to judge and monitor our thoughts, we become "single-minded"—we have no referent from which to judge our experiences. Without this ability for reflection, we are unable to identify even our most obvious dreams.

The definitional problem that arises within this examination of thought, however, is that Rechtschaffen uses the word *consciousness* to describe both streams of thought. He writes that "in dreams, the reflective stream of consciousness is drastically attenuated." He also writes that "it is only during dreaming that most of us regularly lose so completely the road map of our own consciousness." Thus, we possess two streams of consciousness: a reflective stream of consciousness that judges and evaluates a voluntary stream of consciousness.

We now zoom in on the central misunderstanding that has plagued the question of consciousness throughout time: the failure to delineate between these two components of our thought. And it is these two components of thought, when they are active together, that truly distinguish consciousness.

[9]Ibid., 98.

THE DUALITY OF HUMAN CONSCIOUSNESS

Can we isolate the factors that comprise the experience of consciousness? Can we rescue consciousness from the embarrassing lack of understanding that so persistently surrounds the term?

When I worked in sleep research at the National Institutes of Health in Bethesda, Maryland, I once asked sleep researcher Dr. Wallace Mendelson to define human consciousness for me. Much to my surprise, my existential question did not cause Dr. Mendelson to blink an eye. "Consciousness is easy," he explained. "Consciousness is a duality. It is the seemingly paradoxical ability of being able to experience sensation and, at the same time, of being able to experience oneself experiencing that sensation."

When Dr. Mendelson first gave me this definition of consciousness, I was unsure of what I had my hands on. Over the years, however, my appreciation of this definition has grown steadily. It is the best understanding of consciousness I ever have encountered. The definition pierces to the center of the question of consciousness in one simple equation: *Consciousness is a duality.* It is the ability "to experience sensation and, at the same time, to be able to experience oneself experiencing that sensation." If we refer to Rechtschaffen's components of consciousness, we see that same duality: Consciousness occurs when the reflective stream is present in conjunction with the voluntary stream. This, I offer, and this alone, is consciousness.

The discrimination that we must make in our understanding of consciousness is that behavior that is performed without reflectivity—without the duality of attention to experience, without the active effort to experience the experience (and this covers legions of waking behavior)—actually is *un*consciously performed behavior. Until we actively reflect on our experience of sensation, we are *un*conscious. Notice that this is probably a quite different understanding of consciousness than we have ever considered before. But the linkage of consciousness with reflectivity is essential for an informed understanding of consciousness, and as we set out to develop our ability for consciousness, we must work to improve our familiarity with this concept. Because the spontaneous stream of thought is always with us (it is the constant in experience, the voluntary production of our minds), it is our ability for reflectivity that must be developed. Development of the ability to generate and maintain reflectivity *is* the development of consciousness.

But now let us take this new definition of consciousness and see if it will pass the dream test. Do we possess consciousness in our dreams? Do we possess reflectivity, or the duality in dream experience? Are we able to "see" what we are seeing in our dreams? Are we able to "hear" what we are hearing? Are we able to "touch" what we are touching? In short, are we able to experience our experience of sensation as it occurs in dreams? The answer, really, is a resounding no! Indeed, our ability for consciousness—our ability to achieve reflectivity in our minds—is specifically denied us during dream sleep. As Rechtschaffen observes, single-mindedness is a quality that *defines* dream experience. If we had the ability to reflect in a dream, we would recognize instantly that we were dreaming, because our dreams are so obviously incongruent with our waking lives. But this ability for duality is maddeningly elusive in dream experience, for reasons we shall soon discuss. As a result, in our dreams we are single-minded; we no longer possess any referent from which to judge and evaluate our experience. Without our ability to perceive our dream experience as it occurs, we genuinely become one-dimensional. Without consciousness, we are unable to see ourselves. And in a certain sense, with this loss of reflectivity, we, as we know ourselves experientially, cease to exist.

4

The Body
of Time

And the serpent said unto the woman, Ye shall not surely die: for God doth know that in the day ye eat thereof, then your eyes shall be opened, and ye shall be as God, knowing good and evil. . . .

And when the woman saw that the tree was good for food, and that it was a delight to the eyes, and that the tree was to be desired to make one wise, she took of the fruit thereof, and did eat; and she gave also unto her husband with her, and he did eat.

And the eyes of both of them were opened, and they knew that they were naked; and they sewed fig leaves together, and made themselves aprons.

And man called his wife's name Eve; because she was the mother of all the living.

—GEN. 3:4, 6, 7, 20.

Look at your hands, your arms, your legs, your torso. How old is your body? Is it eighteen, twenty-five, forty-five, sixty? Is it however old you are in chronological years, or is it older? Our bodies are indeed a particular age, but if we take a long look at ourselves, we can see our bodies as millions of years old. We did not spring from dust yesterday. Indeed, each of us is a survivor of more time than we can imagine. Long into our past, each of us can trace back literally millions of years of biology. Our ancestors successfully navigated the perils of time, chance, and hard labor to create us as we are today. Each time the handoff of genetic code was made, our bodies blended with another, right up to yesterday, when our parents successfully passed on their genetic code to create us. Each of us is a unique and individual being, the result of millions of years of growth, reconstitution, and transformation. Take another look at those hands.

THE EVOLUTION OF CONSCIOUSNESS

Against the backdrop of millions of years of evolution, the question is often asked as to why consciousness should have evolved. What benefit or advantage does the ability for self-awareness, and the concomitant existential reflection that attends self-awareness, lend to us evolutionarily? As conscious beings, we are partial to consciousness; it is the only way we know ourselves. But as we survey the world around us, we must acknowledge that nearly all other life forms do *not* possess this ability for consciousness. Why, then, are we the exception? If there is a biological reason, then do we come to life on the back of this ancient creature of time, man, merely to take a ride on an existential Ferris wheel? Do we get swooped up to see the stars, only to retire gently, and forever, at the end of the ride? Or has our consciousness evolved for another reason? Are we a most-favored species, selected by the gods to become as we imagine them?

While consciousness bequeaths us the great questions of the living, in the same breath it must be asked what advantage these *questions* lend us. Questions all too often drive men and women into existential quagmires and foster all types of erratic behavior. What benefits the body from the agony of a mind and soul?

The seeming irrelevance of consciousness to biological goals has long puzzled evolutionists and, at the same time, lent support to those who claim a higher or spiritual force present in the universe—which somehow has culled this ability of self-awareness to arise in us, seemingly against the laws of material evolution. Yet in pondering the nature of dream experience and our failure to recall this experience, we soon must ask whether a relationship exists between consciousness and memory. Is it the absence of consciousness during dreaming that causes us to be unable to recall most of our dreams? Our memory of ordinary dream experience, as we know, is uncannily poor. Our memory of lucid dreams, on the other hand, is typically very good. What accounts for this difference?

Try to recollect one of your dreams from last night. If you are unable, try again tomorrow morning. You will observe that nonlucid dreams almost always are recalled via a trace process. That is, we tend to start with a fragment of a memory and then work backward, stringing together as many associations as we are able. Note also that if we do not immediately work to recall the dream or record it on paper, most of the impressions soon vanish.[10] Lucid dreams, however, are recollected more holistically. The first time we observe a lucid dream is when we are in the dream itself. When we "recall" our experience of a lucid dream, this is our second "view" of the dream. As a result, our memory for lucid dreams is superior to that for ordinary dreams. We don't need to work backward, stringing together traces of associations. Instead we are able to move at will to recall the dream. Beginning, middle, and end—the experience is much more firmly impressed in our memory.

Consciousness is a psychological experience, but as with all psychological experiences, it possesses a neurobiologial corol-

---

[10]An exception to this rule is when we are able to recall certain dreams very well without having performed either act of reinforcement. These well-recalled dreams often are very vivid, or emotionally powerful, when we experience them, indicating a greater intensity of experience. Stressful dreams and nightmares fit this category. Our attention is acute; we believe we are about to suffer dire consequences for our actions or inactions. Exceptionally beautiful dreams that are profoundly emotional and moving are also of high intensity and therefore are better recalled.

lary. As suggested in chapter three, consciousness is our ability to experience the experience of sensation as it occurs. When we gain consciousness in a dream, we are able to experience our experience of the dream as it is occurring, which allows us to make the fairly obvious observation that we are dreaming. But notice that with consciousness, we always experience sensation twice: first when it comes over the sensory "wires" to us, and then when we actively observe, or experience, our experience of the sensation. Thus we "see" our seeing, "touch" our touching, and "feel" our feeling. The extent to which we focus our attention on the experience determines the degree to which the experience is impressed in our memory. It also determines the degree to which the experience becomes part of our active awareness—that is, memory that is recalled.

As our experiments with consciousness progress through the course of this book, we will find that a striking relationship exists between consciousness and memory. And to return to our original line of inquiry, this relationship also suggests a simpler answer to why conciousness evolved than, perhaps, does divine intervention. Our ability to reflect radically enhances our ability for memory, which may be one reason why consciousness is valuable from an evolutionary point of view. The relationship that exists between consciousness and memory is most likely the great *advantage* of consciousness. This ability for reflection also ushers us into the paradigm of experiential existence. Welcome to the living.

5

Why We "Sleep" Through Our Dreams

Of all the times when we might most want our consciousness, when we are in the fabulous dreamscape, we find that it is almost categorically denied us! Each night we enter the dreamscape once again, yet each night we enter blind. Without consciousness, we are unable to recognize our dreams. We are unable to *see* where we are, unable to *be* where we are.

Psychologically, the absence of consciousness from dream sleep makes no sense. We are all blessed with a fantastic, natural mechanism for inner illumination, for healing and mental health, yet we are never permitted access to it. To add insult to injury, not only are we unable to interact with our dreams consciously, but our memory of the experience is radically impaired. Unconsciously experienced sensation is very difficult to recall; we routinely forget the overwhelming majority of our dreams. So why do we dream at all?

THE BIOLOGICAL FUNCTION OF DREAMING

From a biological perspective, the experience of dreaming did not evolve for psychological reasons. Dream sleep, as far as anyone has looked, is found in virtually every warm-blooded creature and uniformly *not* found in cold-blooded, or passively heated, life forms. This simple observation has caused researchers to speculate that dream sleep is related to thermoregulatory processes common to warm-blooded creatures. Recent evidence suggests that dream sleep, through its increased neural activity, may help keep the brain warm when our body temperature falls at night. During sleep, our core body temperature falls a full degree and a half centigrade. It is hypothesized that this cooling is one of the restorative aspects of sleep; the body is permitted to relax from maintaining its own warmth. In this theory, the brain is more sensitive to temperature variations than is the body, and thus the brain utilizes dream sleep to stay within a specific temperature window, where it is neither too warm nor too cold. This theory fails to explain dream-rebound phenomena, however, which we will discuss later.

Another theory holds that because we experience dreams unconsciously and because our memory of dreams is so poor, consciousness is obviously not essential to the function of dream sleep. This view, which has little or no regard for the content of dreams, became popular among scientists in the mid-1960s, just as the neurobiological sciences began to flex their muscles.

In his book *Dream Psychology and the New Biology of Dreaming*, Lewis J. West captures the mood of the time: "As I see it, the dream *reflects* a function rather than serving one; passes through awareness as a result of biological energetics or 'work,' rather than doing work itself; is an effect rather than a cause of the ninety minute cycle."[11] That is, our experience of dreaming might actually serve no primary function in and of itself but rather appear to be a side effect of a more primary process.

This vision challenged many of science's most cherished be-

---

[11]Lewis J. West, *Dream Psychology and the New Biology of Dreaming* (Illinois: Thomas Books, 1967), xx.

liefs about dreaming. In 1967, Freud was still mainstream science, and nearly everyone accepted his thesis that dreams ventilated repressed conflicts in the psyche. But West, aligning himself with the newly emerging school of neurobiology, states unequivocally:

> The dream does not exist in order to provide an outlet for the discharge of primary-process or instinctual energy; rather it represents an epiphenomenon of that fundamental periodicity, as yet poorly understood, which perhaps is basic not only to the maintenance of sleep during the night but also the maintenance of alertness during the day.[12]

This new perception of the dream experience brought immediate opposition from the Freudian school, as suggested in chapter two. Freudians saw an elaborate psychological structure in dreams, and they maintained their belief that dreams dictated the accompanying physiological activity being observed in sleep labs at that time. In essence, this was a "which came first, the chicken or the egg?" debate. The Freudians said that physiology followed the dream; West and the neurobiologists decided that the physiology came first.

The new evidence emerging from laboratory experiments with cats, dogs, mice, chimps, rats, and other subjects added fuel to the fire and kept challenging Freud's theories. "But what is the mouse dreaming about?" the neurobiologists asked. The Freudians groped for an answer.

Some scientists carried the new vision of dreams to an extreme. They went so far as to say that dreams actually were undesirable events. All of the hallucinated activity of dream sleep—indeed, all of the "noise," as they grew fond of referring

12Ibid., xx.

to dreams—threatened to disturb the quiescence of sleep. Nightmares, anxiety attacks, dreams of running and falling or of overexerting oneself—who needs them? Indeed, they chirped, if we could just get rid of all of this noise at night, we might all get some sleep.

What a curious idea!

DREAMS AS DISTURBERS OF SLEEP

Of all of the stages of sleep we transit in the course of a night, dream sleep is without question the stage in which we are most active. Our heart rate zooms and slows, our breathing becomes shallow and irregular (not unlike when we are awake), we perspire, and we occasionally speak. Our skin, brain, and core body temperatures all rise in response to the increased activity, while our body is inhibited from responding to our mind's commands for movement. As the experience of dreaming begins, countless billions of neurons begin to fire in rapid, highly excited desynchronized activity, creating the sensory impressions of the dreamscape. Beneath our eyelids, our eyes dart about. We are asleep, but we are watching or waiting for something.

On the inside of these countless billions of neurons, we suddenly come to life. And typically we are in the midst of great activity. We are running down a gray street lined with tall buildings; it is growing dark in the city and we feel we must get home. There is a man chasing us who would do us harm, but the night may work to our advantage. Suddenly we are at the supermarket. We are arguing with a clerk who has overcharged us for some groceries. We settle the disagreement, only to find that we have no money to pay for the groceries anyway. We leave the market, but we carry with us a large stuffed poodle to mark our place in line. Outside, our attention is drawn to an airplane on fire, streaking across the sky. Suddenly we are in the airplane. We are seated by a window and looking at the flames through the window. The poodle is seated next to us. We knew we shouldn't have boarded this plane, we say to ourselves. We call for the stewardess to ask when the next plane leaves, but our mother appears instead. We ask her when she started working for the airline. She corrects us and tells us she works for a cruise line. She shows us her badge—it reads "Cherry Cruise Line." We ask her if she can get us tickets to the animal show tonight on the ship—we saw a poster. Tonight there will be all types of sea animals performing in one of the pools on the boat. She says yes, but cautions us not to swim off the side of the boat at night. There are sharks, and a few passengers have been lost. Then she introduces herself to the poodle, who somehow has changed into an attractive woman. "You must be my son's fiancée," she says as she extends her hand. We are embarrassed that we did not introduce her sooner. And with that, we awaken.

Given the amount of activity that takes place during a dream, we may indeed wonder how we sleep through it all. Dream sleep is like having a three-ring circus perform in our mind each night!

THE DEEPEST STAGE OF ALL

In experiments performed to measure the varying depths of sleep stages, usually involving noises played over loudspeakers next to the subjects' beds, dreamers often do not awaken, even though the tests typically use loud, blunt, annoying tones. Consistently, people in dream sleep snooze right through the noise, even when the volume is increased to ninety decibels—the equivalent of having a subway pass through your bedroom.

Naturally, these tests are something of a lark to perform. This is because there has not yet been a sleep lab designed that can contain a ninety-decibel white-noise signal in a sleeper's twelve-by-twelve-foot room. So at 2:00 A.M., or whenever the test is being conducted, everything within a forty-yard radius of that noise is disturbed. Other night-shift workers come by to see what the ruckus is, security guards come by to check on the "fire alarm" that's sounding, and the only people sleeping are the subjects engaged in stage 4 or dream sleep.

While dream sleep is considered one of the deepest stages of sleep (only stage 4 of synchronous sleep is as unresponsive to external stimuli), it also, paradoxically, is considered to be a light stage of sleep. This is because we are more likely to spontaneously awaken from dream sleep than from any other stage. If we allow ourselves to awaken naturally—that is, without an alarm clock—it is an odds-on favorite that we'll awaken out of dream sleep. If we ever find ourselves awake in the middle of the night, chances are we have been in dream sleep and we are able to recall having just been dreaming.

How can dream sleep be both a deep stage and a light stage of sleep? The answer is simpler than it appears. During dream sleep, the body works very hard to keep itself asleep. At the same time, all of the activity that occurs during this stage—the production of the dreamscape, the physiological changes in the body—perpetually threatens to awaken us. As mentioned in chapter one, all dream sleep periods are punctuated by microawakenings—brief moments when we are pushed toward awakening, either to fall asleep again or to awaken. No other stage of sleep has such regular intrusions, so researchers conjecture that the arousals are a direct result of dream activity.

DREAMS AS GUARDIANS OF SLEEP

Experiments in which subjects sleep through tremendous barrages of noise have shown that dreamers almost always incorporate these noises into the story lines of ongoing dreams. That is, the noise comes to play a part in the dream and then seems to make sense. For example, in the case of a ninety-decibel signal at bedside, one subject might dream she is driving her car when suddenly the horn becomes stuck; as the noise grows louder, she realizes she is driving an eighteen-wheeler, moving quickly, and pulling on the air horn. Another subject dreaming about hunting wild game in Alaska may, upon hearing the sound, suddenly find himself blowing a moose horn; as the noise grows louder, he may find himself encircled by a herd of moose, all bugling at him! Whatever scenario unfolds to accommodate external stimuli, the rule is that our bodies consistently incorporate the sensations into our dreams.

Freud found this incorporating characteristic of dreams so common that, in his *Interpretation of Dreams*, he proposed that in addition to their ventilatory role in the psyche, dreams also served to protect the continuity of sleep. He hypothesized that dreams incorporated external stimuli into their plot lines to allow sleepers to continue sleeping. In this way, dreams provided a means to answer those "questions" that external stimuli posed to our minds in sleep—excessive heat, cold, warmth, hunger, loud noises, and so forth. Freud speculated that if these questions were not answered by our dreams, then we might be compelled to awaken to discover their source. If frequent enough, these awakenings could significantly disturb the continuity of our sleep. In this light, dreams served to guard our sleep by explaining, in dream form, the external stimuli. Thus Freud dubbed dreams "The Guardians of Sleep."

Here is a common example of dream incorporation: A person lives in a building facing a city street, where he hears an unusually loud siren pass by in the night. In his dream, the plot suddenly shifts to accommodate whatever he first associates with the siren. A family member is ill at the time, so the dreamer suddenly finds himself dreaming that he is in the emergency room of a hospital, waiting for an ambulance to arrive. Or perhaps he watched a "cops and robbers" movie on television before going to sleep; he might start dreaming that he is a gangster engaged in a shootout with the police. In the same vein, most of us have probably awakened from dreams in which we are trying to answer a ringing telephone or in which a buzzer keeps beeping, only to find that we actually were hearing the telephone or the alarm clock.

Sensations from our body are readily incorporated into our dreams as well. For example, after a dream about eating or about picking out foods from a cafeteria line, we might awaken with a distinct sensation of hunger. If we drink alcohol before going to sleep, by morning our body will have dehydrated. This sensation may enter into a dream in which we search for water or a soft drink or we drink a glass of water, but our thirst remains unquenched. If the blankets fall off the bed we may dream we are on an arctic expedition. If it is a hot night, we may dream we are in the tropics. Whatever the case, physical sensations regularly enter into or create the story lines of our dreams.

In laboratory experiments, dreaming subjects have been exposed to a wide variety of external sensations, usually auditory, but visual, somatic (touch), and olfactory (smell) stimuli are also used. Shortly after the stimuli are introduced, the researchers awaken the subjects and ask if they recall having been dreaming. Varying with the nature of the stimuli, dreamers usually report that the stimulus was in some way incorporated into their dreams. In one test, cold water was sprinkled onto the back of a person shown by an EEG to be dreaming. As expected, the dreamer did not awaken. But when he subsequently was awakened, he reported that in his dream he was acting in a play, when suddenly the roof of the theater began to leak. When he went over to try to fix the leak, the water dripped onto his back.

THE CHICKEN AND THE EGG REVISITED

The tendency to incorporate stimuli into our dreams is so pervasive that it has, in both past and present times, caused people to question the worth of dream analysis. Many have suggested that this characteristic of dreams may be responsible for most of our dreams' content, previously the exclusive domain of psychoanalysis.

To illustrate, a common experience in dreams is the sensation of restricted movement. Most of us have had a dream at one time or another in which we have tried to strike something or run away from someone, only to find that our hands are unable to land a blow or our legs feel like they are stuck in cement. What is the significance of these dreams? Do we subconsciously perceive ourselves to be ineffective against whatever or whomever our dream antagonist symbolically represents? Or does it mean simply that our body is correctly sending us a signal of immobility because our muscles, owing to the paralysis of dream sleep, are unable to move?

The Russian philosopher Peter Ouspensky once wrote about a recurring dream he'd had for many years, the psychological significance of which he pondered. In his dream, he found himself mired in a muddy swamp, reminiscent of the Russian geography he had known as a child. The dream was accompanied by feelings of restricted movement. It puzzled Ouspensky, and the fact that it recurred puzzled him doubly. Was there an unresolved conflict from his childhood that he was unaware of? One time Ouspensky awoke halfway through the dream. As he began to think about it, he discovered that his legs were tangled in the sheets. This must have been the precipitating cause for the dream! The constriction of the sheets on his legs must have been incorporated into his dream.

It was because of experiences like these that Peter Ouspensky took exception to psychoanalytic interpretations of dreams. His experience with lucid dreaming, which he called "half-dream" states, caused him to write,

> I became absolutely convinced that without these half-dream states no study of dreams is possible and that all attempts at such study are inevitably doomed to failure, to wrong deductions, to fantastic hypotheses, and the like. Most of our dreams are entirely accidental, entirely chaotic, unconnected with anything and meaning-less. These dreams depend on accidental associations . . . there is no consecutiveness in them, no direction, no idea.[13]

As for recurring dreams, Ouspensky offers,

> Even the first observations of recurring dreams showed me that dreams depend much more on the direct sensa-tions of a given moment than on any general causes. Gradually I became convinced that almost all recurring dreams were connected with the sensation not even of a state, but simply with the posture of the body at any given moment.[14]

To an extent, Ouspensky is a modern-day neurobiologist's dream come true. It is evident that he relegated much of dream experience not to the mysteries of an unconscious mind active within us but rather to physical sensations that happen to im-pinge upon the body at the time of dreaming.

Two details included in Ouspensky's account, however, cause one to question whether he ever was lucid during dream sleep. Ouspensky seems to be describing lucidity during hypna-

[13]Peter Ouspensky, *A New Model of the Universe* (New York: Vintage, 1971), 69.
[14]Ibid., 69.

gogic experience—those times when we lie in bed, half awake and half asleep, and watch the dissociated visual impressions that typically accompany sleep onset and offset. Dream experience, however, is distinct from hypnagogic states in many ways. Most dreams, unlike hypnagogic experiences, are very well constructed. They employ themes that endure entire sequences; the plots are not "entirely accidental, entirely chaotic, unconnected with anything and meaningless." Ouspensky says his half-dream states "depend on accidental associations . . . there is no consecutiveness in them, no direction, no idea." These are fine descriptions of hypnagogic experience, but they are woefully inadequate to describe dream experience.

Despite the likelihood that Ouspensky was describing hypnagogic experience, his point regarding recurring dreams nevertheless is well taken. For example, how would a Freudian analyst interpret Ouspensky's recurring dream? Being trapped in a swamp reminiscent of childhood might be seen to reflect the dreamer's repressed experience with the Oedipal complex. The swamp probably represents his mother's genitals, and his feeling of being trapped represents his fixation on his mother as the desire of his emerging libido. The feeling of being stuck further symbolizes his perceived impotence toward attaining his mother, and by extension reflects his repressed anger toward his father, with whom he is in competition for his mother.

A Freudian might well make an analysis like this and then conclude that any attempt to further rationalize the dream, to explain the dream by virtue of bedcovers ("Very interesting . . ."), being stuck in the sheets ("What do you think of when you think of sheets?") was a continuing act of resistance by the dreamer. That is, the riddle was solved, so would the dreamer please admit that the analyst had correctly interpreted the dream? This type of scenario, where the interpretation of a dream as provided by an analyst might be entirely groundless, illustrates the familiar problem that vexes all of the sciences: seeing what we want to see in data, at the expense of maintaining a less biased approach. In a field that is notorious for having to work with unreliable data for its theories, Ouspensky's critique is a valid admonition.

Freud observed that dreams permit us to sleep through noises and other sensations that might otherwise awaken us. This characteristic is indeed valid—our dreams do regularly incorporate, and are influenced by, external stimuli—but it fails to account for why dreams themselves do not awaken us.

For a moment, let us forget about external noises and sensations and instead turn our gaze back toward the dream. Consider that in our dreams, even when we are dreaming in a nice, noise-free room, we still fail to notice even the most bizarre of internally produced sensory environments. Dreams not only are full of physical incongruity, but the comprehensive incongruity of dreams—that is, the general incongruity of dream experience, when compared to our everyday waking experience—is equally striking. Yet despite all of the clues that inhabit our dreams, we still fail to recognize when we are dreaming.

Now I wish to propose something new to the reader: Dreams, in and of themselves, do not guard our sleep. If anything, they ought to be considered "disturbers of sleep." This is because dreams create these fantastic, internally generated sense environments. If we look harder at our experience with dreams, we find that the true "guardian of sleep" is the action that the body takes to dampen our *responsiveness* to dream activity.

THE ATTENUATION OF CONSCIOUSNESS AND INHIBITION OF THE BODY

I once read that sleeping eight hours a night is a relic of our evolutionary heritage. According to this theory, in ancient times sleep was our technique of choice to hide from enemies and predators at night. My first thought was that that makes sense; night generally lasts eight hours, and that's why we still sleep eight hours today. (Or rather, night lasts eight hours after you switch off the television. Something like that.)

I found this theory of sleep interesting because I know that if I were hiding from my enemies, I would rather be awake than asleep. Hiding by sleeping is like an ostrich's sticking its head in the sand when surrounded by lions; we may think we are safer when asleep, but we are not. When we are asleep, we are vulnerable—far more vulnerable than when we are awake. If there is one thing I am fairly certain of, it is that we do not sleep eight hours a day because we are safer sleeping than we are when we're awake.

Both synchronous sleep and dream sleep are essential for the maintenance of the human body. Nature is not superfluous in designing its biology, and we do not sleep a third of our lives without reason. It has been demonstrated in laboratory settings, and is proved every day in our own lives, that we need both types of sleep. Rats that are chronically deprived of all opportunity to sleep die; they are not able to overcome their need for sleep.[15] We may not know *why* we need to sleep, but we do know that we need it, that we need both synchronous and dream sleep, and that we need both of these frequently. Most people do spend eight hours asleep every night.

Researcher Allan Rechtschaffen once said that if sleep is an accident of evolution, it surely is the greatest mistake nature ever made. This is because from an evolutionary standpoint, sleep is costly. Indeed, when I say that most people get eight hours of

---

[15]Sleep deprivation has a rapid compromising effect on the human immune system. It is a medical truism that when we are deprived of sleep, we are far more susceptible to illness. Ultimately it was destruction of the immune system through chronic sleep deprivation that caused the rats to become ill and be unable to recover.

sleep per night, you probably are wishing that you were one of those people. In our lives today, we consider ourselves fortunate to get as much sleep as we do, especially when there are so many other activities demanding our time. We must work, we must provide for ourselves and others. We must eat to provide our bodies with energy. We must bathe and groom ourselves. We need to spend time with our children; we want quality time alone and with our mates. We want and need time to socialize with others. We take vacations; we travel to enrich and broaden ourselves. We play supportive roles to loved ones, which includes meeting obligations to family and friends in need. We do all that is required of us to survive, and there is so much more we would like to do. We may even get a chance to sleep.

Because sleep is such a costly activity in terms of time spent, one thing our body wants to ensure is that when we do sleep, we do it well. There exists great biological pressure for us to accomplish our sleep as efficiently as possible, since during this time we are unable to do anything else.[16] And now dream sleep presents itself. It is such an *active* stage of sleep—an hour and a half of hallucinated dreamscapes, hallucinated activity, hallucinated running, jumping, and thinking we are wide awake. How can we sleep through it all?

The body makes two fundamental responses to dream sleep, both of which are geared to helping us sleep more efficiently. First, the body quiets the activity of dream sleep by inhibiting the motor neurons, disabling them from passing on signals for movement. Essentially the body enters a benign state of paraly-

---

[16]Recent studies show that our bodies would like us to sleep longer than we do. The majority of us today are chronically sleep deprived. People enter sleep labs complaining of exhaustion yet tell their doctors they get only six hours of sleep a night and don't need more. Relieved of the normal cues by which they set their schedules—television, telephone, alarm clocks, children, bed partners—these sleep-deprived people often sleep ten to twelve hours at a stretch. They feel better and are sent home with a prescription to get some sleep every once in awhile.

sis, preserving the quiescence of sleep. Second, the body deprives us of our ability for consciousness during dream sleep, formally known as the attenuation of consciousness. Deprived of our ability for reflection, we become unable to view or step back from our experiences in dreams. Without this ability for reflection, we become single-minded, unable to identify even the most obvious of our dreams. Thus, the body successfully dampens its response to dream sleep, eliminating the aspects that would cause us to awaken. In this way the body ensures that it can achieve sleep as efficiently as possible—that is, without waking every five minutes.

The need for dampening of the reflective ability during dreams is curious. As chapter six explains, sustained experience with lucid dreams shows that consciousness *is* compatible with the sleep stage, albeit a rare guest. When we observe that the immediate result of gaining consciousness during a dream typically is that we awaken ourselves, then we can see why consciousness generally is an undesirable accompaniment to dream experience. Most often when we perceive we are dreaming, the realization startles us and we disturb the physiologic balance of dream sleep, causing us to awaken shortly thereafter. Put simply, we notice we are dreaming, and then we wake ourselves up. First our mind wakes up in the dreamscape, then our body wakes up, and we make that quick transit from dream sleep to being awake again, with the dreamscape but a memory. This is the famous "Oh, shoot!" of lucid dreaming. In attempting to prolong periods of consciousness in the dreamscape, all lucid dreamers first learn not to startle their bodies *out* of dream sleep once they recognize they are dreaming.

So, we arrive at a perplexing juncture in our search. The dreamscape is very nearly categorically denied us. But enjoy, for a moment, the paradox that attends this grail: It is ours, but we are not permitted access to it. We are responsible for its creation, but we know not whence it comes. We spend an hour and a half a day, ten hours a week, twenty-one days a year in the dream-scape, but we rarely get a chance to visit. We walk in it, we talk in it, we feel it, we touch it, and we ask it questions. It touches us, it holds us, we are enveloped wholly within it. Every night we walk the corridors of our mind. Feel and touch the walls!

Consciousness: We exist without it; we do not exist without it.

6

Consciousness in the Dream Lab

What, for instance, is the meaning of a critical remark found so often in dreams: "This is only a dream"? Here we have a genuine piece of criticism of the dream, such as might be made in waking life. Quite frequently, too, it is actually a prelude to waking up; and still more frequently it has been preceded by some distressing feeling which is set at rest by the recognition that the state is one of dreaming.

—FREUD,
THE INTERPRETATION OF DREAMS

I have in my sleep gained a kind of habit of reflecting how the case stands with me, and whether I be awake or asleep. This generally ends in the discovery of the truth of the case; and when I find it to be a dream I then am easy, and my curiosity engages me to see how the fantastic scene will end with the same kind of indifference that the spectator receives from a theatrical entertainment; but being all along an actor in this scene, the reality of the representation is perpetually obtruding itself upon me; so when the scene, as it often does, grows too troublesome to be borne, I can at any time, by making a certain effort, which I can in no way describe to you, awake myself.

—AN "EMINENT DIVINE," EARLY 1800s

Early one morning in 1975, a young graduate student named Keith Hearne hovered anxiously over his EEG machine. On the other side of his laboratory wall, Hearne's research subject had just entered a morning period of dream sleep. He studied the EEG tracing intently. Hearne had arranged a series of eye movements for the subject to perform if he became lucid during a dream; these eye movements would be visible on the EEG tracing. The graduate student was attempting to prove that it is possible for consciousness to enter the dreamscape. If successful, the experiment would rewrite entire chapters in psychology and psychiatry texts. Many people had talked about such experiences, but no one had ever proved it under laboratory conditions.

Suddenly Hearne's heartbeat quickened. A series of eye movements was signaled on the graph, followed by another series. Hearne recognized the patterns, and in a flash realized that his patience and hard work had finally paid off. On the morning of April 12, 1975, at Hull University in England, Michael "Keith" Hearne became the first person in the world to receive a message from a lucid dreamer documented by an EEG to be in unambiguous dream sleep.

Hearne describes his work as follows:

My thoughts turned to the question of whether a suitable channel of communication could be established between a lucid dreamer and the outside world, so permitting the dream to be studied "from within" for the first time. A method using ocular signalling, which circumvented the general bodily atonia of REM sleep, was found to work beautifully.[17]

Five years later and a third of the way around the world, another young graduate student was wrestling with the same

[17]M. Keith Hearne, "Lucidity Letter," Vol. 1, No. 3, 1982, 3.

problem. At California's Stanford University, Stephen P. LaBerge wanted to demonstrate empirically the presence of consciousness during dream sleep. One morning at Stanford's Sleep Research Center, LaBerge arrived at nearly the same solution as Hearne had five years before him. Using a Morse code consisting of fist clenches and eye movements—again to circumvent the muscular atonia of dream sleep—LaBerge recorded himself spelling out his name while he was recorded by an EEG as being in dream sleep. LaBerge became the second individual in history to empirically demonstrate the presence of consciousness in the dreamscape.

A COOL RECEPTION

In the world of dream research, Stephen LaBerge's name is almost a household word today. Since his first clinical demonstration of consciousness in the dreamscape, no one has worked harder, and with more patience, to put lucid dream experience on the psychological "map," proving it to be a valid, even frequent phenomenon among the general population. Paradoxically, however, LaBerge's discovery—and its enormous implications with regard to access to the unconscious mind—was not warmly embraced by the established psychological community. To be sure, lucid dreaming was an intriguing proposition. The ability to enter the mysterious dreamscape equipped with one's consciousness was any psychologist's "dream." Still, there were many questions surrounding the experience.

As a rule, dreams are *un*conscious experiences. Therefore, the notion that a person could be conscious during a dream, be it a lucid dream or any other, seemed flawed from the start. Historically, sleep and *un*consciousness had been perceived as inseparable. After all, sleep is the benchmark by which we define the experience of unconsciousness. Sleep *is* our unconsciousness; it is the opposite of waking, it is the existential no-man's-land, it is the mistress of death. Western science—out of habit if nothing else—invariably sought other explanations for reports of lucid dream experiences. Typically scientists questioned the credibility of such reports—after all, how much credence could be lent to stories by dreamers in dream states? And who were these people who claimed to be conscious while dreaming? Were they unstable? Were they religious?[18]

Then there was the intriguing question of whether the dreamers really were lucid or whether they merely dreamed that they were lucid—the old dream-within-a-dream theory. On the other hand, if these individuals actually were conscious, then were they conscious during what is known as unambiguous (unequivocal) dream sleep, or merely during hypnagogic experience, those dreamlike sleep onset and offset experiences? Perhaps more than anything, though, the mainstream scientists needed more proof—more empirical demonstration of consciousness in the dreamscape.

Dream study has always been criticized for its flawed scientific methodology, concerned as it is with an experience that is, by nature, subjective. Indeed, this is a fact of dream experience. Dreams *are* completely private experiences, and there is no way to circumnavigate this feature. As a result, the field is criticized because its raw data are irreplicable—that is, it is impossible for anyone else to directly experience, examine, and evaluate a subject's dream. By extension, then, all dream reports given by subjects are necessarily of questionable validity. Specifically, who really knows what went on in a dream? There is no way to externally corroborate the interior experience of a dream, and

---

[18]Frequently they were religious. Saint Augustine stands on record as one of the first to give a detailed account of a lucid dream, and it is a mystical experience that he describes. Similarly, the Buddhist *Tibetan Book of the Dead* is a virtual guidebook to lucid dreaming. The Christian Gnostic gospels are also on this terrain.

until some high-technology device comes along that will allow us to videotape our dreams, the field of dream study remains helpless before this obstacle. And while the EEG has helped to make the study of dreams more credible, the instrument can still yield only surface and exterior characteristics of the dream phenomenon. An EEG can tell us whether or not a person is dreaming, and it can tell us when and for how long a person dreamed. But for the real, inner experience we seek, we must rely on the subjective reports of dreamers.

Now add to this initial distance from the data the enormous difficulties that people characteristically have in recalling their dreams, and a researcher is faced with an equally troubling set of questions. What do dreamers remember and what do they forget? What do they invent and what do they confuse with other memories and experiences in their lives? Do dreamers modify their accounts to please themselves or the researcher? Do they leave out certain parts that they are embarrassed about? Do they fill in gaps in dream plot lines with new parts, so that the dream has better continuity and makes more sense?

These are reasonable questions to ask of any dream report. For example, ask yourself the following questions: When you relate a dream to a friend or acquaintance, do you routinely tell them *all* of your dream? Do you tell your friends your most personal dreams, or your most embarrassing ones? I, for one, do not. Indeed, when I tell a dream to a friend, I routinely edit the dream to exclude parts I would rather the other person not know, and I do so without hesitation. While I consider myself a relatively open person, it is also my opinion that there is material in dreams that is nobody else's business.

In the same vein, have you ever wondered about a dream all day, only to suddenly recall an entirely different aspect of the dream? Or as you record a dream in your journal, have you ever

begun to recall more of it as you write? These are common experiences. Our memory for dreams is poor generally, and even
when it improves so that we feel we can remember a dream
quite well, it remains elusive. Bearing this in mind, then, we are
advised to be cautious of the fullness and validity of people's
dream reports, even under the best conditions.

There are still other methodological questions involved with
dream reports. For instance, most reports collected for scientific
analysis are recorded as words on paper, so that a blind reviewer
may look at them objectively. But how well do words describe a
dream experience, which involves all of the senses, plus emotions, intuitions, and thought processes? Is the report prepared
by a trained introspectionist? If so, by whom, and what might
have gotten lost in the translation? Ultimately, who is best qualified to report on dream experience? Given the obstacles we
have just described, we may have the most confidence in our
own dream reports. But if scientists prepare their own dream reports, they irreparably bias the validity of their sample group.

Taken together, these are all reasons why the study of dreams
is such a difficult scientific endeavor. Compared to the empirical
sciences, with their numbers, equations, and ability to replicate
experiments and quantify variables, the study of dreams is a
methodological nightmare (pardon the pun). In light of these
concerns, we can see why an empirical demonstration of consciousness during dream sleep would prove so valuable for the
field.

Curiously, it was LaBerge's, not Hearne's, work that alerted
psychologists to the compatibility of consciousness with the
dreamscape. For unexplained reasons, Hearne did not make his
work public. LaBerge, on the other hand, immediately sought to
publish his findings in physiology journals—only to find that,
even with empirical data, it was difficult to get people to accept

the idea. After awhile, however, the scientific community slowly
began to grasp the significance of the work. Today the ability to
possess consciousness during dream sleep is recognized as a valid
ability of the human mind. Indeed, it is not possible now to discuss the topic of dreams without considering the psychological
significance of lucid dreaming.

As the psychology community reoriented itself to the new
findings, new categories of speculation opened, to be addressed
seriously by research psychologists. As the initial research was
replicated in sleep labs around the world—most notably by
LaBerge, who continues his work to this day, and by West Ger-
man researcher Peter K. Tholey—reports in historical literature
regarding consciousness during dreaming were validated. Aristotle had written about lucid dream experiences, as did Saint
Augustine, Freud, and countless others. Now lucid dreaming
had been clinically demonstrated as well.

Lucid dreaming, or lucidity, as it came to be called, was a
newborn child on the horizon of research into the conscious-
unconscious interface. Many in the scientific community began
to speculate as to its significance. Lucidity was intriguing precisely because it broke down the barrier that had seemed to
exist for so long between two discrete states of mind, of waking
and dreaming. There now were so many questions to ask and
answers to be found.

For instance, if an individual can consciously interact with
his or her unconscious mind, as represented in the creation of
the dream, is this a new level of communication between the
two elements of the mind? If the ability can be harnessed, can it
be a tool for increased awareness and understanding of the unconscious mind and of dreams? Will consciousness, in turn,
learn more about itself? Can lucidity harmonize relations between the ego and the unconscious? Are there hazards to be

avoided? Is it advisable to open up—to conscious interference—
what up to now was an unconscious process? How broadly dis-
tributed a phenomenon is lucid dreaming in the general
population? Can lucid dreaming be learned or taught? Who are
these lucid dreamers, and what have they discovered?

LUCIDITY AND THE MEDIA

While lucid dreaming was virtually unknown and given little
scientific or lay attention prior to 1968, since that time there has
been a steadily increasing stream of information on the subject.
Lucid dreaming has been the topic of television documentaries,
the subject of the 1984 feature film *Dreamscape*, and the subject
of numerous stories in leading news and scientific magazines. In
the past ten years alone, several books have been published on
the subject.

Although most of this coverage has been accurate, the mass
media commonly present one aspect of lucid dreaming inaccu-
rately. Frequently the ability to lucid dream is referred to as a
gift. This implies that only certain people can perform this feat
of consciousness. There is no evidence to support this claim. Indeed, nearly all research has shown precisely the opposite, that
lucid dreaming is a learned progression. The occasion of the
spontaneous, regular lucid dreamer is far and away the exception. Use of the word *gift* may be incidental, it may be poetic, or
it may be purposeful—to mystify dream experience yet again.
However, this error does a great disservice to honest discussions
of the nature of lucid, and by association other, dream experiences.

Dream experience is already overburdened with mystical associations and unrigorous investigations. There is no need to at-
tach yet another misleading appellation to the promising arena

of lucid dreaming. Dreaming isn't mysterious; it is a regular neurobiological function in our mind and body that makes sensorially manifest the structure of the unconscious mind. In the same light, the ability to dream lucidly is not a gift but a simple function of consciousness.

7

Myths and Truths
About Dreams

Empirical research into sleep and dreaming has rapidly invalidated many old "pop" theories that enjoyed debate for so long among dream enthusiasts. Recently even a few of Freud's theories have taken some hard hits. Before looking at what is now known to be true of dreams, let's review some common misperceptions.

DREAMS ARE ONLY IN BLACK AND WHITE

In the 1950s in Europe and the United States, it suddenly became popular to debate whether people dreamed in color or only in black and white.[19] Some contended that we dream in black and white but *remember* our dreams in color—that is, we "paint them in" afterward. What is interesting about this debate is not the question itself but rather the time that the question came to be asked. The debate was popular in the late 1950s. Prior to this time, however, in all of the literature that exists that pertains to dreams, the question of color *never* came up. Freud

---

[19] That this question could even arise and interest dream scientists is testimony to how poor human memory for dreams truly is.

did not raise it, nor did Jung or any other psychoanalyst of the early twentieth century.

If you had never seen a black-and-white world, it would be hard to imagine one—wouldn't it? The cause for this debate appears to be the widespread diffusion of black-and-white television in the United States and Europe in the 1950s! It is true that people *can* dream in black and white; for that matter, there is no reason to discredit anyone's claim to occasionally dream in black and white—or purple, or Technicolor, or Day-Glo. Much as our brains effortlessly re-create our outside world with all of its vivid colors, so too can they re-create the black-and-white world we see in films, on television, and in photographs. No one hears much about the black-and-white theory today. Most people have color TV sets. Now the only time we might dream in black and white is after spending long weekends watching old movies on cable.

DREAMS ARE ACCELERATED TIME EXPERIENCES

Another pop theory is that time in dreams is somehow different from time during wakefulness. It was once popular to argue that dreams that seemed to have endured great lengths of time—ten or twenty minutes, or even all night—actually transpired in only a few seconds. This misconception is older than the one about black-and-white dreams. In the 1800s there were many anecdotes about people who dozed off for the briefest moment—at a symphony, during a conversation, or even while riding a horse—only to find upon awakening that they could recall a long and elaborate dream. When the dreamer awoke, the orchestra still was playing the same piece, the friend was finishing his sentence, or the rider was still atop her mount. Freud legitimized this theory of accelerated dream experience, and the idea still endures today.

In *The Interpretation of Dreams*, Freud recounts the famous "guillotine dream" of a Frenchman named Maury. As the story goes, Maury was awakened when a bed railing fell onto the back of his neck. When he awoke, he recalled a long and particularly disturbing dream in which he was led around "Guillotine Square" during the Reign of Terror. As Freud describes it,

> After witnessing a number of frightful scenes of murder, he was finally himself brought before the revolutionary tribunal. There he saw Robespierre, Marat, Fouquier-Tinville and the rest of the grim heros of those terrible days. He was questioned by them, and, after a number of incidents which were not retained in his memory, was condemned, and led to the place of execution surrounded by an immense mob. He climbed onto the scaffold and was bound to the plank by the executioner. It was tipped up. The blade of the guillotine fell. He felt his head being separated from his body, woke up to extreme anxiety—and found that the top of the bed had fallen down and had struck his cervical vertebrae just in the way in which the blade of the guillotine would actually have struck them.[20]

What a way to start the day! Nevertheless, while Maury's dream appears to be simply the incorporation of an external stimulus—that is, when the railing struck his neck, he answered the question posed by the stimulus by dreaming he was being guillotined—it was quite lengthy and full of detail, all very

[20]Sigmund Freud, *The Interpretation of Dreams* (New York: Avon Books, 1965), 60.

neatly *leading up* to the guillotine. How could Maury have known in advance that the railing was going to fall?

As Freud saw it, there were two possible explanations. First, it was probable that in recalling his dream, Maury committed an error of memory. Freud theorized that the true order of the dream was the railing falling, which caused Maury to dream about being guillotined, and then the events that led up to the guillotine. All of this, posited Freud, was easily managed by the dream's incorporative tendencies, with which we are familiar.

Continuing along this line of reasoning, however, the question of time in dreams now became an issue. Freud took into account that probably only a few moments had transpired between Maury's being struck by the railing and his subsequent waking. Could Maury have dreamed such an elaborate dream in only a second or two? In the dream he was led around Guillotine Square, the crowd taunted him, he saw the famous nobility of the time, and he was questioned by the revolutionary tribunal. He was led to the chopping block, he was strapped to the plank by the executioner, and his head was lowered. By all accounts, Maury experienced a lengthy and "complete" dream. If Maury's account was true, then Freud deduced that the entire dream had to have transpired in only a few seconds. From this deduction, Freud seriously entertained the possibility that dreams (if this dream, then why not all dreams?) might be accelerated experiences in sleep.

Freud said that there could be another explanation. During the brief period between Maury's being struck by the railing and his subsequent waking, instead of dreaming at superspeed, Maury might have merely recalled an old fantasy from years before. Freud speculated that, probably in conjunction with his reading about the Reign of Terror, Maury had possibly imagined this elaborate (and even romantic?) fantasy of himself being executed. Maury fantasized what he later reexperienced as a dream!

Imagine it for yourself. You are a young college student, reading about the French Revolution. As you learn about the Reign of Terror, with its noble and stoic bravery in the face of death, your mind wanders idly into fantasy. You imagine yourself before the revolutionary tribunal, where you are accused of crimes you did not commit. You are condemned to die, yet as you are led to the block, surrounded by great figures of the time, you maintain your dignity. Before a mob clamoring for your death, you retain your grace, wit, and humor. As you prepare to place your head on the chopping block—a block already smeared with the blood of the other nobles—you see a young maiden out of the corner of your eye. She is marveling at your bravery. You stand and, in one final gesture, your eyes meet and you bow before her.

Freud said Maury would not need to "re-dream" his fantasy. Rather, the "ready-made" fantasy need only be recalled by the associated stimulus of the bed railing. The fantasy could be reexperienced very quickly; it did not have to unfold in dream time.

The discovery that all people dream about one hundred minutes a night certainly put the damper on the accelerated time theory. There was no longer a need to compress dream experience—which by its nature is condensed already. We now know that dreams unfold in real time. In experiments performed with lucid dreamers attached to EEG machines, the dreamers count to ten or twenty, using eye movements and/or fist clenches to demarcate the intervals of time. In such experiments, dream time has been found to be congruent with real time.

TIME AND TIME AGAIN . . .

One of the ways time *is* different in dreams is that events occur faster and transitions between events are abrupt or lacking. In many ways dreams are like films. There may be long, complicated story lines, but we don't have to wait on the laws of real time for the events to unfold. In fact, if there is a single physical law that is broken most consistently in dreams, it is the law of time. Dreams consistently collage our diverse memories and experiences. They move abruptly from one scene to the next, often without logical connection. In this sense, dreams violate the continuity of time, but they seem to obey our sense of time within episodes.

"I HAD A DREAM"

Another misconception refuted by laboratory research and by lucid experience with dreams is the notion that dreams are self-contained "units." For example, when we talk about dreams we typically say "I had the strangest dream last night," or "You wouldn't believe the dreams I've been having." We imply that dreams exist as isolated events, with a beginning, middle, and end. But clinical studies have shown that no matter when we are awakened during dream sleep, we always tend to report dreaming. That is, no particular part of dream sleep is more heavily associated with dreaming, although studies show higher incidences of dreaming when subjects are awakened during bursts of rapid eye movement. But while eye movement is associated with particularly intense dreaming, dreaming takes place throughout dream sleep. Thus, dreams do not begin and end like a series of short plays at a drama festival. When they are able to maintain consciousness for extended periods during dream sleep, lucid dreamers uniformly report that dreaming occupies *all* of their time in dream sleep. So the familiar concept of a dream, with its implied beginning, middle, and end, is an arbitrary distinction made on the behalf of the dreamer. In all probability, a "dream" actually refers only to that portion of dream sleep that a dreamer is able to remember.

SEX IN THE DREAMSCAPE

When lucid dreamers become aware they are dreaming, their orientation to the dreamscape naturally changes. Usually, whatever tension or immediacy which was present in the dream dissipates, and lucid dreamers are able to relax in the knowledge that the experience, after all, is only a dream. In this state of relaxed awareness, a playful curiosity inevitably develops. Lucid dreamers compare dream objects against waking experience. They strike up conversations with dream characters to see how these characters of their own creation will respond. Lucid dreamers fly and explore their dreamscapes. They pray, meditate, and ask for spiritual guidance with problems in their lives. Camouflaged representations are asked to identify themselves. Lucid dreamers also try to share dreams, to "leave their bodies" and enter into the world of astral projection. And, of course, lucid dreamers explore fantasies in their dreams.

GREAT SEX

It probably comes as little surprise to learn that many people, upon becoming lucid in a dream, seize the opportunity to act out sexual fantasies. (Freud is smiling in his grave.) But for many people, lucid dreaming represents an unique opportunity to act out, and to fulfill, some heartfelt sexual desires. In the dreamscape, we can be as uninhibited as we dare in our sexual explorations. We can have sex with abandon and without con-

sequences. The dreamscape is a place where we can all attempt
to consummate some of our most private sexual fantasies.

The fact that dream sex is widely reported to be *great* sex—
that is, that the experience of orgasm in dreams is widely reported to be especially intense—adds an intriguing dimension
to lucid dream sex. The ability for people to achieve powerful
orgasms in dreams probably is due, at least in part, to the fact
that our bodies during dream sleep are profoundly relaxed—far
more relaxed than during any "quiet" or resting awake time.
Psychologically, one must also consider this: Is there anything in
life more private than a dream? The truth of dream experience
is that we can do whatever we want in our dreams, and no one
excepting ourselves will ever be the wiser. This freedom from
inhibition coupled with the relaxation of the body most likely
explains the powerful orgasms of dream sex adventures.

SEX IN THE DREAM LAB

Men and women both become sexually aroused during dreams.
As a rule, men develop erections during each of their dream
sleep periods; women respond similarly, as the vagina becomes
flush with increased blood flow and the clitoris becomes "erect."
Arousal of genitalia is a regular feature of dream sleep. Each
night we all cycle through periods of arousal and relaxation, coincident with these periods.

Does this mean, as Freud suggested, that our dreams really
are about sex, whether or not we want to admit it to ourselves?
Do we all dream about sex every night, even if it is in highly
camouflaged form, and do our bodies belie this truth? Interestingly, in tests performed in sleep labs where men and women are
awakened during periods of sexual dream activity (measured
with tumescence gauges and other devices for monitoring response), erotic dream imagery is not often associated with peri-

ods of arousal. That is, when aroused men and women are awakened and asked to report on the content of their dreams, their reports typically do not reflect direct sexual activity. A man with an erection who is awakened might just as well report dreaming of being stuck in traffic as reporting some sexy dream scenario. The same holds for women. Thus, evidence shows that there is not a strong correlation between these periods of arousal and our attending dream images. Rather, what is suggested is that these periods of arousal operate at a quieter level in our bodies and may be more of a physiological function, rather than reflecting, or having much influence upon, our psychological state.

This finding, however, should not be interpreted to read that no correlation exists between our minds and bodies during sleep. As we know from personal experience, if we experience an overtly sexual dream we often awaken to find that we also were physically aroused. In the same way, when we are lucid in a dream and then direct the dream toward sexual activity and to climax, we learn that our bodies respond accordingly. And while it is reported that people can "dream" of orgasm without physically experiencing it (particularly in men, who can dream of orgasm without experiencing ejaculation), one must observe that as often as not, men do ejaculate in response to their perceived dream experiences. This is the proverbial "wet dream," common to both men and women alike.

When men experience difficulty maintaining an erection or achieving climax in their waking lives, they often are sent to sleep labs to help determine the nature of their difficulties. For a doctor, knowledge of whether a patient is able to achieve an erection during dream sleep allows the doctor to determine whether his patient's impotence is physically or psychologically induced. If the test, called a nocturnal penile tumescence study, shows he is able to achieve an erection during dream sleep, then the difficulty with achieving erection in waking is diagnosed as being related to psychological factors inhibiting arousal—for example, estranged relations with his partner, sexual boredom, or fear of performance. If a man does not become erect during dream sleep, then he is ruled to be physically impotent; that is, there is a problem with the plumbing, as it were, and not with the head. Given this information, a physician can decide whether to concentrate on the physical or psychological factors contributing to the patient's difficulties.

Throughout medical history, far more attention has been focused on male impotence than on female impotence. Because the female orgasm is not necessary for reproduction and, no doubt, because research has been influenced by the traditional male bias of the medical profession, an environment of vague ignorance persists regarding the question of female orgasm. Current research informs us that roughly 10 percent of the female population is *anorgasmic*—that is, physically unable to achieve orgasm. Of the other ninety percent who are able to achieve orgasm, however, only fifty percent report that they regularly do. What accounts for this discrepancy?

It seems that one may, with caution, relate to women the same findings made with regard to men and impotency. For example, if a woman found she was able to achieve orgasm in her dreams, then this should reassure her that her ability to achieve orgasm physically is intact. If she nevertheless does not experience orgasm in her waking sexual life, this evidence suggests that perhaps she needs to reexamine the psychological conditions of her waking sexual relationships. Is the excitement gone between her and her lover? Is her lover clumsy, insensitive, uninterested in her orgasm? Is she able to relax enough to allow herself to orgasm? Does she have preconceptions about a woman's role in sex that prevent her from asserting and enjoying herself? Is sex associated with a negative experience from her past that causes her to become tense, uneasy, or afraid? Can she orgasm when she masturbates, but not with partners? These are sensitive questions for anyone, but they need to be asked when someone is experiencing difficulty with his or her sexual satisfaction.

SEX AND FREUD

A nascent lucid dreamer's early fascination with sex in the dreamscape is a familiar stage of development through which many lucid dreamers pass. And while we may feel in a certain sense that this early preoccupation with sex is only natural—that is, maybe we would expect that this is what people, especially younger people, would do in their fantasies—it once struck me how uncannily this fascination with sex in the dreamscape does coincide with one of Freud's theories.

A fundamental psychodynamic principle of Freud's is that our sexual drive, encompassed within the "id" in our psyches, is pervasive. Indeed, one of the things people have found so objectionable in Freud over the years is his contention that the overwhelming majority of behavior is sexually motivated. To a certain extent, Freud said that people, under the surface pretense of "nice," "conventional," and "civilized" behavior, actually are wild animals in heat *at all times,* and that but for the "civilizing" influence of society, we would act upon these sexual drives. One of Freud's basic premises is that the primitive and basic urges existing in the human animal are repressed, and it is precisely this repression that allows us to maintain a functioning society. Thus we don't all run around raping, pillaging, and living like brutes; we don't sleep with family members, we don't kill competitors for mates, we have sex only upon consent, and so on. In society, these deeper drives and urges, while still present within us, are constrained. But the price we pay for all this repression is that, to varying degrees, we all are *extremely* sexually frustrated. And Freud attributed many of the imbalances and neuroses that he saw in everyday life directly to this frustration of basic drives in the psyche.

If we look again at people's fantasies in the dreamscape, it is interesting to note that for many, the first thing they seek to do upon gaining consciousness in this fantasy world is to engage in sex. As soon as the "apparent" rules are lifted in the dream-scape—as soon as the dreamer ceases to mistake the dream for reality and realizes he doesn't have to obey any "rules" any-more—it is amazing how quickly he begins to behave just as Freud theorized. I regularly speak with people about their lucid dreaming experiences and am always amused at how readily lucid dreamers will admit to performing all sorts of acts in the dreamscape that society would condone as extremely morally reprehensible. Women speak of wanton lust, of trying to achieve orgasm with anyone or anything they can find. Men freely speak of "grabbing the first woman I see," with no care whatsoever expressed for their dream partner's consent. The sexual drive is so great and the sexual frustration so high that dreamers experience no hesitation in dropping all their inhibitions and pretenses to "decency" or "civilization." When a dreamer knows she is dreaming, she knows there are no real repercussions to her acts. She knows she will not be caught and punished, and she knows that no one else will ever know of this behavior. And in this type of environment, just as Freud said, some pretty basic drives take over the human animal. *Interesting . . .*

THE TRUE NATURE OF DREAMS

Dreams are not as bizarre and other-worldly as some pop theorists have led us to believe. They actually are a lot like waking experience. The first time we are lucid in a dream for any length of time, we can determine the nature of dreams for ourselves. Lucid experience allows us to see that we do dream in color, that our sense of time is the same as it is in waking hours, and that dreams continue for as long as we are able to stay conscious within them, or until we awaken ourselves from dream sleep.

With greater dream experiences, however, come new and more challenging questions. Indeed, experience with lucid dreams quickly raises a new category of questions about dreams, questions that make the above "surface characteristic" debates— of color, time, and length of dreams—seem almost trivial by comparison. In particular, lucid dream experience challenges a habit of our familiar self-identification process. But this, I venture, we will find to be a positive experience.

THE CONSTRUCTION OF THE DREAMSCAPE

A primary characteristic of all dreams is that they are sensory environments created by our mind. And in these sensory environments, we find ourselves engaged to some extent. Our dreams embrace characteristics of our external world yet also embody characteristics distinct to dream experience. That is, our dreams contain the subtle detail, sophisticated associations, and metamorphoses common to dream experience, while breaking an assortment of natural laws.

Before investigating the dreamlike characteristics of dreams, however, consider for a moment the ability of dreams to faithfully re-create our everyday environment. All too often we focus on the fantastic or bizarre elements of dreams and overlook the fact that even our most ordinary dreams are extraordinarily good re-creations of our waking world.

Artists in the Night

All dream researchers have observed that in dreams we are *hypermnesic*—that is, we possess a memory that is vastly superior to our waking memory. Thus, in dreams we frequently encounter people and objects presented in sharp detail that we have seen only casually while awake. We find that incidents from childhood or other past experiences suddenly emerge, often powerfully. Indeed, the entire construction and content of dreams defy the ability of our waking powers.

Lucid dreamers regularly express amazement at the apparent reality of their dreamscapes. The very real nature of a dream frequently makes it difficult to identify a dream as a dream. The re-creation of the external world, with its three-dimensional space, its physical appearance, and its friendly faces, is so extraordinary, so complete and detailed, that we often misidentify the dreamscape, even when we suspect we are dreaming.

Dreams are not rough outlines and vague visual impressions. Nor are they mainly visual and auditory constructions, as many dream researchers have suggested. Rather, dreams are completely "drawn in"—they are fully constructed sensory environments. While they may be subject to peculiar exaggerations and distortions, our dream images are created with more detail than one could ever hope for in our waking imagination. Thus we encounter dreamscapes whose construction is so perfect and complete that we are hard-pressed to claim that we created them. Yet we all possess this extraordinary ability. You need only look to your dreams tonight to see that this is true. We are all accomplished artists in the night.

But wait! We have only begun to explore our abilities in the dreamscape. For example, how many dreams can you recall in which you were only an observer? Not many, I venture. This is because it is the nature of dreams that while we are observers, we also are actors. We *participate* in our dreams. Because of the interactive nature of dream experience, possessing consciousness in a dream causes us to interact with the dream in new and otherwise impossible ways. Instead of reacting automatically to what happens, we can *choose* how to respond. Our dreams also respond to our choices within them, and entire dreams are changed as a result.

But let us address this experience with a bit of intellectual hardness. With what, or with whom, are we interacting in our dreams? Granted, a dream is a hallucination, but it is a hallucination on a grand order. Intelligence, wit, perception, sentience, keen observational skills, incredible memory, a towering talent for metaphor and symbolism, an awesome facility for creation and synthesis—these qualities and many, many more are effortlessly displayed in our dreams. Dreams speak an uncanny yet beautiful, uniquely personal language. Our dreams are fabulous creations, often displaying a sophisticated sense of humor. We interact with our dreams through voice, thought, emotion, and action. But from where does this fantastic ability arise? Who, or what, creates our dreams?

PLEASED TO MEET ME: THE EGO MAKES THE ACQUAINTANCE OF THE UNCONSCIOUS MIND

Typically there are five stages of awareness through which a nascent lucid dreamer progresses. These stages of development revolve around the increasing awareness we gain of the presence of unconscious processes within us. These five stages are outlined on the following pages.

1. We Become Aware of the Unconscious Mind

The memory problems associated with ordinary dream experience can prevent us from ever knowing much about dreams. Indeed, our dream life can be relatively nonexistent unless we develop it.

Perhaps better than any other experience, lucid dreaming illustrates the fundamental dichotomy of human experience—that we possess both conscious and unconscious abilities. Nowhere is the unconscious mind more powerfully tangible than during a lucid dream, where the creations of the unconscious are dramatically represented for us to touch and feel, to spend time with, to interact with, to engage in dialogue, and, as our memory for the experience is restored, to reflect on. Lucid dreams bring home the verite of the unconscious mind like no other experience.

Recognizing that there are unconscious processes is a large first step for most of us. People are inherently resistant to attributing processes of the mind to anything other than ordinary awareness. Lucid dream experience, however, illuminates the conscious and unconscious elements of the mind. This fabulous display liberates us from a fundamental ignorance of our own nature. It is the first psychological significance of lucid dreaming.

2. We Become Familiar with Our Unconscious Mind

Because consciousness gives us the ability to purposively interact with our dreams, we can perform tests and make detailed observations of our dreams. This type of hands-on experience, when contrasted with ordinary dream recall processes, gives us a fantastic introduction to the nature and validity of the unconscious mechanism within us.

As our famliarity with dream experience improves, we will gradually learn the language of dreams and be able to begin using this psychological fluency in our everyday lives. The artistry and subtlety of dreams, the hypermnesic aspect of dreams, the insights that dreams afford into our experiences and relationships—as they are rearranged, put into dreamspeak, and projected back toward us in the dreamscape—these are abilities that our dreams regularly and effortlessly perform. When we discover that dreams exhibit coherence, reflect strong perceptive abilities, access a wealth of memories, and revolve around themes central to our well-being, then dreams become illuminated as powerful tools for self-understanding that we can use to assist our evaluations of, and decisions in, waking experience. Dreams, especially lucid dreams, enable us to have increasing access to the abilities of our unconscious mind.

3. We Recognize the Unconscious as a Partner in the Self

One of the wonders of lucid dream experience is to be aware, during a dream, that you are creating the dream with which you are interacting. Lucid dreamers quickly find themselves asking, "How can that be me over there, creating this dream, when this is me over here, doing my best to respond to it?"

It's a good question.

In ordinary dreams, we do not recognize the internally generated sensory environment as being self-created. Our mind is fooled, and we interact with our dreams as if we were interacting with the familiar outside world. But in lucid dreams, we are aware that despite all of the apparent separateness, the dream is self-created. After all, a dream *is* but a dream. Who else could be responsible for creating it? And while we typically possess very little control over the construction of our dreams, and while we may, especially in nightmares, feel decidedly alienated from our dreamscapes, ultimately we must take responsibility for their creation. Herein lies the essential challenge of lucid dream experience. We are challenged to overcome the error that identification only with the ego represents. While we may not feel at home here yet, we are both our conscious and unconscious elements. We—in the fullest sense of the word—are on *both* sides of the dreamscape. Self-identification only with the conscious is an error—a familiar error, even a natural error, but an error nevertheless.

Lucid dreaming is an incomparable demonstration that we are broader beings than we ordinarily know—we are dualistic beings. In this stage, ordinary awareness—the ego—joins the unconscious as an equal partner. The self, as we now understand, is composed not only of ordinary awareness but also of the unconscious mind.

4. We Accept the Relationship Between the Ego and the Unconscious

One of the more confusing experiences encountered by nascent lucid dreamers in their progressions with lucidity is the discovery that they do not possess as much control over their dreams as they might like. Initially lucid dreaming holds out to dreamers the prospect of being in an ultimate sort of fantasyland, a place where conscious dreamers, because they are aware that they are *only* dreaming, are able to act out all of their conscious fantasies. Much of the literature about lucid dreaming caters directly to this desire. "Control your dreams," books promote. "Realize all your fantasies."

Experience with lucid dreams, however, does not heed such a simple agenda. Lucid dreamers consistently find that attempts to manipulate dreams according to conscious whim frequently meet with unanticipated resistance, or with some turn of events over which consciousness has no control. The point is that consciousness in no way dominates the dreamscape. It is able to influence the course of events, but consciousness quickly learns that it is in relation with another force.

In the reorganization of self-understanding that lucid dreaming encourages, ordinary awareness and the unconscious are seen as partners in the construction of the whole being. Each is different and has its own properties and qualities, yet each is an indispensable element of the whole.

To find within ourselves such a powerful display of our unconscious mind, and thus of our duality, is potentially destabilizing. Carl Jung once wrote, observing the reaction of the ego to its discovery of the unconscious mind, that "it seems a positive menace to the ego that its monarchy can be doubted." Dreams serve only to heighten an individual's awareness of the unconscious mind. Nevertheless, there is no need for terror or fear. The main concern is that we not deny the validity of the unconscious mind once we have become aware of it. Denial is a familiar defense, against which the unconscious will only press more determinedly for recognition. The key to unity is to learn to assist these two elements to work in concert. We must achieve a resolve within ourself not to engage in the psychologically unsound habit of repression. We must will to unify ourselves.

5. We Learn the Mechanism of Consciousness in Ourselves

In the final stage, we learn to distinguish among the plethora of definitions of *consciousness* that compete in the world of ideas and choose those that coincide with our personal and experiential understanding of consciousness. Because it is the only doorway through which we can enter the dreamscape, lucid dreamers must become fluent with the mechanism of con-

sciousness within themselves. Thus, we learn to distinguish between reactivity and consciousness, between internal dialogue
and consciousness, between being self-referented and being
conscious, between ego and consciousness, and between being
awake and being conscious. We learn that consciousness is not
merely being awake, but rather it is the ability of the mind to actively experience its experience of itself. In this new understanding of consciousness, the true sense is liberated from the
tangle of other definitions and we are able to achieve far greater
control over, and thus enjoy more, the benefits of this remarkable ability. We learn that we are dualistic beings, and we learn
that we are either conscious, or we are not.

8

Techniques for Awakening Consciousness in the Dreamscape

I came to think that to be conscious during a dream, I first had to be conscious during the day. Now that sounds silly! We're all conscious during the day, aren't we? No! Most of us are not. Most of the day, we're always involved in something, doing this or that, then still something else; we're just as busy as in our dreams. Never do we stop to think: I am here, now. I'm perfectly conscious that I exist. I hear this noise, now. I see this thing, or these things, now. I smell whatever, now. I know who I am, where I am, what I'm doing and why, where I live, and all my memory is available to me, now. . . . Either we do things without being really conscious of doing them, either we're so focused on our own thoughts, that we are no more aware of what is around us.

Anyway, what I did was write a big "C" for "conscious" on my left hand to remind me as many times as possible to be conscious during the day. I'd see it every time I looked at my watch, and many other times too. After one week of this training, I had my first lucid dream, and ever since then I never went under an average of one lucid dream per week!

—OLIVER CLERC,
IN THE *LUCIDITY LETTER*

When consciousness dawns on us in a dream, it is as if we *materialize* in the dreamscape. One moment we didn't exist, the next we do. The transition is dramatic. The experience is very much like the *Star Trek* depiction of people who "beam" through space and who suddenly arrive on new and distant planets. The difference is that when we gain consciousness in a dream, we *emerge* into the sensory environment of the dreamscape. Prior to gaining consciousness, it is as if we did not exist in the dream at all, at least not in any present-tense sense of the word. But once we are conscious, suddenly we can *see* where we are—we are able to see our seeing, hear our hearing, touch our touching, and feel our feeling. With consciousness we can *be* where we are. Consciousness is the doorway through which we enter the dreamscape.

If we wish to awaken our consciousness during dream sleep, we first must learn to awaken our consciousness while we are *awake*. Then we can teach ourselves how to bring consciousness into the dreamscape. The entire process is at once this simple— and this difficult.

CONSCIOUSNESS IN WAKING EXPERIENCE

Consciousness, as we have explored, is a phenomenon of the mind that most people associate with being awake. Indeed, most of us assume that when we are awake, we are conscious. After all, what else could we be? It extends from this observation that most people also assume that consciousness is a *continuous* characteristic of waking experience—that when we fall asleep, we lose consciousness, but when we awaken from sleep, we regain our consciousness and are conscious again all day long. This seems obvious, but is it true?

If we keep in mind that *consciousness* refers specifically to our ability for reflectivity, then we need to reevaluate our assessment of consciousness in waking experience. For example, in many ways, thought itself is continuous. When we are awake, we always seem to be occupied with thinking about something. We think of one thing, then another; we think back to an experience we had, then our attention is summoned by a task in front of us, and so on. But these thoughts do not in themselves constitute consciousness.

Consciousness is our ability to observe our thought—to keep track of it, to watch its course of associations, and to see all of the ideas that either complement or compete with the primary thought. When we are conscious during these meanderings of our mind, we are aware of our thought experience as it occurs. Remember, the "as it occurs" part of this definition is vital; consciousness is a *now* experience. It is not looking back on a train of thought that we had a moment or two ago.

But consider ordinary waking thought and behavior. We do many things, think many thoughts, and perform many behaviors without making an effort to observe or experience the process. The truth is that we spend far less time actively reflecting on our experience than we might believe. Only occasionally do we watch and experience our experience of sensations as they occur. If we pursue this observation, we soon find that the periods of consciousness in our waking hours are the *exception*, not the rule! Much of the time that we are awake might be better described merely as periods of experiencing thought or, more dramatically, having a thought happen to us. This implies a passivity in our orientation to experience, and this implication is fully intended.

The primary reason consciousness is misidentified in waking experience, again, is because of the voluntary stream of thought. This continuous thinking, our attention focused on the road in front of us, on the lighter, on the speedometer, on the rear-view mirror, on that conversation last night with a friend—this inner progression of thought, which dominates so much of waking experience, has its own momentum. Much of the time, we do not watch or monitor this stream of thought.

For example, have you ever been driving a car and suddenly realized you can't recall the past five or ten minutes? It is a peculiar, but common, experience. What happens to us during these periods? Does our mind go completely blank? Clearly not, for the car remains on the road and we are still driving. What does happen is that for an extended period of time, we lose—and this is what causes the event to be significant to us—our reflective stream of thought. Our mind was "drifting," and we were being carried in the stream of voluntary thought. And we still were able to perform some very complex behavior. We handled a one-and-a-half-ton vehicle at speeds of up to sixty miles per hour and maybe even changed lanes and passed other cars, all without reflecting on our experience at all. Pretty neat trick!

Or did you ever find yourself thinking about something unusual—some event long in your past—without recalling what prompted your thinking about it? The peculiar nature of the thought draws our attention to it. At this point we may be surprised and wonder how we got to thinking about it. If we are able to remember, we can trace our thoughts back to the original thought. But notice that, often as not, we are unable to recall what ticked off the association. If we can step back from ourselves, we can see that our minds were drifting and we weren't necessarily watching what was going on. We were being carried along in a stream of voluntary thought. Notice also the characteristic lack of memory for these types of occurrences. Failure of recall for unobserved experience is extremely common; as a rule, we possess poor memory for unconsciously experienced sensations.

In his investigation into the nature of consciousness, researcher Julian Jaynes writes that it is natural to perceive consciousness as a defining characteristic of waking experience. Historically, consciousness always has been confused with myriad other activities and abilities of the mind.

We feel it [consciousness] is the most self-evident thing imaginable. We feel it is the defining attribute of all our waking states, our moods and affections, our memories, our thoughts, attentions, and volitions. We feel comfortably certain that consciousness is the basis of concepts, of learning and reasoning, of thought and judgement, and that it is so because it records and stores our experiences as they happen, allowing us to introspect on them and learn from them at will. We are also quite conscious that all this wonderful set of operations and contents that we call consciousness is located somewhere in the head.

On critical examination, all these statements are false. They are the costume that consciousness has been masquerading in for centuries.[21]

Jaynes is not the only one to have arrived at this evaluation of the nonrole of consciousness in waking experience. Oliver Clerc, whose letter to the American dream journal *Lucidity Letter* is excerpted at the head of this chapter, made similar observations about consciousness in waking hours. Clerc was successful in inducing consciousness in his dreams because of his daytime efforts at greater consciousness. To bring consciousness into the dreamscape, we first must be able to identify consciousness in waking experience. Then we must learn how to cultivate and sustain these periods of consciousness. Finally, as we become facile with our consciousness, we can learn how to bring it into our dreams.

The distinction between wakefulness and consciousness has seldom been drawn by philosophers throughout history; fewer still have explored the significance of such a distinction. Philoso-

---

[21]Julian Jaynes, *The Origin of Consciousness in the Breakdown of the Bicameral Mind* (Boston: Houghton Mifflin Company), 1976, 21.

pher Peter Ouspensky, however, who spent most of his formative years under the tutelage of another great Russian philosopher, G. I. Gurdjieff, wrote extensively about the need to develop consciousness in waking life.[22] In an occasionally brilliant book, *In Search of the Miraculous*, Ouspensky writes,

> By observing in yourself the appearance and the disappearance of consciousness you will inevitably see one fact which you neither see nor acknowledge now, and that is that moments of consciousness are very short and are separated by long intervals of completely unconscious, mechanical working of the machine. You will then see that you can think, feel, act, speak, work, without being conscious of it. And if you learn to see in yourselves the moments of consciousness and the long periods of mechanicalness, you will as infallibly see in other people when they are conscious of what they are doing and when they are not. Your principal mistake consists in thinking that you always have consciousness.[23]

Once again, our attention is brought back to the misidentification of consciousness in waking experience. Consciousness is *not* the same thing as wakefulness. Remember, all members of the animal kingdom routinely alternate between waking and sleeping states, but for this we do not assign the ability for consciousness to these creatures. Consciousness is different.

---

[22]Ouspensky spent fourteen years studying with Gurdjieff, and one of Ouspensky's major achievements during this period was to record Gurdjieff's philosophical beliefs, many of which were based on observations of the role of consciousness—and its absence—in human affairs.

[23]Peter Ouspensky, *In Search of the Miraculous* (New York: Harcourt Brace, 1965).

One reason why consciousness is difficult to identify in waking experience is because it is, in a word, subtle. Consciousness flickers in and out of our waking experience. We become conscious briefly as something demands our attention, but then just as quickly our consciousness disappears. This alternation between consciousness and single-mindedness is one of the great illusions of life. Because we more readily possess the ability for consciousness when we are awake, we are misled into believing we are always conscious when awake.

Ouspensky was told to actively practice *self-remembering*. Self-remembering, as he describes it, was his attempt to improve the frequency and duration of periods of consciousness within himself, thus improving the general consistency of his consciousness. Ouspensky's description of self-remembering parallels our definition of consciousness: It is our ability for reflection and duality, our ability to do two things at the same time.

Ouspensky's self-remembering process was as follows:

I am speaking of the division of attention which is the characteristic feature of self-remembering. I represented it to myself in the following way:

When I observe something, my attention is directed towards what I observe—a line with one arrowhead:

"I" ─────────────────➤ the observed phenomenon.

When at the same time, I try to remember myself, my attention is directed towards the object observed and towards myself. A second arrowhead appears on the line:

"I" ◀─────────────────➤ the observed phenomenon.

Having defined this I saw that the problem consisted

in directing attention on oneself without weakening or obliterating the attention directed on something else. Moreover this "something else" could as well be within me as outside me.[24]

Ouspensky might just as well have written in his first sentence, "I am speaking of the duality of attention which is the characteristic feature of self-remembering." He continues his observations with an amusing anecdote describing his first attempts at self-remembering, of learning how to "divide his attention." Maintaining consciousness—maintaining the division of our attention for extended periods of time, even during waking experience—can be difficult. If we practice this focus, we immediately see what a unique state consciousness really is. Ouspensky says:

The very first attempts showed me how difficult it was. Attempts at self-remembering failed to give any results except to show me that in actual fact we never remember ourselves.

I was once walking along the Liteiny towards the Nevsky, and in spite of all my efforts I was unable to keep my attention on self-remembering. The noise, movement, everything distracted me. Every minute I lost the thread of attention, found it again, and then lost it again. At last I felt a kind of ridiculous irritation with myself and I turned into the street on the left having firmly decided to keep my attention on the fact that I would remember myself at least for some time, at any

[24]Ibid., 119.

rate until I reached the following street. I reached the Nadejdinskaya without losing the thread of attention except, perhaps, for short moments. Then I again turned towards the Nevsky realizing that, in quiet streets, it was easier for me not to lose the line of thought and wishing therefore to test myself in more noisy streets. I reached the Nevsky still remembering myself, and was already beginning to experience the strange emotional state of inner peace and confidence which comes after great efforts of this kind. Just round the corner on the Nevsky was a tobacconist's shop where they made my cigarettes. Still remembering myself I thought I would call there and order some cigarettes.

Two hours later I *woke up* in the Tavricheskaya, that is, far away. I was going by *izvostchik* to the printers. The sensation of awakening was extraordinarily vivid. I can almost say that I *came to*. I remembered everything at once. How I had been walking along the Nadejdinskaya, how I had been remembering myself, how I had thought about cigarettes, and how at this thought I seemed all at once to fall and disappear into a deep sleep.

At the same time, while immersed in this sleep, I had continued to perform consistent and expedient actions. I left the tobacconist, called at my flat in the Liteiny, telephoned to the printers. I wrote two letters. Then again I went out of the house. I walked on the left side of the Nevsky up to the Gostinoy Dvor intending to go to the Offitzerskaya. Then I had changed my mind as it was getting late. I had taken an *izvostchik* and was driving to the Kavalergardskaya to my printers. And on the way while driving along the Tavricheskaya I began to feel a strange uneasiness, as though I had forgotten something.—*And suddenly I remembered that I had forgotten to remember myself.*[25]

Ouspensky's remarks as to being in a state of deep sleep echo what Allan Rechtschaffen would describe as single-minded. It is the alternation between single-mindedness and duality that Ouspensky describes.

If it is still difficult to grasp this idea of unconsciousness, perhaps the expression "space out" will bring the experience closer to home. People "space out" all the time, having fantasies and meandering in streams of voluntary thought. Single-minded thought does not mean we are unable to do things or that we become paralyzed; to the contrary, we are capable of performing extremely complex tasks when single-minded. But we are reacting and interacting with our environment without observing our experience—as Ouspensky would say, performing our thoughts and behaviors "automatically" and "mechanically."

Rechtschaffen acknowledges that rarely in waking experience do we enjoy the sustained periods of single-mindedness that we do in dreams:

> Although the data indicate a massive failure of reflective awareness during dreaming, the distinction from waking mentation is certainly not absolute. Fragmentary dream-like experiences which lack reflective awareness do occur during wakefulness, although at a substantially lower rate than during nocturnal dreaming. . . . Not only is the incidence of nonreflectiveness much lower during wakefulness than during nocturnal dreaming, but the Foulkes and Fleisher report also indicates that waking nonreflectiveness tends to be momentary and interspersed with reflective evaluation. The very extended

[25]Ibid., 118, 120–121.

periods of nonreflectiveness which characterize most dreaming is rarely achieved during wakefulness.[26]

The clinicians agree with the philosophers. The study that Rechtschaffen refers to is the 1975 Foulkes and Fleisher report "Mental Activity in Relaxed Wakefulness."[27] The researchers found that 15 percent of their subjects reporting spontaneous mentation during waking fit the category of being nonreflective, in that (1) they were not controlling their thoughts, (2) they had lost awareness that they were in the laboratory, and (3) their mentation was hallucinatory. These subjects were lost in thought or fantasy, and their imaginations were accompanied to some extent by visualization. An additional 22 percent of subjects were found to be nonreflective because they (1) were not controlling their thoughts and (2) had lost awareness of being in the lab, but these subjects did not report their mentation as hallucinatory. This adds up to an astonishing 37 percent of subjects whose mentation during waking was found to be nonreflective, or single-minded. In assessing the presence or absence of consciousness in waking experience, we are reminded of Ouspensky's words: "Your principal mistake consists in thinking that you always have consciousness."

To improve our ability with consciousness, we first must be able to identify the alternations between single-mindedness and consciousness that occur so regularly in our minds. To gain entry to the dreamscape, we must discriminate between these two subtle yet profoundly different types of cognitive orientation to our environment—the unobserving, reactive stance of nonreflectiveness and the self-observing, dualistic approach of consciousness. Only then can we unlock the door to conscious-

[26]Allan Rechtschaffen, "The Single-Mindedness and Isolation of Dreams," *Sleep* Vol. 1, No. 1, 1978, 98–99.
[27]D. Foulkes and S. Fleisher, "Mental Activity in Relaxed Wakefulness," *Journal of Abnormal Psychology* 84 (1975), 66–75.

ness in our dreams. Only then can we stabilize the duality in our-selves and allow this candle in our mind to illuminate our lives.

RECOGNIZING THE DREAMSCAPE

Step One: Know Your Sleep Cycles

One of the first observations we can make about human sleep is that it is *regular*. When we fall asleep, we transit the same stages of sleep over and over. First we fall into deep sleep, then we rise into light sleep, then we move into a period of dreaming. At the completion of ninety minutes, the cycle repeats. This is the fundamental structure of all human sleep. The quiet stages of synchronized sleep are followed by the active stage of dream sleep. As mentioned earlier in this book, an easy way to become more aware of your nightly sleep cycles is to count the number of cycles you sleep each night.[28] Look at your clock before you go to sleep at night, and when you awaken during the middle of the night or in the morning, check the clock again to see how long you have slept. For example, if you go to bed at 11:00 P.M. and wake at 5:00 A.M., then you have slept for six hours, or four ninety-minute cycles.[29]

---

[28]This is useful not only to get in touch with our biorhythm but also to figure how much sleep we should allow ourselves when we are short on time. Depending on how much reserve we have, sometimes only a few cycles of sleep can carry us through some very long days. But remember, drawing on your sleep reserve is like drawing money out of the bank: Eventually you must pay it back. The best way to pay back sleep deprivation is to get some sleep. If you deprive yourself of sleep for too long, you run your body down and soon will feel cold and tired and be susceptible to illness. Getting sick is a time-honored method our body employs to make us slow down.

[29]If that is enough sleep for you, then in addition to being an early riser, you also are a short sleeper—you manage well on forty to forty-five hours of sleep per week. If, on the other hand, you wake at 5:00 A.M. and can't wait to roll over, you are more like everyone else—you need fifty to sixty hours of sleep per week. At the far end of the spectrum, if you think at the end of seven and a half hours of sleep that it would be time well spent to pack in another cycle or two, then you are a long sleeper, one who enjoys sixty to seventy hours of sleep a week.

The second observation to make about sleep is that just be-fore we awaken, we all enjoy long stretches of time dreaming.[30] During the night, the amount of time dreaming grows progres-sively longer with each cycle. By morning we are spending up-ward of thirty to forty minutes dreaming within each cycle. These are the long, consistent periods of dream sleep that you want to target for lucidity.

As you become more aware of your sleep cycles, and as you learn when your dreams come during the night, you can pre-pare mentally and physically for those times. When you awaken early in the morning, before you roll over and close your eyes for another cycle, be confident that your dreams are on their way. In the early morning hours, you stand on the brink of thirty- to forty-minute blocks of nonstop dreamscape action. The trick, of course, is to recognize the dreamscape.

Step Two: Remember Your Dreams

To recognize our dreams, we must be acquainted with dream experience itself. To do this we must assist our memory for dreams.

We have discussed at length the failings of human memory for dreams. Conservative estimates for retention of dream expe-riences run to 10 percent. A fairer, more accurate figure is prob-ably closer to 1 percent. Do we comprehend the implications of these figures? Do we realize how removed from our dream life we truly are? Think of how underdeveloped our dream life is!

---

[30]Dream sleep is linked to the circadian rhythm of our body's temperature cycle. As ex-plored in chapter five, we dream most when the core body temperature is at its lowest. In fact, the propensity for dream sleep is so strong at the nadir of the temperature cycle—at about 4:30 A.M.—that synchronized sleep, which we have said as a rule always precedes dream sleep, can be displaced. We can have "sleep-onset" dream periods at this point in the circadian temperature cycle. This is a useful physiological characteristic to know, especially if you wish to bring consciousness directly into dream sleep from wak-ing. We will talk more about these and other curiosities of sleep physiology shortly.

On good mornings, most of us can probably recall about a minute or two of our most recent dream. These are fairly long, "healthy" recalls, as far as memory goes, and they would fill a good page or so of paper if we were to write them down. In well-recalled dreams there are plot development and theme, changes of events, different characters. There is metamorphosis and there are scene shifts. If we recall a dream well, we notice the details—the colors, the sizes and shapes of rooms, the scenery outdoors. We recall specific conversations, what people were wearing, and how it felt to be walking around in the dreamscape. These are well-recalled dreams.

But consider our more typical recall. Most often, especially if we do not write a dream down, all we retain are fragments—small snippets and elusive visual snapshots. We say things like, "I was with some friends of mine, and we were at an amusement park, and one of the rides was broken, but I don't remember much else." And have you ever tried relating your dreams to a friend? Often it ends up a little embarrassing because the friend doesn't find your dream as interesting as you do, largely because you aren't able to describe it very well. You wind up saying, "You and I were at the bowling alley, and Billy was there, and there was something about one of the waitresses, and then, I don't know, suddenly we were at your grandmother's house, and we were inside, and I had mud on my feet and I was worried about tracking it through the house." If we do not work to develop our memory for dreams, our dream life is about as good as having no dream life at all.

A common characteristic of dream experience that regularly dupes us into believing we possess greater command of our dream life than we do is that upon awakening, we are frequently able to recall our last dream quite well. At this point we still have pretty good access to the dream. We give it a review, ponder the events momentarily, and then turn our attention to the tasks of the day. Though we don't know it at the time, we have just crossed the point of no return. We may *think* we will recall that dream later, but we're wrong. We will be left scratching our head, wondering "just what it was" we dreamed last night. Or we'll begin telling someone else about this really interesting dream, and it will be nothing more than a string of dull fragments and discontinuities.

To develop your memory for dreams, learn to write them down. This means devoting five to ten minutes at the start of your morning to recording your dreams. Consider this habit a practical aspect of improving your dream life; however, be forewarned that this practical aspect is often the single most difficult hurdle to surmount. When you awaken in the morning, you need to be able to calmly, actively, and receptively peruse your mind for the fragments and memories that are still lingering with you. The process of dream recall demands your undivided attention. You need quiet; you cannot be distracted—no television, no radio, no small talk about the day.[31]

Recording dreams is the *only* way to learn more about your dreams. The process of writing makes you organize your thoughts, helps you focus on the events in the dream, and clarifies the sequence of events. As you write, you will recall more details. Writing improves your recall of dreams, even of dreams you think you remember fully. Associations pop into your mind as you write, and these associations are significant clues to the connection of events. They will help you identify how your mind associates some of the more confusing aspects of the dream.

---

[31] If you're a college student and there is no one to disturb your sleep in the morning, it should be relatively easy to perform this exercise. If you are working, you may have some problems of adjustment. Also, if you're married or living with someone, try to get your mate involved. You must find the time to attend to your dream life. It's not a strenuous effort; it's really more of an organizational skill.

Writing is also the only way to retain the depth and richness of recall that you possess when you first awaken. Once you put a dream on paper, you can later, at your leisure, reflect on its meaning. Also, if you awaken in the middle of the night and do not write down the dream, it is almost guaranteed lost. By keeping a dream journal, you will later be able to review dreams that you otherwise would have forgotten. Without a hard copy, the overwhelming majority of our dreams are lost forever.

Think of the times you have awakened from a dream in the early morning hours and thought, "Well, that dream didn't make any sense; it was about driving the kids to school back in my hometown, and I didn't even have kids then. It couldn't have been very important." Having made such an assessment, you decide not to write down the dream. Remember that when you awaken, you are not in the best condition to appraise the relative merits of your dreams, especially very early in the morning. More often than not, dream interpretation requires focused attention and good recall. It also requires a sensitivity to nuance and detail that eludes most people at 4:00 A.M. Often the real significance of a dream will not strike you until you review it much later, when your mind is fully awake. But if you have not written it down, you'll have little or nothing to review.

While reaching for pen and paper can be wearisome or loathsome so quickly upon awakening, I guarantee that you will be pleasantly surprised at what you learn about your dreams. You will educate yourself not only about dreams but also about yourself, about how your mind works. And when you become familiar with this elemental component of your physiology, you enhance the prospect of recognizing the dreamscape.

As a final suggestion, when writing down a dream, record but keep separate the thoughts you are having as you record the dream, such as the symbolism of the dream, which objects or characters have particularly strong associations, what events from your past the dream causes you to recall. Jot these side notes quickly in the margin and concentrate intently on the dream itself. What were your thoughts during the dream? What was the sequence of events? Who said what when? Transcribe the original as fully and as objectively as possible. Then review the dream report and ponder its different aspects, starting a new entry with your comments or continuing to write in the margins. You want to get the first recall on paper before it vanishes.

I am amazed at the resistance so many people show toward recording their dreams. I have heard every excuse: "I can remember my dreams; I always have been able to." "I only record prophetic dreams." "I had a dream, and I was going to write it down, but it wasn't significant. I can tell the difference between them." "I wanted to write it down, but I didn't want to wake myself up to do it."

It is true that awakening from sleep to record a dream can wake us up too much, so that we feel unable to return to sleep. The activity of writing down the dream can leave us wide awake in the middle of the night. In the end, when and how we choose to record our dreams is a personal decision. Nevertheless, there is no hope of learning anything about your dreams unless you *write them down*!

Step Three: Recognize Incongruity in Dream Experience

Dreams generally are incongruous experiences when compared with our everyday lives. This is why, upon awakening in the morning, we often are baffled at the events that transpired in the night. As a rule, dreams speak a peculiar, often wildly constructed language. Nevertheless, despite the clues that regularly appear, identifying our dreams remains a challenging task.

As discussed in chapter five, the primary reason we experience difficulty identifying our dreams is because our ability for consciousness is biologically impaired during dream experience. Now I wish to draw attention to yet another reason why identifying dreams can be difficult.

If we reflect on our experience with dreams, we see that most often we do not notice incongruity. That is, we tend to navigate the paradox and incongruity of dreams as if the entire experience, with all of its convoluted symbolism and breaches of familiar laws, makes sense. Because we relate to our dreams at this unconscious level, where the content of dreams seems to be experienced for its unconscious values, it is difficult for us to see incongruity in the experience.

Dreams routinely take liberties with the laws of time and space. Even mundane dreams—those of swimming in the ocean or of driving the children to school—regularly violate continuity. For example, it would not be uncommon to be at a beach resort you visited as a child at one moment and the next moment be back in your current home after having given a large party, with no connection or bridge between the two scenes. Dreams, at least manifestly, pay no heed to continuity, both temporal and physical.

When I say a dream "manifestly" pays no heed to continuity, there is the implication that the events actually do possess a connection, but that the connection is not visible, or manifest, immediately. In essence this is Freud's theory that dreams, while appearing to be jumbled nonsense from divergent times and places in our life, actually are coherent, if only we could understand the connections. Indeed, a fundamental thesis of psychoanalysis is that dreams, despite their appearance, are coherent, that they speak to us, and that what they have to say is worth listening to.

In psychoanalysis, this is the difference between the latent and the manifest content of dreams. The *manifest content* is the surface story told by the dream. The *latent content* is the message that lies beneath—the true meaning of the dream. It is, perhaps, this dichotomous nature of dreams that explains why we consistently overlook such seemingly flagrant violations of continuity and of temporal and physical laws. It may very well be that while we are interacting with a dream, the dream makes sense in a symbolic and temporally and physically liberated way. This is another reason why recognizing incongruity in dream experience can be such a tricky endeavor.

For example, let us say that you frequently dream of driving various different automobiles, or autmobiles that you once owned but no longer possess. Perhaps because in your waking life you drive only one automobile, you feel that driving a strange automobile is a good clue with which to associate dreaming. So you work to create the association in your mind that if you are driving a car in a dream other than the one you own, then you must be dreaming. The problem, however, is that if you are reexperiencing some earlier stage of psychic development, which somehow is associated with that older automobile, then it is going to make perfect sense, in the dream, to be back behind the wheel of that older car. Conversely, if you are contemplating a change or a decision in your life, you may find that in your dreams you have just purchased a new car or you are taking a car for a test drive.

The point is that these symbols, from an unconscious perspective, may make a great deal of sense. Thus, we seem to understand the logic in the jump from being at a childhood beach house to being back in our present residence after having given a large party, and we similarly understand the more comprehensive incongruities of dream experience, like driving cars we don't own or haven't driven in years.

As you chronicle your dreams, you will discover many dream experiences you can use to help you recognize a dream while it occurs. For example, the common experience of fly-ing—dreams in which you flap your "wings"—is a good clue with which to associate the awareness of dreaming. Clues like this are violations of physical law, such as possible only in dreams. Ultimately you wish to associate flying with dreaming; then, next time you find yourself soaring, you will wonder what it was you were supposed to remember about flying. If you are lucky, you will recall that flying implies dreaming, and with a flash of recognition, the adventure of lucidity will begin.

Other clues frequently involve the body in some way. For example, people often recognize they are dreaming when they realize they can see clearly in their dreams without wearing their eyeglasses. People who have quit smoking cigarettes, simi-larly, often startle themselves when they find themselves puffing away in a dream. "What am I doing with this cigarette?" the dreamer asks herself. If she is clever, she may figure out the an-swer. The same holds true for dreamers on diets, dreamers "on the wagon," and dreamers who have extricated themselves from certain relationships.

Of course, negative dream experiences can also be associated with the thought that one must be dreaming. If we are experi-encing recurrent nightmares or negative experiences in dreams that focus on or revolve around a particular theme—always being attacked or always being chased through a dark forest, for example—then we can work to create the association that the only time we encounter this persecution is when we are dream-ing. If we concentrate on creating this association in our mind, then chances are the next time the antagonistic dream scenario unfolds, we will wonder whether this isn't vaguely familiar and will ask ourselves if we are dreaming.

Whatever you choose as a clue to identify your dreams, the association *will* carry over to your dreams. As you keep a dream journal and familiarize yourself with the content of your dreams, you can experiment with clues. Before long, next time you take off in flight or are pursued by some familiar tormentor, there is an exceptionally good chance that you will have the associated thought, "Oh! I must be dreaming." And with this awareness, you will have successfully identified the dreamscape.

Step Four: Scary Dreams

The association between stressful or frightening dreams and lucidity is longstanding. Many dreamers have taught themselves to be lucid as a direct result of negative experiences with nightmares. Nightmares, as we all know from personal experience, range from dreams involving persecution, where we dream we are being attacked or pursued by some person or thing who wishes to do us harm, to full-blown horrifying experiences, where we not only see, but feel and hear terrors we would not wish to view at a horror film. While nightmares most commonly afflict young children, they are by no means restricted to them.

One aspect of nightmares not often considered is that people's *days* are also affected by these dreams. Nightmares can be deeply disturbing, often in ways the dreamer does not understand. A dreamer may be left wondering why, when his daily life seems normal and well composed, his nightlife is subject to such dark dreams.

In a selection from literature that pertains to lucid dreaming, philosopher Thomas Reid describes the circumstances that caused him to teach himself to be lucid. As a youth, Reid frequently experienced nightmares. The nightly ritual began to haunt him, until the budding philosopher began to wonder

> if it weren't worth trying . . . to recollect that it was all a
> dream and that I was in no real danger. I often went to
> sleep with my mind as strongly impressed as I could

with this thought, that I never in my lifetime was in any real danger, and that every fright I had was in a dream. After many fruitless endeavors to recollect this when the danger appeared, I effected it at last, and have often, when I was sliding over a precipice into the abyss, recollected that it was all a dream, and boldly jumped down. The effect of this commonly was that I immediately awoke. But I awoke calm and intrepid, which I thought a great acquisition.[32]

After awhile, Reid was no longer bothered by his dreams, which suggests that the fear embodied in them was overcome by his lucidity. This indeed is a hallmark of nightmare experiences: When dreamers are able to summon the courage to defeat their persecutors, their nightmares end.

Other lucid dreamers have experienced similar progressions of events. Another dreamer, also bothered by nightmares, gives the following account in the *Lucidity Letter*, a dream journal:

I started to lucid dream in my teens. I had reoccurring nightmares since my childhood and by my early teens I had learned to wake myself. I soon then learned that I didn't have to wake myself but rather could alter my dreams so as to have a pleasant outcome.

With practice I soon became totally aware that I was dreaming and yet conscious. I exercised this control carefully at first since I found if I "pushed" the dream I would awaken. With practice, however, I learned to "push" the dream further and further without waking up.[33]

---

[32]Thomas Reid, in Frederick Seafield, *The Literature and Curiosities of Dreams*, Vol. 2 (London: Chapman and Hall, 1865), 194.
[33]A. Mitrevics, *Lucidity Letter*, Vol. 2, No. 3, 1983: 4.

Frightening or threatening dream experiences are familiar ways in which lucidity enters the dreamscape. We encounter something frightening or stressful in a dream, and this shakes us into a suddenly observant frame of mind. With our attention on the alarming circumstance or event, we correctly perceive that we must be dreaming. Unfortunately, upon making this recognition, people sometimes dismiss the validity of the aggression or conflict and seek to escape the situation.

When we are lucid in our dreams, we can fly away from troublesome scenes, or we can choose to ignore the conflict and concentrate on realizing our fantasies. This type of response is OK—whatever we choose to do in the dreamscape is entirely our own business—but in doing so, we turn our dream toward fantasy and the persecutor disappears, wiping out any potential for insight into the conflict. Dreams, especially those that involve conflict, are significant. While we may not recognize the design, these disturbing people or situations almost surely represent tensions and fears of which we may or may not be aware in our waking life. In this light, these dream experiences are opportunities to learn about unconscious concerns, so that we may address them in our everyday life. Dreams often illuminate our fears and imbalanced relationships; they routinely represent feelings and awarenesses we have failed, for whatever reasons, to perceive consciously. They should be recognized as *allies* to our awareness. Conflict in our dreams is one arena in particular that we should not be averse to exploring. When we do experience conflict, our first concern should be to understand why it is there. Indeed, if we hone our dream responses so that we pay attention to disturbing experiences, then we will quickly address—and get past—whatever conflict is there.

Step Five: Curiosity Leads to Lucid Dreaming

The occasion of lucidity is not limited to incongruous or disturbing material. It is evident from many lucid dreamers' experience that only casual interest in dreams can be sufficient to induce subsequent lucidity. The following three accounts, one from a dreamer who heard about lucid dreaming from an unidentified source, another from one of the more famous lucid dreamers in history, the Marquis d'Hervey de Saint Denys, and the third from Nobel Prize–winning physicist Richard Feynmann, illustrate how the ability for lucid dreaming grew from simple curiosity.

The first, a casual lucid dreamer named Edith Gilmore, reports:

> Some years ago I had my first lucid dream after having learned that such a phenomenon does exist. I have since then recorded such dreams. . . . Like others, I find the experience positive, with a sense of joyous altered state of consciousness during the dream. I customarily awake with a cheerful "afterglow" which carries through the day. And, like others, I do carry out "experiments" in the dream, though I am usually too happy and fascinated to be systematic.[34]

By contrast, notice how the marquis' intense concentration on his dreams while he was *awake* helped him identify his dreams. The marquis was an avid chronicler and drawer of his dreams.

> These activities [the chronicling of dreams] became part of the store of memories of waking life on which my

---

[34]Edith Gilmore, *Lucidity Letter*, Vol. 3, No. 1, 2

mind drew during sleep. Thus one night I dreamt that I was writing up my dreams, some of which were particularly unusual. On waking, I thought what a great pity it was that I had not been aware of this exceptional opportunity while still asleep. What a golden opportunity lost! I would have been able to note so many interesting details. I was obsessed with this idea for several days, and the mere fact that I kept thinking about it during the day soon resulted in my having the same dream again. There was one modification, however: this time the original ideas summoned up by the association the idea that I was dreaming, and I became perfectly aware of this fact. I was able to concentrate particularly on the details of the dream that interested me, so as to fix them in my mind all the more clearly on waking.[35]

In a final example, Richard Feynmann, in his best-selling book *Surely You're Joking, Mr. Feynmann*, describes how he accidentally taught himself to be lucid. As a student, Feynmann received the assignment of describing what happened to his thought processes when he fell asleep at night. His professor wanted to know if thought went slower and slower until it finally stopped, or if it went full speed and suddenly cut off. Feynmann was to observe his thought processes as he fell asleep. Ultimately his self-observation led him to be lucid in his dreams.

So every afternoon for the next four weeks I would work on my theme. I would pull down the shades in my room, turn off the lights, and go to sleep. And I'd watch what *happened*, when I went to sleep.

[35]Hervey de Saint Denys, *Dreams and How to Guide Them* (London: Duckworth, 1982), 44.

. . . I kept practicing this watching myself as I went to sleep. One night, while I was having a dream, I realized I was observing myself in the dream. I had gotten all the way down, into the sleep itself!

In the first part of the dream, I'm on top of a train and we're approaching a tunnel. I get scared, pull myself down, and we go into the tunnel—whoosh! I say to myself, "So you can get the feeling of fear, and you can hear the sound change when you go into the tunnel."

I also noticed I could see colors. Some people had said that you dream in black and white, but no, I was dreaming in color.

By this time I was inside one of the train cars, and I can feel the train lurching about. I say to myself, "So you can get kinesthetic feelings in a dream." I walk with some difficulty down to the end of the car, and I see a big window, like a store window. Behind it there are—not mannequins, but three live girls in bathing suits, and they look pretty good!

I continue walking into the next car, hanging on to the straps overhead as I go, when I say to myself, "Hey! It would be interesting to get excited—sexually—so I think I'll go back into the other car." I discovered that I could turn around, and walk back through the train—I could control the direction of my dream. I get back to the car with the special window, and I see three old guys playing violins—but they turned back into girls! So I could modify the direction of my dream, but not perfectly.

Well, I began to get excited, intellectually as well as sexually, saying things like, "Wow! It's working!" and I woke up.[36]

---

[36]Richard P. Feynmann, *Surely You're Joking, Mr. Feynmann* (Bantam Books: New York, 1986), 34.

One observation we can draw from these accounts is that these lucid dreamers, though motivated by different goals, taught themselves how to be lucid in their dreams simply by developing their reflective abilities, which is the development of consciousness itself. Whether it was an active effort like that of Reid or a casual effort like that of Gilmore, there was an attempt to be more discriminative, to watch for dreams, or, in Feynmann's case, to observe the experience.

Step Six: Physiological Tricks

Awakening and Returning to Sleep

Another technique for inducing lucidity is to awaken from sleep and then, after some time passes, return to sleep. How much time people let go by varies greatly. Some dreamers find it helpful to space as much as five or six hours between blocks of sleep, while others advocate only a fifteen-minute period. The latter is easier for most of us to fit into a normal schedule, of course, but if afternoon naps are possible, then long breaks can be employed.

During these periods between sleep cycles, it is important to do something that awakens you a bit. That is, just lying in bed for fifteen minutes is not recommended. Instead you should get up, feed the dog, or watch the sunrise. Enjoy the time by yourself, stretching and doing a little yoga, meditating, brushing your teeth, getting a bite to eat—anything you want so long as you clear your head a bit before going back to sleep.

The common element in technique is that it allows us, close to the event of dreaming, to awaken ourselves mentally. This facilitates our ability, when something in a dream strikes us as incongruous, to have the associated thought, "Hey! This must be that dream I'm expecting." The trick, of course, is to still be sleepy enough to go back to sleep for a few hours after you have awakened yourself sufficiently to be lucid in your next dream.

Remember, sleep cycles are ninety minutes long. Even in the early morning, a period of deep sleep will typically precede dream sleep. This means you need a full hour and a half for the entire dream cycle.

A variation on this technique was offered by a woman who discovered that making love early in the morning frequently induced lucid dreams. What a discovery, eh? It seems that this technique is particularly effective for inducing lucidity because it achieves the awake-asleep dichotomy. In the morning, making love will wake us up, but it can also make us sleepy afterward. It's certainly worth a try.

Using Advanced Technology

Recently devices have been invented to assist in all types of body alignment. A few devices are designed specifically to induce lucid dreams. New Age bookstores may have such items in stock that you can try out, or may be able to refer you to a mail-order catalog that carries these tools. One popular design is a pair of eyeshades worn during sleep to detect rapid eye movements. When dream sleep begins, the glasses blink a red diode. The flashing red light is incorporated into the dream, and the dreamer recognizes the light as the clue that he or she is dreaming, thereby gaining consciousness in the dream.

Other popular devices incorporate both sound and vision. About the size of portable cassette players, these devices come equipped with eyeglasses and headphones. A synchronized signal allows users to hear sound and see light at the same frequency. Through this dual-sense modality, these devices seek to entrain the synchronous firings of the neurons in the brain, or simply, to modify the brainwaves.

For example, as you read this book, your neurons are firing in a desynchronized rhythm. Nevertheless, the basic frequency is about 15 to 18 hertz, or cycles per second. When you get drowsy and fall asleep, the frequency slows. These are the stages of sleep. These devices are programmed (you can program the unit yourself, adjusting it to your individual pace) to flash the lights and pulse the tone of white noise at the same frequency associated with each stage of sleep. You put the headset on and lie down in a quiet room, and soon the light flashes and the white noise pulses slow. When I tried it, I could feel my body going into sleep, though I was conscious, watching the process. It is a fun unit. The only problem I could see was its price, which was prohibitive but which may come down in the future.

Taking Advantage of Dream Physiology

One of the more interesting characteristics of dream sleep is that our body has a memory for this sleep—that is, it knows when we've been getting dream sleep and knows when we've been missing it. We mentioned in chapter two that early experiments with dream sleep deprivation did not show psychological instability in the subjects; rather, researchers found it increasingly difficult, as the subjects went for longer and longer periods without dreaming, to keep their dream-deprived bodies from entering dream sleep. On the first night of a week-long test, only four or five awakenings were necessary to keep the subjects from dreaming. But by the sixth and seventh nights, the subjects had to be awakened an average of thirty-five times in a single night—or about once every fourteen minutes—to prevent them from slipping into dream sleep. This led to the discovery of what today is called *REM pressure*.

What intrigued these early scientists was that the body seemed to keep track of how much dream sleep it had missed— for several days, even. That is, not only would a dream-deprived body, once allowed to sleep, enter dense dream sleep and then dream profusely for one night, but it would continue for several nights to make up for lost dream sleep.[37] Even after we awaken, feeling like we have now had as much sleep as we needed, our body continues to make up for lost dream sleep. For a reason that no one understands, the body wants and gets a requisite quantity of dream sleep.

Keeping these characteristics in mind, then, REM pressure is a fun variable for those of us who wish to manipulate the dream sleep cycle. For example, if you experience an exceptionally busy week and average only five hours of sleep a night even though you are used to getting eight hours, you can know that on the weekend, when you can sleep a bit more, you will be dreaming an exceptional amount to compensate. This is a particularly good time to roll over and sleep an extra cycle, practicing your lucid dreaming—perhaps after making love, if possible. If the REM pressure is particularly high, your dream sleep periods will be long, intense, and deep.

Remember, when our bodies are tired and when we are deprived of dream sleep, it becomes more difficult to disturb or bump ourselves out of dream sleep when we are lucid. This means we can have long, very active lucid dreams. As they say in sleep labs, we will be "locked in" to the dream sleep period. This is when some of the best experiences with lucidity occur.

Another feature of REM pressure worth knowing about is that when it is sufficiently high, it can cause us to immediately fall into dreaming sleep. This is known as the displacement of quiet sleep. In chapter one we said that quiet, or synchronized, sleep always precedes dream sleep. The exception to this rule occurs under conditions of extreme sleep deprivation.

---

[37]Dream sleep density is measured in sleep labs by counting the frequency of eye movements in a dream sleep period. Periods of dreaming typically are marked by occasional bursts of eye movement, followed by periods of relative quiescence. Greater density dream sleep refers to sleep with lots of REM.

If we are sleep deprived and lie down during the day for a brief nap or to begin our sleep, we often have the experience of immediately entering dream sleep. If we are attentive, we can transit the first stage of drowsiness—stage 1 sleep—and then watch the light visual imagery of hypnagogic experience. If we can hold on to our consciousness, we soon will find that our light mental imagery has turned into a full sensory environment, and we will be conscious in the dreamscape.

STABILIZING CONSCIOUSNESS IN THE DREAMSCAPE

The Stages of Partial Lucidity

The active suppression of consciousness during dreaming explains the partial lucidity that frequently characterizes dream experience. Owing to the generally incongruous nature of dream experience, we have a sense of disbelief. We may suspect that we are dreaming but still be unable to achieve the realization, even though there are obvious clues. For example, dream researcher G. Scott Sparrow shows how this critical or reflective inertia can prevent a dreamer from recognizing a dream:

> I am with two friends outdoors, looking at the night sky. I notice that there seem to be two moons, each not full, but about one-half or three-fourths full. I decide I must be dreaming, but I think that it's too real to be a dream. I don't want to say anything about there being two moons because, if I am mistaken, it would be a laughable mistake.[38]

[38]G. Scott Sparrow, *Lucid Dreaming: Dawning of the Clear Light* (Virginia Beach, Va.: A.R.E. Press, 1974), 19.

Clues like seeing two moons in a night sky are critical. We *must* train ourselves to recognize them if we ever wish to be lucid. When we see two moons and think, "I must be dreaming," we must then leap to the realization that we *are* dreaming. But it's hard. Our ability for consciousness is impaired, and we are not yet operating at full mental capacity.

Another lucid dreamer, occultist Oliver Fox (the pen name of Englishman Hugh Calloway), also wrote about these prelucid stages. Notice that Fox, writing in 1897, chooses virtually the same words as Allan Rechtschaffen does nearly a hundred years later when describing the "completion" of consciousness during dream experience. (Rechtschaffen writes that "the reflective stream of consciousness is drastically attenuated" in dreams; Fox refers to this reflective stream as "the critical faculty.")

> In order to attain to the Dream of Knowledge we must arouse the critical faculty which seems to be to a great extent inoperative in dreams, and here, too, degrees of activity become manifest. Let us suppose, for example, that in my dream I am in a cafe. At a table near mine is a lady who would be very attractive—only, she has four eyes. Here are some illustrations of those degrees of activity of the critical faculty.
>
> (1) In the dream it is practically dormant, but on waking I have the feeling that there was something peculiar about this lady. Suddenly I get it—"Why, of course, she had four eyes!"
>
> (2) In the dream I exhibit mild surprise and say, "How curious, that girl has four eyes! It spoils her." But only in the same way I might remark, "What a pity she has broken her nose. I wonder how she did it."
>
> (3) The critical faculty is more awake and the four eyes are regarded as abnormal; but the phenomenon is

not fully appreciated. I exclaim, "Good Lord!" and then reassure myself by adding, "There must be a freak show or a circus in the town." Thus I hover on the brink of realization, but I do not quite get there.

(4) My critical faculty is now fully awake and refuses to be satisfied by this explanation. I continue my train of thought. "But there never was such a freak! An adult with four eyes—it's impossible. I am dreaming."[39]

In dreams, we continually exhibit faulty logic or are unable to think critically. In Fox's first three scenarios, we see the emergence of the reflective stream. Fox's credulity is taxed; he seeks an explanation for the observed anomaly. Yet he is unable to step back from his experience to identify his dream. What should be an obvious indicator remains unrecognized.

Unquestioning acceptance of dream events typifies ordinary experience with dreams. If you record your dreams tonight, you will make at least ten noncritical observations in any sustained nonlucid sequence. Yet even when you recognize something in a dream as impossible or anomalous with your waking life, you will often fail to make the connection that you must be dreaming. Thus, you "hover on the brink of realization."

Occasionally some event in a dream will tax our credulity to the extent that we question ourselves and try to "explain" the event. Yet even in these circumstances we can come away without identifying the dream. We arrive at some explanation that satisfied us in the dream, but when we awaken, it appears positively feeble. Sparrow's failure to identify his dream, even when there were two moons in the night sky, attests to this faulty logic.

---

[39]Oliver Fox, *Astral Projection* (New Hyde Park, N.Y.: University Books, 1962), 35–36.

False Awakenings

When dreamers become suspicious that they are dreaming, they usually perform various tests of the dreamscape. They look for violations of physical laws, such as gravity (dreamers sometimes leap into the air to see if they can fly or hover), or watch to see if objects or people metamorphose. If the tests are successful, they are satisfied that they are dreaming. These tests of the dream-scape, however, reveal two interesting characteristics of dream experience. The first is a state of mind so enfeebled that it cannot readily discriminate between dreams and reality. The second is the excellence of the re-creation, by the dreamscape, of our external environment.

When dreamers suspect that they are dreaming, they often conclude that they are awake owing simply to the "real" quality of the dreamscape. Because we perceive dreams through the same medium we perceive the outside world—our brain—our dreamscape appears phenomenally real. When we convince ourself that we are awake, we experience what is known as a *false awakening*. They are common. Sparrow's dream is an example of a false awakening. Although he had doubts, Sparrow convinced himself that he was awake.

False awakenings are peculiar experiences. I recall a particularly impressionable dream in which I was in the bathroom of my college dormitory. I was standing at the sink, running water over my hands, when for some reason I became suspicious that I was dreaming. I stopped and looked around me. My first thought was, "This can't be a dream. This is all too real." Besides, I thought as I further assessed the dreamscape, "Everything's in its place." The toilet was where it always was, at the far side of the bathroom, and two towels were folded and hanging on the rack to my left. The window at the end of the bathroom was open. Outside I could see it was a sunny day, with sunshine on the green grass. I dismissed the thought that I was dreaming and resumed washing my face, when all of a sudden that strange feeling came over me again. "What a ridiculous idea," I thought. But this time the suspicion made me uneasy.

It is a queer feeling to be unsure if you are awake or dreaming. I turned away from the sink and looked carefully around me again. "Everything is where it always is," I thought. I studied the counter. There were water glasses, toothbrushes, deodorant, curled tubes of toothpaste, and toilet kits. All of the colors, all of the dimensions were right. My gaze fell to the sink: The water was flowing. There was no way, I decided, that this could be a dream. I studied my reflection in the mirror; I looked as I always do. I could feel the floor with my feet. I was in the bathroom, and I was wide awake. Convinced that I was awake, I became alarmed for my mental health. I realized that I had just suspected I was dreaming, when actually I was wide awake. I wondered if I was going crazy, and I reproached myself to get a grip on myself. Then I woke up.

I learned from my experience how good the production of the dreamscape can be. When we are able to experience them consciously, our dreams will defy all previous expectations. Despite what we have been able to remember of dreams in the past, when we are conscious in a dream, the realism of the experience is simply amazing. I also learned not to be fooled by false awakenings—most of the time. When we become lucid in a dream, we should try to strengthen our sense of consciousness rather than become involved in tests of the dreamscape. The problem with testing the dreamscape is that we often prove ourselves wrong. That is, we try to put our hand through a wall, because if we are dreaming, we ought to be able to do that sort of thing, but lo and behold, in the dream we find the wall solid as a rock. So we decide we are *not* dreaming. Wrong!

Remember that when we are awake, we never seriously entertain doubts as to the validity of our sensory environment. Perhaps in philosophy or psychology or spirituality we might ponder these thoughts, but for the most part, when we are awake, we are confident that we are not dreaming. False awakenings are so common that, in defense, there ought to be a first law of lucid dream experience: If you ever become *suspicious* that you are dreaming, take it as a given that you *are* dreaming. This way, we save valuable time in the dreamscape and move past these false awakenings into conscious exploration of our dreams.

MAINTAINING CONSCIOUSNESS IN THE DREAMSCAPE

The first few times we gain consciousness in a dream, we usually can maintain it for only a brief period. This is because we either are so excited and surprised that we inadvertently startle our bodies and awaken ourselves physically, or else our consciousness is "swept away" by the current of events in the dream. Accordingly, upon successful identification of the dreamscape, we must take care not to awaken ourselves physically. At the same time, we must work to keep ourselves "awake" in the dream—we must maintain and stabilize our consciousness so that we do not lose it. This is the delicate balance of lucid dreaming. Beyond this primary goal, we must work to develop our consciousness while still in the dream. In essence, the lucid dreamer must strive to become a *sophisticated* lucid dreamer.

Consciousness is difficult to awaken during dream experience, and it also can be difficult to maintain. This is amply supported by well-documented reports from lucid dreamers. And occasionally we awaken from sleep able to recall having had a lucid dream for some time, but also realize that in the course of the dream, we lost consciousness—there was no continuity of consciousness from the dream to the subsequent awakening. In these cases, either we forgot to remind ourselves that we were dreaming or our attention was drawn to the activities in the dream and, at some crucial point, away from our experience of the dream.

I frequently am reminded of Peter Ouspensky, who says he found self-remembering to be characterized by a division of attention. A major part of self-remembering is to focus on two things at once: the dreamscape and ourselves—our experience of the dream and how it feels. We must actively self-inventory if we wish to maintain consciousness.

Writer Carlos Castenada has described how he learned to focus his attention on his hands as a way of stabilizing his consciousness. Scott Sparrow learned to meditate to stabilize his consciousness. Others have repeated verbal reminders, such as, "This is a dream. This is a dream. Everything I see is a dream." Everyone finds a technique that works for them. At this point, earlier explorations of the frequency or infrequency of consciousness in waking and any attempt to increase consciousness in waking experience prove valuable. Actually, we learn most about this by losing consciousness in a dream a few times. Next time, we work actively to keep that consciousness.

SOPHISTICATED LUCID DREAMERS

Our goal is to become a sophisticated lucid dreamer, but what does this mean? If people look back on their experiences with lucid dreaming, they find that even when able to maintain consciousness through lengthy dream sequences, often their awareness is not balanced or focused. That is, even when they are successfully able to maintain consciousness in a dream, they find that they viewed the dream very much as if it were real. When this happens, dreamers miss the opportunity to respond to their dreams as creatively as they can.

The following account of a lucid dream illustrates the relative change in orientation that often comes with lucidity. The dream is recounted by a Frenchman named Yves Delage.

> I am in a situation which may be troublesome or unpleasant, but I know very well that it is completely unreal. From this point of my dream, knowing that I cannot run any risk, I allow scenes to unfold themselves before me. I adopt the attitude of an interested spectator, watching an accident or catastrophe which cannot affect him. I think: over there are waiting for me people who want to kill me; I then try to run away; but suddenly, I realize that I am dreaming and I say to myself: since I have nothing to fear I am going to meet my enemies, I will defy them, I will even strike them in order to see what will happen. However although I am sure enough of the illusory character of the situation to adopt a course of action which would be unwise in real life, I have to overcome an instinctive feeling of fear. Several times, I have in this way thrown myself on purpose into some danger in order to see what would come of it.[40]

Delage is still very much involved with whatever dream plot he found himself in upon becoming lucid. It's an okay dream, but couldn't he have responded to it more creatively? In many ways Delage is still testing the dreamscape, getting into fights and throwing himself into illusory danger. Why was he running around striking people? Why did people wish to kill him? What if instead of fighting these people in his dream, he tried to speak with them? What would they have said? How would the dream have responded if Delage had responded *to* the dream rather

[40]Green, Celia, *Lucid Dreams* (Oxford: Institute for Psychophysical Research, 1968), 142–43.

than trying to direct it? Could he have at least tried to figure out what was going on in this dream of his own creation?

Delage's dream is not without merit. But it is useful to show what many lucid dream experiences are like. Often, instead of working to further develop our consciousness and awareness of the dreamscape, instead of responding critically or creatively, we immediately perform some fantasy or let the events of the dream buffet us about. It is important to *develop* our consciousness in the dreamscape.

By contrast, notice how in the following dream, Dr. Ram Narayana, an Indian physician, engages his dream characters in some pretty interesting dialogue once he realizes he is dreaming. Narayana realizes that the dream is self-created. He therefore decides to inform the people he finds populating his dreamscape that they are not real—that they are illusions created by his mind.

> In his state of dream he addresses an assembly of men, the majority of whom are his friends and acquaintances. During the course of his speech he explains to his friends that it is a dream and all the people before him are creatures of his dream. Some of the audience ask him what proof he has to give then that he is right in what he asserts. To this he replies that he will think over the question when he wakes up and will explain his reasons when he meets them next time in his dream. At this explanation they all laugh at him and call him a lunatic. When he wakes up he finds himself very puzzled, and even in his waking state he is unable to know how he can convince those creatures of his dream, during the dream state, that it is really a dream.[41]

---

[41]Ram Narayana, *The Dream Problem and Its Many Solutions in Search of Absolute Truth*, Vol. 1 (Delphi, India: Practical Medicine, 1922), xiii.

Narayana remains perplexed regarding how to demonstrate to his dream characters that they are products of his creation. In a later lucid dream, he encounters a group of dream sages and explains his dilemma. The sages render an astute explanation of the situation:

> Another elderly figure from amongst the dream crea-
> tures rose from his seat and overawed the assembly with
> his long grey beard and yogi's staff. He began his oration
> in a curious and amusing manner, though with an au-
> thoritative tone, his voice quivering with anger and his
> gaunt finger pointing toward the dreamer: "What reason
> have you to call us your dream creatures and yourself the
> creator of us all? If you are our creator we say equally
> emphatically that so are we the creator of yourself. We
> are all in the same boat, and you can claim no sort of
> higher existence than ours. If, however, you want to be
> convinced of my statement, I can show you the creator
> of us all, that is, of yourself as well as ours." With these
> words he struck the dreamer on the head with his heavy
> staff, who, in consequence, woke up and found himself
> lying in bed with his mind extremely puzzled.[42]

In the initial phases of lucid dreaming experience, dreamers tend to exercise their fantasies in the dreamscape; it is perceived as an escape into some sort of ultimate playland. Early fantasies typically center on sex and flying, which according to some dream theorists amount to the same thing. What makes you a *sophisticated* lucid dreamer, however, is allowing your uncon-scious to produce some material rather than exploring your conscious fantasies.

[42]Ibid., 305.

When we are conscious in a dream, we are interacting with something quite spectacular—a full-blown sensory environment created by our unconscious mind. The dreamscape is richly decorated; it speaks a beautiful language of metaphors and collages. We should use the opportunity to learn more about our dreams and about ourselves. Ultimately this orientation to the dreamscape will prove far more psychically fulfilling.

If we merely perform in "minidramas" of our conscious direction, then ultimately we come away from the experience without having learned anything. In the long run, we have acted out a fantasy we already knew we possessed. This is not to say that there is not worthwhile satisfaction in acting out one's fantasies, for there genuinely is. But if we take the time to attentively interact with our unconscious mind—to study it, to increase our ability to respond to whatever events arise in the dream, to try to learn from our dreams and understand them—I guarantee we will come away fascinated, intrigued, challenged, and proud to be in possession of such a wonder. Take time to explore the dreamscape! The sophisticated lucid dreamer is someone who wants to learn.

9

The Language of Dreams

The procedure is easily described, although instruction and practice would be necessary before it could be put into effect.

—FREUD,
ON DREAMS

In chapter seven we observed that lucid experience with dreams would challenge some familiar habits of self-identification. Once we acquire conscious experience with the dreamscape, the real mystery is *who* is responsible for creating the dream.

The dichotomy we sense between our self and our dreams is quite real. Even when we know, somewhere in the back of our mind, that we are creating the dream we are simultaneously interacting with, the dream maintains its structure and identity apart from "us." It is impossible to totally control the events of a dream, as the transformations and symbolism continually surprise us. Thus, even though we are the creators of our dreams, we find we exercise only tenuous control over them. We may truthfully say that we are engaged with another element that insists on its own identity. Paradoxically, however, we also *are* this other element—who else could it be? So if we both experience the dream and create it, what does this reveal about our true self?

DREAMS ARE REPRESENTATIONS
OF THOUGHT

In large measure, the gap we sense between our self and our dreams is a communications problem. It is as if our ego, our active, everyday awareness, speaks English and our unconscious, that nightly producer of dreams, speaks Japanese. If dreams truly are "letters" sent from one part of our self to another, then we are receiving lots of letters, but perhaps not understanding them.

Dreams, despite their nonsensical appearance, obey a few simple principles of construction. The sooner we can learn these principles, the sooner we will learn to speak the language of dreams. When we do, we will find a faithful correspondent within our self, and also a great ally. Dreams, once we are able to understand them, complement our limited waking abilities. They give us access to levels of awareness that we otherwise might never know exist.

Because dreams are self-constructed, understanding them is a personal, self-interactive process. We must begin by asking ourselves, "Why did *I* dream what I did?" We also must recognize that dreams are *representations of our thoughts.*

For example, let us say that as you are falling asleep one night, your mind courses through several thoughts. You may think about friends you know, you may review events of the day, or you may think about tasks that await you tomorrow. When you are awake, you experience these as thoughts. As you drift toward sleep, however, a transition occurs. Instead of thinking about your boss, suddenly you are *talking* with her on the telephone! Your boss answers in her familiar voice. The dream shifts and now you are with your boss in her office, continuing the conversation. Your thoughts have become represented in a dream.

Although waking thought is often accompanied by visualization, visualization is different from representation in dreams. When we are awake and think of a friend or loved one, visual pictures may appear in our minds. Or as we review the events of a day, we may have visual memories of things that happened, or fantasies and imaginations of what might have occurred had the day gone differently. But in dreams, thought makes the transition from being mere thought and imaginings to being represented in three-dimensional sensory environments, and experienced as actual events.

Two Types of Dreams

Often we awaken from dreams that are obvious reflections of recent concerns. For example, if you dream of not being prepared to take a test when in real life you are concerned about an important business presentation, or if you dream of missing a plane or of losing your luggage when you actually are scheduled to take a family vacation, you intuitively understand these dreams. Typically you awaken with feelings of anxiety, which are relieved by your discovery that you only were dreaming. Upon awakening, you may immediately identify the cause of the dream: "That darned business presentation!" you think to yourself, or "I'd better get those travel arrangements confirmed with the agent." These dreams, in the jargon of dream interpretation, are known as *transparent dreams*. In transparent dreams, the thoughts and concerns that created the dream are readily apparent to the dreamer.

Transparent dreams are common—we experience them every night, whether we remember them or not. On occasion, however, we experience dreams that do *not* immediately make sense to us. Since dreams can also represent thoughts and feelings that concern us unconsciously, we will not be aware of these thoughts and feelings and, possibly owing to our repression of them, we may be actively avoiding them. Because dreams that represent our unconscious concerns are harder for us to grasp, we need dream interpretation skills to understand them.

CONSTRUCTION OF THE DREAMSCAPE

Just as a good poem must be read carefully to absorb all of the meanings that lie embedded in it, so too must dreams be "read" carefully for subsurface meanings. A dream's meaning is couched in pictures and symbols, in condensations and associations, and hidden behind displacement and other techniques of camouflage. Just as a poet chooses certain words that carry a nuance, combine to follow a desired rhythm, and convey an overall sensibility, dreams also have a diction, a rhythm, and a tone that reflect their meaning. To succeed in understanding our dreams, above all we must learn to *listen* to them.

Representation of Unconscious Thinking

We think about events, relationships, and experiences all the time, without necessarily being aware that we are thinking of them. These thoughts also show up in our dreams. For example, let us say that the other day, while you were in a doctor's office waiting for your appointment, you read a magazine article titled "Fifty Great Ways You Can Help Plan for Your Parents' Retirement." You realize suddenly that, indeed, your parents are growing older. The thought that someday you will be taking care of them dawns on you. This is peculiar, since most of your life they have been taking care of you. Your mind quickly fast-forwards to the thought that you too are getting older, and that your parents are going to die one day.

When the doctor calls you into her office, your attention is drawn away from these thoughts. She says she's glad to see you, and you put down the magazine. After you leave, you are so absorbed in the remaining errands of the day that your thoughts don't return to parents or old age. But Freud would say, and what is evidenced in your dreams, is that unconsciously you continue to think about these things. Even though you aren't aware of it, you may be mulling over these new realizations.

In our example, the unconscious thoughts and feelings center on a recognition that the time with your parents is growing short. Your immediate feeling may be that you want to spend more time with them. You may feel frustrated with your lifestyle because it does not permit greater and fuller interaction. You may also fear the unknown. These are logical, stable, and reasonable reactions to this awareness, but because you have not had the time to think them through, the feelings and awarenesses *remain* unconscious. More accurately, you are distracted from your feelings.

Now let's construct a dream using this material as the basis. How would a dream represent these currently unconscious feelings and awarenesses about your parents growing older? Recall that dreams speak in representations. While most researchers label these representations mainly as visual and auditory, we may expand the descriptions to include all our senses. The dream is going to construct a full sensory environment to express these feelings and awarenesses.

Condensation and Association

The dream will reflect all thoughts that commingle with the primary thoughts and concerns. This is what is referred to, in dream talk, as *condensation and association*. So in relation to the thought of your parents getting older, you experience the following thoughts:

1. You love them and miss them very much;
2. You miss being a child;
3. You miss your old dog; and
4. You used to love the family trips to the beach when you were a kid.

Not too dramatic, right? But it also sounds like you may be missing your childhood in reaction to all of the changes and demands that come with being an adult. Indeed, your primary reaction appears to be regression. You are wishing you were a child again, when you would not have to deal with such problems.

Synthesis

To represent these feelings and awarenesses, the mind sends the family on vacation. You go to the beach where your family used to go when you were young, and your dream portrays one of those nights you used to spend playing charades. In the dream it is your turn; you are your age now, trying to act out the title of a film, *Natasha*, a very difficult one for your group to figure out. But suddenly your father jumps and shouts, "*Natasha!*" You give him a big hug, and everyone claps.

A very simple dream. You awaken and say to yourself, "How strange!" You write in your dream journal:

Dream w/family. At some house, like a beach house— nighttime. Playing game of charades. Other people are there; indistinct. It is my turn, I am acting out title of film—some Russian film named *Natasha*. Dad gets answer and we give each other big hug at end of dream. Nice vibes in dream. Wake up. 6:07 A.M.

What is the meaning of this dream? How did you get from your unconscious feelings and awarenesses to this dream representation?

Deconstructing Dreams—The Principle of Free Association

Now we arrive at one of the great simplicities of dream experience. Invariably all dreams can be deconstructed through one simple but challenging technique pioneered by Freud: *free association*.[43]

To illustrate this process of free association, consider Freud's description in *On Dreams*. He explains how he would ask a patient suffering from a phobia to free associate on that phobia, so that Freud might learn what the phobia was associated with in the patient's mind.

> The procedure is easily described, although instruction and practice would be necessary before it could be put into effect.
>
> If we make use of it on someone else, let us say on a patient with a phobia, we require him to direct his attention on to the idea in question, not, however, to reflect upon it as he has done so often already, but to take notice of *whatever occurs to his mind without any exception* and report it to the physician. If he should then assert that his attention is unable to grasp anything at all, we dismiss this with an energetic assurance that a complete absence of any ideational subject-matter is quite impossible.

---

[43]There exist countless techniques for dream interpretation, and the author is not endorsing one technique over any other. It is the author's opinion, however, that all dream interpretation schools have the principle of free association at the core of their technique.

And in fact very soon numerous ideas will occur to him and will lead on to others; but they will invariably be prefaced by a judgement on the part of the self-observer to the effect that they are senseless or unimportant, that they are irrelevant, and that they occurred to him by chance and without any connection with the topic under consideration. We perceive at once that it was this critical attitude which had prevented the subject from reporting any of these ideas, and which indeed had previously prevented them from becoming conscious. If we can induce him to abandon his criticism of the ideas that occur to him, and to continue pursuing the trains of thoughts which will emerge so long as he keeps his attention turned upon them, we find ourselves in possession of a quantity of psychical material, which we soon find is clearly connected with the pathological idea which was our starting point; this material will soon reveal connections between the pathological idea and other ideas, and will eventually enable us to replace the pathological idea by a new one which fits into the nexus of thought in an intelligible fashion.[44]

With practice we can become adept at using free association to help us understand our dreams. When we free-associate on the various elements of a dream, we allow whatever thoughts, feelings, or memories we expereince in relation to the dream to "come up." We want to see the link between the surface representations of our dreams and the subtler feelings and awarenesses that lay beneath.

For practice, let's apply this free-associative technique to the dream just constructed. Let's say that you were more or less un-

---

[44]Sigmund Freud, *On Dreams, The Complete Psychological Works of Sigmund Freud* (London: Hogarth Press, 1953), 635–36.

aware of the feelings stirred up the day before with regard to your parents. Or perhaps more accurately, you became aware of them momentarily but then forgot about them. You awaken from this dream of playing charades and think, "That's odd. Why would I dream about being at the beach and playing a game of charades, and what the heck is the significance of a film named *Natasha*?" The surface, or manifest, content of the dream seems far removed from current themes in your life. But you have learned that dreams speak in metaphors, so you are willing to give this one some effort. You reread what you wrote. You see that your father was in the dream, which you had already forgotten. Nevertheless, why would you be dreaming about your father and charades and being on the beach? You free-associate a bit, allowing yourself to feel all of the emotions and memories that the dream causes you to experience. You think that the dream certainly reminds you of when you were growing up and your family was together at the beach—and you used to play charades all the time. You also take note of the good feelings you had in the dream. It was a nice dream; it felt good. In thinking about this, it occurs to you that you miss your dad; indeed, you miss your family.

Then it clicks. You suddenly recall being in the doctor's office and reading that magazine article. You think, "That's it! That's what I was thinking about yesterday, and that's why I dreamed about my family last night." Then you think about the feelings you had yesterday with regard to your parents growing older— how you miss them, how you would like to see them, and how you are concerned about them. The dream, as it shows you what you have been thinking about unconsciously, brings you back in touch with your feelings. You make a mental note to phone your folks and you plan when you may be able to see them.

That taken care of, your mind returns to the dream. The beach, the charades—you get all that. But what about the film

Natasha? You draw a blank. "Did we ever see Russian movies together as a family? We didn't know any Russian people, and I can't think of any people I know named Natasha." So you sit, allowing your memory to wander for whatever might come up in association with Natasha. Then it pops into your mind. Natasha was a cat you had when you were six years old. You had a black cat named Natasha who was "your" cat. You peruse the memories this brings up—of being six, of the cat, of your house at the time, of your old dog, and of petting and carrying the cat. For a moment you flash back to being a six-year-old. A collage of memories washes over you. With a smile, you start your day. As you get dressed, you marvel at the construction of the dream. The metaphor of playing charades in front of your family—trying to communicate with them—was beautifully constructed.

Just as we would not suspect two foreigners engaged in conversation of speaking nonsense simply because we do not understand their language, likewise it is an error to presume that dreams speak nonsense simply because we do not understand their language. Dreams characteristically are straightforward representations of our thoughts. Just as we enjoy a well-constructed morning crossword puzzle, we can relish our dreams—if we apply ourselves to the task. Dreams are straightforward and able to be unraveled only when we assist our memory for them by recording them upon awakening.

In addition to learning the rules of dream construction, we must also improve our free-associative skills. The process of free association is vital to understanding the myriad associations and influences that go into dream construction. This process requires us to *feel through our memory* for the associations aroused by a dream. And for this we need time and privacy to inventory our mind. Indeed, dreams are not billboards at which we can glance quickly and register meaning. When we set out to understand a dream, we need to focus our attention on it. The psychoanalytic couch is a fixture in therapists' offices for precisely this reason: It helps us to engage in this highly personal and self-interactive process.

To understand why we build our dreams as we do, we must inventory ourselves. Each dream is a riddle or anagram that we alone are able to unravel. This is why no psychiatrist, no psychoanalyst, no dream dictionary, no collection of one thousand dreams interpreted can ever successfully interpret our dreams for us. All dreams are unique, personal constructions. Others more experienced with dream construction can illuminate typical dreams and guide us through interpretive techniques, but ultimately it is the individual dreamer who holds the key to understanding.

Thus in the dream example, there may be some elements your analysis has missed, but all in all you feel comfortable with your understanding of the feelings and awareness that lay beneath its creation. You are aware that you miss your family, that you miss your childhood, and that you miss those times you had when everyone was all together. You also are confident that if there's anything particularly important in the dream that you did miss, it will come up later in another dream. Dream thoughts that go unrecognized, if particularly pressing, recur in later dreams. So you will get another chance to make yourself aware of whatever feeling or awareness was represented.

Disguised Dreams

Though most dreams can be understood quite readily once we possess the proper tools with which to decipher them, not all dream constructions unravel so easily under trained eyes. Some dreams, even after we have applied free-associative technique, remain elusive. Either we are unable to draw any associations that "ring true" or the language the dream has chosen is suddenly beyond our repertoire. We are left with the unmistakable feeling that the dream meant something, but its meaning remains hidden.

In *disguised* dreams, the meaning of the dream—or rather the identity of the unconscious feelings and awarenesses that gave rise to the construction of the dream—remains obscured. Of course, at some level nearly all dreams are disguised. The basic means of dream construction—representation by environment, condensation and association—excludes those who do not understand at least some of the principles. But some dreams do disguise their meanings from us, for the express purpose of hiding their unconscious feelings and awarenesses. These are the famous disguised dreams of psychoanalytic experience.

At first glance this appears an inherent contradiction—why might we disguise something from ourselves? If we're attentive, however, we will see this mechanism of disguise operating all the time in dreams. We will also learn to pay particular attention to dreams that employ these disguised representations.

Repression Is the Source of Disguise in Dreams

Probably all of us are familiar with the term *repression*. In its simplest sense, it is the process whereby one attempts to avoid, or *not to admit to oneself*, thoughts, feelings, and awarenesses that are painful to recognize and address. Another way of describing repression is to say that it is how we avoid feelings and awarenesses that contradict how we would *like* or *imagine* our lives to be. Repression sounds simple, and essentially it is.

Before you become overconfident, however, be forewarned that of all the psychological mechanisms used by the ego to structure its idealized vision of the world, repression is by far the most subtle, and the most surprisingly pervasive, defense. The great subtlety of repression is that it is an *unconscious* defense mechanism. Indeed, for repression to be successful, it must operate without our being aware of it. It's a catch-22: When we truly are successful at avoiding a painful feeling or awareness, we will be naively unaware of our avoidance.

As beings who operate on two levels of consciousness, we can avoid feelings and awarenesses on the conscious level, but this does not mean that we necessarily can avoid them on the *un*conscious level. When we do possess contradictory awareness—when we avoid acknowledging thoughts, feelings, or awarenesses that we are aware of unconsciously—then herein lies the seed for contradiction within us. The paradox of repression is that we already know, at the unconscious level, what it is we are trying to avoid knowing at the conscious level.

Distortion in Dream Experience Is a Reflection of Distortion in Waking Experience

Now let's draw the link between repression and disguised dreams. When we avoid feelings and awarenesses—be they conflicting feelings about family members, good friends, or ourselves—we are trying to *create* our conscious world the way we would like it to be rather than as we know it to be. And in this game of creation, unpleasant feelings and awarenesses are denied, avoided, transformed, re-created, and reimagined in our mind. Excuses are made and defenses are erected to justify the shortcomings. Attenuating circumstances are employed to rationalize the behavior of ourselves and others who have hurt us. All of these transforming mechanisms help us to shape reality as we *wish* to see it.

Not surprisingly, the repressed feelings and awarenesses that we avoid in our waking life emerge in the story lines of our dreams. And when we dream of topics or concerns that we are not allowing ourselves to see and recognize directly and honestly in waking experience, our dreams reflect this distortion accordingly. Disguised dreams are a sign to us that our feelings and awarenesses in *waking experience* are distorted.

A Strange, Emotional Dream

To illustrate, let's say a woman learns in her waking life that her lover of two years' time is being unfaithful to her. But to make this situation more difficult to decipher, let's say she learns of this infidelity only unconsciously—that is, something her lover did recently tipped her off that something was wrong, and the vibes between her and her lover are different. Unconsciously she suspects—indeed, she is *aware*—that her lover is being unfaithful. But let's also say that she is repressing this awareness, that she hasn't allowed it to become conscious yet, because at a certain level, she doesn't want to know. She wants the relationship to be different from how it is.

A day or two after becoming unconsciously suspicious of the infidelity, she dreams that she is with her lover on an ocean cruiser, far out at sea. She is at the bow of the ship, looking forward at the broad expanse of ocean, and holding on to the railing; a gentle breeze brushes against her cheek. Suddenly the boat develops a huge gash in its hull. She rushes to the side and peers over the edge. She sees that a giant fish with a red, pointed collar around its neck has hit the boat, and the boat is now sinking rapidly. The fish, killed by its collision with the boat, floats alongside. Suddenly she is at the bow again, but her lover is gone. She looks about anxiously to discover where he is. Down a walkway she sees one of her lover's old friends, someone she met once at a college reunion. At this point she forgets about her lover. The ship is listing badly, and this distant acquaintance is having difficulty climbing toward her. Interestingly, she does not try to help the person. Rather, she watches intently as she

tries to move toward her. The individual is grabbing the railing
and crying out for help. The dreamer says to herself, "If she had
worn the right shoes, she wouldn't be getting wet." With this
thought, she awakens.

Given the framework in which this dream is presented, we
can read the writing on the wall. The dream is about infidelity
and about the best-laid plans going wrong; it is about moral positions, so to speak, as outlined by the positions of the characters
in the dream. But to interpret a dream from this vantage point is
to quarterback a football game the day after it was played. To be
fair we must retreat a few steps and view the dream from the
dreamer's perspective.

From the start, the dreamer is not conscious of any infidelity
in the relationship. In fact, her lover recently surprised her with
a present, a new blouse from her favorite store, plus a red long-
stemmed rose.

She wakes from this dream in a strange, emotional state and
thinks, "How dramatic." The dream was powerful in a way she
doesn't really understand. Boat at sea, lover there, then this other
person—lots of drama. But she wakes up disturbed. The dream
leaves her with the distinct sense that something is drastically
wrong. She works to recall the dream, then records it. Intuitively
she does not want to miss this dream. She writes:

> On ship at sea, w/ R. Up on bow, big boat, looking out
> over ocean. Hands on railing. Then big whole [sic] in
> side of ship. Look over edge of boat and see giant catfish,
> with red, pointy collar on, floating on ocean top. Boat
> hit fish and whole now torn in hull. Boat sinking. Turn
> back to look for R., can't find. Suddenly see R.'s friend
> P., from party last May. P. is coming up side of boat, try-
> ing to reach where I am. P. is wearing my new blouse! Is
> having very difficult time getting up to where I am. Boat

is listing dramatically, but I still stand up straight. P.—
hands on railing, calling for help. I notice P. has cheap,
slippery plastic shoes on. I think if P. had worn proper
shoes, wouldn't be getting wet. E.O.D.—6:30 A.M.

She reads her journal entry. She can't make heads or tails of
it but knows the dream affected her deeply—that disturbed feeling is lingering. But there is no time at the moment to analyze
the dream, so she gets up, takes a shower, and goes to work.
Though she thinks of the dream from time to time throughout
the day, she generates only vague feelings about it. That evening,
though, her mind returns to the dream and she retrieves her
dream journal.

"Ah!" she says as she rereads the dream. "R. and I were *together* on the boat. I'd forgotten that. We were on the bow of a
ship, a big ship, way up high, looking forward off the bow as it
crossed the ocean." She remembers the dream better now. The
sky was bright and sunny, and she could feel the breeze blowing
on her cheek as she stood at the front of the boat. Her hands
were holding on to the railing. She reads on:

Then big whole in side of ship. Look over edge of boat
and see giant catfish, with red, pointy collar on, floating
on ocean top.

That's right, she recalls, some huge catfish sank the boat. It
had a collar on that was red and pointy. The points on the collar
had ripped the side of the hull. Then she notices that she misspelled the word *hole* both times she wrote it. Interesting. She
rereads those two passages: "big whole in side of ship. . . . Boat
hit fish and whole now torn in hull. Boat sinking."

Now comes an interesting time in dream interpretation.
That disturbed feeling the dream left this morning is beginning
to return. Indeed, she may not like what she is beginning to re-

alize about this dream. Unconsciously she may be sensing that she is entering a sensitive area. Remember, she has a lot invested in the relationship. She may be engaged or hoping to marry someday. The relationship may be important to her sense of self-esteem or important to her socially. Or it may simply break her heart to find this person, with whom she had felt so close, being dishonest with her. In a different scenario, she may be financially dependent on her lover, or she may have children. Does she really want to know what this dream is telling her?

Careful! Sometimes when we get near sensitive awarenesses, we react without thinking. We can be so fearful of what is threatening us that we slip into "automatic pilot" for weeks, months, or even years, before we return, usually by force, to the threatening awareness we hoped to avoid. In this case, the woman may suddenly find that there are many things she should be doing today instead of interpreting a silly dream (resistance). So she misspelled a word—it happens all the time (denial). Dream interpreation is dumb. She never should have started this deciphering of unconscious thoughts as represented by her dreams (resistance). Her relationship is the most important thing in her life (resistance).

Simplex or duplex? Are we willing to hear out the fears and strange feelings that arise within us as we rethink our dreams? Are we willing to investigate the feelings we experience in the morning, or are we going to ignore them? Do we really want to know what our dreams seem to be telling us? Think twice about this last question, because the message may change your life.

"Nonsense," the woman says to herself, "it's just a dream." She reads on:

> Turn back to look for R., can't find. Suddenly see R.'s friend P., from party last May. P. is coming up side of boat, trying to reach where I am. P. is wearing my new

blouse! Is having very difficult time getting up to where
I am. Boat is listing dramatically, but I still stand up
straight. P.—hands on railing, calling for help. I notice P.
has cheap, slippery plastic shoes on. I think if P. had worn
proper shoes, wouldn't be getting wet. E.O.D.—6:30 A.M.

An interesting transformation occurs in the dream. Right
after she discovers the "whole" in the boat, the main character in
the dream (besides herself) shifts from being her lover to being
her lover's old friend, whom she met once at a party. Why
should this person suddenly appear, and why should she just as
suddenly cease to wonder as to the whereabouts of her lover?
This other person seems so arbitrary. She tries to think of what
she associates in her mind with this person that might cause her
sudden appearance in the dream. After awhile, the only thing
the woman can think about is that when she met her lover's
friend, she was a little jealous of their old friendship—a natural
enough feeling. She recalls wishing at the party that her lover
would pay more attention to her.

But the new blouse! Why is this person dressed in her new
blouse? What is the connection? Is she jealous of this person?
Does she think her lover would rather have given the shirt to
this other person? She allows these thoughts and others that
come up to float around in her mind awhile, then decides no,
that's not it. None of those associations rings true.

An absurd thought comes into her mind: "This other person
is substituting for my lover! This other person is my lover in disguise! But that can't be it. That doesn't make any sense." But it
has an irresistible logic about it. She and her lover were together
on the boat, then suddenly they were apart. Then she saw this
other person, who's vaguely associated with her lover and her
earlier fears of other people interfering in her relationship. "It's
like this other person is a blend of my lover and my fears about

our relationship, and she also is this person from the past," she says to herself.

And that blouse! What does that blouse have to do with all of these associations? She tentatively decides to explore this line of reasoning. She doesn't want to jump to any conclusions. Cautiously, she returns to the blouse. She recalls that she thought it nice when her lover gave it to her; indeed, it was unusually nice. And the rose too. And now she suddenly thinks of the catfish that sank the boat. In the dream, the fish wore a red, pointed collar; the identification with the rose suddenly becomes unmistakable.

Now she is becoming genuinely disturbed. What is going on? She may get upset at her unconscious for trying to make her think her lover is cheating on her. She may also be confused, and rightly so, and may just want to drop all of this for a while. Nevertheless, after thinking about this dream, she is left with renewed concerns as to the fidelity of her lover. She thinks her lover may be having an affair with an old friend from college.

Let's wind this dream up. Say she has all of these thoughts and suspicions, and she confronts her lover about it. There is a terrible fight, and her lover vehemently denies everything and makes her feel horribly guilty for even thinking such thoughts. Then her lover says he needs time to think, he never knew she harbored such doubts, and now he is uncertain of her character. Now she really feels lousy and guilty, and she swears off dream interpretation forever. A week later she learns that her lover was seen recently with an old flame from college.

Soon enough she remembers the dream that set off the chain of events. She rethinks the dream and concludes that she actually became suspicious the night her lover gave her the blouse and rose. Suddenly all of the pieces fall into place. "We went out to dinner that night, and R. ordered catfish. We talked about what a strange name that was for a fish, and whether it tasted good or not. R. told me that catfish taste great even though they are bottom fish that feed on sludge and garbage on the bottom of rivers. I thought that was gross and that people shouldn't eat fish that eat garbage, but I didn't say anything. Then I remember thinking how the whole night was a little queer, how R. was nervous, but I attributed it to work and that we hadn't seen each other for a while." She reviews the whole dream and thinks, "What an incredible metaphor." The boat, heading out over the ocean—the journey of life. She's with this other person, and they're both holding on to the railing. (Every time we read "railing," we should think wedding band.) Then there's this "whole" torn in the hull of the ship by a catfish with a red, pointy collar. And then the lover disappears and this distant person from the past, with whom she associates fears of interference, appears. This person plays a neat role in the dream construction because she at once represents the dreamer's lover, her suspicions, and the clue to the infidelity that set her mind thinking in the first place: the blouse.

As she peruses the dream further, she realizes another thing: it certainly is clear how her unconscious perceives her ex-lover. In the dream, she stood at the bow of the ship and was able to stand up straight, while this other person was clutching at the rail for balance. In the dream, she was safe; she felt no concern for her safety. This other person was crying for help, and all she could think was that it was this person's own fault, because of the shoes. In connection with the shoes, she thinks of "idols that have feet of clay." She had two specific thoughts with regard to the shoes: They were cheap and they were slippery—two connotations that not only are uncomplimentary but describe a person who is sleazy or dishonest.

She is willing to make a further prediction based on this dream: Her lover is going to come back to her. He will crawl up that sloping deck, but from the looks of it, she's not sure those shoes are going to carry him.

What a strange transition! This dream was warning her. Even though it was about something she was afraid to learn, even actively did not want to know, at another level of her awareness, she had discerned that her lover was being dishonest. She even pinpointed the time and location of the infidelity. The dream warned her about someone with whom she was investing a lot of time and energy, heart and soul. Something inside of her picked up the clue that something wasn't right—indeed, that something was dramatically wrong—but she wanted so much for the situation to be otherwise that she actively overlooked the clues. She gave her lover the benefit of the doubt, and she nearly made a big mistake.

Why do dreams choose to speak in such convoluted language? For example, why wouldn't the woman dream that she was visiting her lover on his old college campus, say, only to find him involved with another? She very well could have had a dream like this, but *distortion* in dreams is a function of how much we want or do not want to admit an awareness. If she was openly suspicious of her lover, then she might very well experience such a transparent representation of her thoughts. If our dreams are representing areas about which we feel great anxiety, then *out of deference to the desires of our conscious perceptions*, dreams invariably transform themselves.

The scenario of the boat receiving a "whole" cut into its side and sinking is a metaphoric displacement from the dream thought that the woman's relationship has suffered serious injury. She is highly resistant to the thought that her relationship is in peril, so instead of representing this thought directly, the dream picks a metaphor. Likewise, once the ship started to go down, she no longer saw her lover needing to be rescued; instead she saw a virtual stranger who was nevertheless associated with the definite thought in her mind.

The end result of distortion is that we are able to experience dreams that manifestly appear unthreatening but that we sense are laden with meaning. Hence the dream that appears trivial yet haunts our waking hours. Or the nightmare that leaves us disturbed but whose origin eludes us entirely. The cause of distortion in dream representations is our maintenance of contradictory awarenesses.

Do we *really* want to know what our dreams are telling us?

UNCONSCIOUS AWARENESS IN THE DIVIDED INDIVIDUAL—A TWO-TIERED ABILITY FOR AWARENESS

Dreams can "tell us" things we do not already know? What a curious idea! It's as if there are two "pools of awareness" or "stores of knowledge" within a single individual.

Perhaps the single most important psychological insight that dream experience has revealed about the human mind is this two-tiered ability for awareness. Accordingly, when we speak of awareness, we need to distinguish between the two types. A helpful way to view the conscious–unconscious interface is in terms of active and inactive awarenesses. *Active awareness* is characterized by its accessibility to consciousness. It is all the thoughts, feelings, memories, and experiences we possess to which we have unimpeded access. Take a moment to peruse all of what you know of yourself. This is "you"—who you are. Active awareness is commonly referred to as the ego.

Now let us consider the other side of the equation. *Inactive, or unconscious, awareness* is characterized by the thoughts, feelings, memories, and experiences that have been lost to us, either owing to the passage of time or because we have purposely tried to forget them.

This two-tiered awareness was one of the most radical of Freud's propositions about the mind. Essentially he said that it is possible for us to be aware of something without us necessarily being aware of it. Needless to say, this runs contrary to popular thinking about the nature of awareness. To describe an awareness as unconscious seems manifestly wrong, for how can an awareness exist if a person is not aware of it?

As confusing as Freud's idea of unconscious awareness appears at first glance, it is critical for anyone wishing to understand the human mind. That we routinely become aware of tremendous amounts of information *unconsciously* is a quality of our mind that dream experience will illuminate again and again. We are also able to *react* to this unconscious awareness without being aware that we are reacting to it. This is how one is said to be moved around by unconscious forces. We see and feel things without being aware that we are seeing and feeling them, and we react to these perceptions.

Freud observed that unconscious awarenesses exist in the mind as do conscious ones, except that the former do not enjoy the same access to consciousness, or the ego, as do the latter. He observed that repression is a mechanism that enables us to keep these two realms of awareness segregated. As your experience with dreams progresses, you will discover that Freud's thesis is borne out by experience: Dreams regularly provide access to information stored in our unconscious.

Of course, not *all* unconscious awarenesses are repressed. While there typically exist many unconscious awarenesses we would like to avoid, some are, comparatively speaking, neutral or value free. These awarenesses are not being avoided by the ego but rather, most likely because they are not perceived as vital to the needs of the individual, they have not made their way to consciousness, or active awareness.

Unconscious Awarenesses in Everyday Experience

In everyday experience, we often become unconsciously aware of information, only to later become actively aware of what we have known unconsciously for some time. Say a few nights before you are planning to leave on a car trip, you have a disturbing dream. You are on a highway heading off to some mountains in the distance, when suddenly the car swerves and fishtails. You barely miss having an accident. In the dream, you were aware that one of your tires had gone bad, and this was the cause for loss of control. Because of this dream, the next day you inspect your tires. Much to your surprise, you find that one of your tires is indeed bald. Was the dream portentous? Was it a communication from a guardian angel? Perhaps, but another explanation is that, at some point in the past, you became aware unconsciously that the car was steering poorly at high speeds. Or perhaps you noticed the tire one morning when you entered the car but didn't devote any thought to it then. As you began to anticipate your trip, this significant detail of information became represented in a dream. Thus you became *actively* aware of information you were already aware of *inactively*.

In another illustration, you see one of your coworkers at your desk one morning. You do not notice anything awry. You speak with your coworker briefly, and accomplish the tasks of the morning. That night, however, you have a vivid dream that your coworker is in a fight with his lover. The following day, you tell your coworker of the dream and express concern for their relationship. Much to your surprise, you learn that your dream identified your coworker's situation precisely. Are you psychic? Maybe, but an equally plausible explanation is that you perceived something wrong the previous morning. During that brief encounter, you may have recognized emotional stress and even succeeded in identifying the source. But while you absorbed this information, at the time you were concerned only with whatever work detail brought you together. The information you held unconsciously made the transit from inactive to active awareness through a dream.

In yet another example, you meet someone only casually at a party. Later you dream of being romantically involved with that person. The dream takes you by surprise. You think, "I met this person only once, and I never even thought about him (or her) again." But apparently that's not true. When you think it over, you admit that you did find the person attractive.

Or maybe an old friend comes to town, and you spend a night out on the town together. You have dinner and some drinks, and later visit a nightclub. The following week you dream your friend is arrested for driving while intoxicated. You make some casual inquiries and find out that your friend actually has been having problems with alcohol. You didn't notice it the night you went out, but maybe at the time you were giving your friend the benefit of the doubt.

While the idea of unconscious awareness appears paradoxical at first, as you become more familiar with dreams, you will be more comfortable with the concept. You'll find that dreams are frequent conveyers of information between our conscious and unconscious awarenesses. This is the primary reason why, throughout time, dreams have been considered valuable psychologically: They reveal our unconscious awarenesses.

Do dreams really show us things we do not already know? The answer is twofold. Dreams show us that there are two stores of knowledge within our mind. Consciousness contains everything we are actively aware of, while the unconscious—and this is the tricky part—contains everything else we *also* are aware of. The mystery is how we can maintain unconscious awarenesses without being aware of this knowledge at the conscious level. At this point, however, we should be able to overcome our conscious bias enough to recognize that unconscious awarenesses are as valid as are conscious ones.

Dreams do *not* show us things we do not know. In fact, precisely the opposite is true. Indeed, the revelatory capacity of dreams attests to the fact that at some level in our beings, we must already know whatever it is that our dreams are reflecting. Accordingly, the real question to ask of dream experience is whether we are aware *yet*, on the conscious level, of the knowledge that dreams make manifest.

For example, in the dream of the unfaithful lover and the sinking ship, if we examine the sequence of events, at some point we must acknowledge that *prior to the dream*, our dreamer was already aware that her lover was being unfaithful. This awareness is what gives rise to the construction of the foreboding dream. The distinction in this case is whether she allowed this awareness to become conscious—whether she allowed herself to *feel* this unconsciously possessed awareness. In the above circumstance, we said that our dreamer did *not* allow herself to become actively aware of this suspicion (prior to her dream) because, quite simply, she did not *want* to become aware of it. Even though she was aware of the infidelity at an unconscious level, she avoided acknowledging or addressing this gut feeling, sixth sense, intuition, or nervousness—or however else this awareness manifested itself during waking experience. To have acknowledged her suspicions would have been painful, so she resisted its becoming part of her active awareness. In simpler terms, she saw what she wanted to see and she did not see consciously what she did not want to see. Yet as her dream shows, her unconscious awareness of the infidelity persisted.

10

Duality and Unity

It seems like an empty wrangle over words to argue whether mental life is to be regarded as co-extensive with consciousness or whether it may be said to stretch beyond this limit, and yet I can assure you that the acceptance of unconscious mental processes represents a decisive step towards a new orientation in the world and in science.

—FREUD,
INTRODUCTORY LECTURES ON PSYCHOANALYSIS

For more than fifty years we have known, or could have known, that there is an unconscious as a counterbalance to consciousness. Medical psychology has furnished all the necessary empirical and experimental proofs of this. There is an unconscious psychic reality which demonstrably influences consciousness and its contents. All this is known, but no practical conclusions have been drawn from it. We still go on thinking and acting as before, as if we are simplex and not duplex. . . . It is frivolous, superficial and unreasonable of us, as well as psychically unhygienic, to overlook the reaction and standpoint of the unconscious.

—JUNG,
THE UNDISCOVERED SELF

At the end of the last chapter, we introduced a new element that we said is able to influence the construction of both our dreams and our vision in our waking worlds. Repression, we said, is an ability we each possess that allows us to avoid recognizing or addressing difficult feelings and awarenesses within us. The function of repression is easy enough to understand: Avoiding unpleasant feelings and awarenesses in waking life creates a more comfortable psychic environment for the individual.

But the human mind is not such a simple mechanism. In the last chapter we saw what we thought was a fundamental law of awareness—that we cannot be aware of thoughts or feelings of which we are not aware—turned on its head. Indeed, we saw that not only is it possible to be aware of thoughts and feelings of which we are "not aware," it is even common. Dream experience regularly shows us that we maintain unconscious awarenesses. In this light, the success of repression as a defense against awareness became suspect. While repression does enable us to avoid feelings and awarenesses at an immediate level of awareness, the avoided material persists within us nevertheless. From this observation we deduced that there genuinely are two types of awareness in the human mind: those that are conscious, or active to the individual, and those that are not immediately accessible—unconscious, or inactive, awarenesses. Repression is a technique the ego utilizes to maintain this artificial division, this duality of awareness, within each of us.

THE LESSONS OF DREAM EXPERIENCE

This chapter concerns itself, in a general sense, with the type of relationship we maintain with ourselves. More specifically, we wish to explore the relationship between our conscious and unconscious levels of awareness. But before we begin this discussion, it will help to review three simple lessons that dream experience teaches us about our mind.

The Unconscious Is Aware

The first quality of our mind we want to recognize is that we all possess great unconscious ability. Dreams, in their representa-

tions of our inner and outer worlds, demonstrate the unconscious to be a sensitive, able, and perceptive chronicler of experience. Contrary to its popular name, it is our experience that the
unconscious mechanism actually is *acutely* aware. Instead of *unconscious,* the unconscious mechanism might more appropriately
be called *superconscious* or *superawareness.* The solution to this
riddle was discovered in the previous chapter, where we saw that
it is the ego that, utilizing the mechanism of repression, *limits
what it allows itself to become aware of,* according to a type of "pleasure-unpleasure" principle, as Freud described it. As a rule, the
ego tends to avoid feelings and awarenesses it finds difficult to
integrate, while it seems ever willing to indulge itself in feelings
and fantasies it finds comforting and pleasing. As a result, the
unconscious becomes, in part, a repository for feelings and
awarenesses that the ego, in its effort to mold and protect the
image of the self, excludes from its realm of awareness.

The Unconscious Is a Part of the Self

Earlier we said that a central challenge of lucid dreaming is that
it asks us to take ownership of, and responsibility for, unconscious mental activity. Conscious ownership of unconscious
ability is a paradox, but this dichotomy of talent, nevertheless, is
a fact of our beings. Dream experience is dramatic testimony to
our unconscious mental ability. It also shows us that both
"minds" are partners in the composition of the self. Identification only with our conscious ability is an error—it is a familiar
and even natural one, but the psychologically educated individual learns to identify with both abilities.

Resistance to Awareness

A third quality of our mind that we want to recognize is that
our conscious and unconscious abilities often exist in a relation-

ship of resistance to each other rather than in a state of harmony and cooperation. The culprit in this antagonistic relationship is the error of the conscious element's identification only with the conscious (the ego). When the ego avoids recognizing feelings and awarenesses that nevertheless exist within the being, the avoided material is forced to remain *un*conscious. This is the failure of the "simplex" identification process, which both Jung and Freud, in the passages excerpted at the head of this chapter, are addressing.

In this chapter we will focus our attention on the curious defense mechanism of repression. What we will find is that while repression is often functional as a tool for coping with difficult feelings and awarenesses, invariably it is also a two-edged sword. Repression is functional in extreme cases of shock and trauma, when difficult experiences threaten to overwhelm our ability for comprehension. It is functional in younger years as well, when psychological sophistication and more mature management skills lie beyond our grasp. But in almost all other cases, the use of repression as a coping skill proves itself to be powerfully *dys*functional. This is because repression succeeds in an individual only by severely compromising that individual's ability to perceive reality.

It is the negative consequences of repression that cause us to pay it such careful attention. Repression divides our beings into conscious and unconscious compartments of awareness. It surrenders conscious management of our knowledge and awareness to an unconscious mechanism. And repression causes us to participate in unconscious behaviors of avoidance. This last characteristic is perhaps the most damaging, as it has an ultimately bewildering effect on our sense of personal validity. For all of these reasons, a working knowledge of the defense is desired.

I have one final thought before we embark upon our discussion. Separation between conscious and unconscious awareness is really an illusion. In all cases of repression, recall that we already know what it is—what feelings or awareness it is—that we are avoiding. The avoided feelings and awarenesses are already inside us. We are already feeling them and are already aware of them—unconsciously. Indeed, all dreams that reflect avoided feelings and awarenesses show us that unconsciously we are intimately acquainted with the material. In this light, the goal of self-unification becomes a simple process—conceptually at least—of training our mind and body to learn to listen to themselves, and to identify, accept, and resolve nonintegrated feelings and awarenesses. The knowledge and practice of this simple triad of mental health skills is the path by which we learn progressively to unify ourselves, to repair the duality of awareness that exists between our conscious and unconscious minds.

WHY REPRESSION IS SO HARD TO SEE— REPRESSION IS AN UNCONSCIOUS DEFENSE

In the last chapter, we saw a fairly common example of how it is possible for a person to avoid recognizing feelings and awarenesses that, nevertheless, are present within. We observed that our .dreamer was actually aware, unconsciously, of infidelity in her relationship before she became consciously aware of this knowledge through the medium of a dream. Until her dream puzzled her sufficiently, our dreamer was able to avoid her unconscious awareness simply by not thinking about it, or perhaps by finding something else to do whenever she came near to it in her mind. For various reasons, our dreamer did not really want to know or understand her feelings.

Avoidance of troublesome awarenesses is easy enough to understand. One way we can avoid difficult feelings is by simply refusing to recognize them. And while we all may acknowledge the limitations of this strategy for "feelings management"—

avoided material does not go away, but rather remains merely avoided—we can also see how, if our avoidance was consistent, the illusion might prove effective. "What feelings?" we might soon ask ourselves.

If repression were only this simple a defense to understand, there would not be volumes of psychoanalytic texts dedicated to its explanation in minutiae, nor would there be the countless thousands of hours dedicated to its discussion, each week, in therapy sessions around the world. The reason why repression is far more subtle than it first appears, and why it is fabulously more effective, is because it is an *unconscious* defense. What this means is that repression operates without our being aware, consciously, that it is operating. When we are successful at avoiding feelings and awarenesses, we are unaware that we are avoiding anything.

Repression Is a Response to Anxiety

Freud explained repression in terms of anxiety. He said that repression is a response to anxiety—the body's inborn way of protecting itself against overload. According to Freud, the sequence of events that occurs in repression is that we momentarily become consciously aware of feelings and awarenesses, and if this new material generates sufficient anxiety, then it can, through the technique of avoidance, be prevented from entering into conscious awareness again, where we would be forced to recognize it and which might cause unbearable strain on the psychic mechanism. These feelings and awarenesses are now identified as being anxiety producing, and our psychic mechanism works as best it can to avoid encountering them in the future.

To understand what an unconscious defense mechanism entails, however, we need to suspend for a moment nearly all of our assumptions about conscious decision making in our lives.

For example, it is entirely incorrect to understand repression as a defense we *choose* to engage in—as an option we choose to employ from our cache of self-management skills, as it were. To the contrary, repression is an *unconscious* defense; it is something that *happens to us*. Because of this, the only way we can identify repression within us is secondarily, after the fact, by identifying the symptomologies of repression that invariably trail in its wake. Before we discuss symptomologies, though, the question of unconscious avoidance—how we actually avoid feelings and awarenesses without even knowing that we are doing so— looms before us.

As an introduction to our discussion of avoidance techniques, I offer to the reader that if repression were not such an ingenious defense mechanism, it couldn't be so phenomenally successful. As we peruse the upcoming list of avoidance techniques, the principal thing to remember is that repression does not want us to be aware that we are avoiding anything. Why? Because if we know we are avoiding something, then we will wonder what it is we are avoiding, and then the purpose of repression would be compromised. Indeed, we quickly learn that the key to repression's success is its ability to operate beneath a shroud of unconsciousness. The more parts of the avoidance process that repression can hide from us, the better its chance of succeeding. Another thing to remember is that while repression is not powerful enough to *erase* feelings and awarenesses, it is exceptionally powerful in its ability to hide this material from us— even when we're looking.

Sound challenging? It is.

THE MERRY-GO-ROUND OF REPRESSION: HOW REPRESSION CAUSES US TO AVOID FEELINGS AND AWARENESSES

Distraction and Confusion

Distraction and *confusion* are two of repression's most faithful friends; there is nothing like them to keep us chasing our tails. But consider the process. If I can make certain feelings inside you confused and muddled, and then can constantly distract and interrupt your ability to concentrate every time you set yourself upon the task of examining your feelings, then what are the chances that you will get any serious work done on yourself? This is one of repression's best tricks, and it does it to us all the time.

Confusion of feelings is probably something we are all familiar with. Distraction, on the other hand, can be more difficult to see. For example, when was the last time you had a job to do that you really didn't feel like doing, like taking out the overflowing trash can or preparing your taxes? It's amazing all the things we can do to avoid doing the job.

I remember when I was in college that my roommate and I invented a game of bouncing a rubber ball off our dormitory room walls. We played this game for hours. It was obvious that we were procrastinating, putting off the inevitable hour when we would have to get to work or jeopardize our grades, but our game, in the meantime, was captivating. We put different spins on the ball, bounced it higher and lower, and commented on and discussed in great detail the ball's response. It was much better than doing our schoolwork.

Procrastination is similar to unconsciously motivated desires for distraction, but it is different in one key regard. When we procrastinate, we usually are aware of what we are doing. We know we're putting off something and that eventually we'll have to attend to the avoided task. When procrastination becomes unconsciously motivated, however, when we crave distraction unreasonably or when our distraction becomes a type of desperate attempt to avoid reality, usually it is because the emotional stakes have climbed higher. It's not a term paper, taxes, or uncut lawn we want to avoid; now it's something really difficult, something we really do wish would just go away. Most likely we are not confident in our ability to manage some of our feelings consciously. Like feelings of unhappiness in our marriage or feelings of shame and failure in our own life. What would be the consequences of acknowledging these feelings? We might really have to change our life. We might have to split up, move on, and tend to the broken pieces afterward. A lot of hard work. Do we really want to open this Pandora's box?

But the truth is, we don't have to think about all this. There's so much else to do. We need to go to the store, the bills need to be paid, and we have our party next weekend with the Joneses to think about. There are probably some important shows on television tonight, too.

Single-mindedness

Repression and consciousness keep getting in each other's way. Repression seeks to limit our awareness, while consciousness brings to light all material that crosses its path. If consciousness had free access to all feelings and awarenesses in our being, then no feelings or awarenesses would be unconscious, at least not for long. But the fact is that we don't possess such easy access to our feelings. How does repression rein in the wandering eye of consciousness?

Have you ever had one of those "off days"? Where you'd lose your head if it weren't attached to your shoulders? Where you misplace your hat and gloves, you leave your purse at a restaurant, you stay one stop too long on the subway, your mind keeps drifting off at work? "What a hassle," you think. "I'm really spacey today."

Walking down the sidewalk, we find ourselves lost in thought, having imaginary conversations in our minds. We may even speak out loud or gesture in response to our conversation. This makes us notice how lost in thought we are, and we try to snap out of it. We didn't even *see* the street we just walked down! We try to pay attention for a moment, noticing, observing, but soon the urge to continue in our conversation is irresistible, and we fall back in.

Repression and *single-mindedness* are close bedfellows. This is because if repression can cause us to be unreflective for extended periods of time—if it can keep us spaced out, muddling along in streams of fantasy and automatic thought and behavior—then it has an easier time guiding the course of our thoughts. We may be distracted and confused and helplessly "lost in thought," but if we are unreflective, we also will be unable to identify our symptomology, much less work to understand its causes. We will be on autopilot, a curious, strangely silent navigation of our lives. Moments of self-awareness startle us as we regain our outward orientation, but our surfacing is short-lived. When we are unreflective, we also are instantly forgetful. We begin a task and five minutes later wonder what it was we were about to do. Single-mindedness makes our life blurred and discontinuous. Without reflection, we have no alternative but to just move along. But *we* aren't driving; repression is.

Tension

In psychoanalytic schools, repression is viewed as an active process in the body. When we repress a feeling or awareness from becoming conscious, we do not just repress the feeling at an unconscious level and then not worry about the consequences. To the contrary, we constantly worry about the consequences. We feel threatened by the repressed material and continuously guard against it becoming conscious.

Avoidance of feelings and awarenesses requires energy, and this energy expenditure creates psychic *tension*, which is soon translated into a generalized physical tension. Our muscles tense and we get headaches. We feel stressed and anxious, often without even knowing we are carrying all of this around. There is a sense of unease whose origin is difficult to identify. But consider how this unease benefits the goals of repression. When we are stressed and anxious, it is difficult for us to do any real thinking or working or fixing of ourselves. We're just tense. Distracted. Confused. Frustrated. And when we feel like this, we are primed for other behaviors of avoidance.

Regression

Regression is a formal psychological term that describes the process whereby an individual uses coping skills learned earlier in life to manage stressful experiences in the present. There is nothing wrong with this in principle; all knowledge, after all, is cumulative. But when regression operates within us, it usually is an indicator that our coping skills (involving particular feelings) are not very well developed. For example, young adults frequently regress to previously learned patterns of behavior when they rejoin the company of their parents. The reason is because it is easier and less stressful to go back to old behavior patterns than it is to assert oneself and establish new behavior patterns that more accurately reflect the nature of the changing relationships. For the same reason, old friends easily fall into behavior patterns learned many years previously. Lovers too, avoiding difficult changes, awarenesses, and decisions in relationships, can slip into childish behaviors.

Regression does not function only in the context of relationships. All of us, as we face novelty and uncertainty in our life, seem to carry a strong nostalgic wish for our past as children, when decisions, for good or ill, were made for us and we possessed little or no responsibility for our fate. Adulthood requires thinking, effort, decision making, and responsibility. Bridging the chasm between dependence and independence is hard work, and no one has left a road map. The rewards of maturity are fabulous, but every once in awhile, we shrink from the challenge.

Reactivity and Compulsion

When we commit feelings and awarenesses to unconsciousness, we commit ourselves to obeying consistent patterns of avoidance with regard to them. If we want the material to remain unconscious, we cannot allow our gaze or feelings to settle too long in one place or allow our train of thought to proceed too far in certain directions. As a result, we live on guard against feelings and awarenesses.

How do we avoid feelings and awarenesses? It's easy enough: distraction, confusion, tension, loss of consciousness, automaticity, *reactivity*. The avoider hops on the merry-go-round, and there's always a horse handy. Throughout this process, however, the avoider is merely a passenger. We perform these behaviors without perceiving the unconscious motivations controlling them.

Avoided feelings and awarenesses are secrets that we harbor even from ourselves. Because our secrets involve difficult feelings and awarenesses, we become frightened of them—frightened of the confusion, doubt, and irresolution that hover about them. We really wish they would just go away. Avoidance may be an unrealistic option, but the overwhelming majority of us are willing to give it a try.

When experiences in our life push us near areas of hurt, observe our reaction. We become skittish, jumpy, and nervous. And when we draw near to the orbit of our pain, the first thing the ego wants is to get away—*now.* So we act now. Our behavior becomes *compulsive,* insistent, and irrational. We crave distraction. We crave avoidance. We crave blindness. Fear of encountering painful feelings and awarenesses is the foundation of all compulsive behavior.

Camouflage

"Tell me lies, tell me sweet little lies," croons the voice in a popular song. It's a familiar theme. We all live with lies, decorations we place on the past, present, and future to make our life more palatable. The question we need to ask ourselves, though, is how many lies, and to what extent are we willing to deny reality in order to maintain these pretty pictures? For example: Are we willing to wipe clean the slate of our childhood feelings by asserting that our childhood wasn't really traumatic or didn't affect us much? Are we willing to deny feelings that tell us something's wrong in order to keep our marriage together? Will we continue to deny a drug or alcohol problem when it's already affected our friends, family, and health?

To distinguish *camouflage* from blatant untruths (which many of us would find impossible to maintain), let me propose that camouflage is more subtle than patent falsehoods, and most successful when an element of uncertainty is introduced into assessments. For example, if we are experiencing residual pain from growing up in a family in which we received inadequate attention or approval from a parent, maybe we will balance the portrait of our childhood by citing our adult accomplishments as evidence that our family life was nurturing. In the recoil of hurt from an abusive act in a relationship, we may revise our assessment of the act by listing to ourselves all of our partner's good qualities—qualities that overshadow the abusive act, until it happens again. The alcoholic who is able to hold on to his job has "proof" that he has no problem. We forgive the "friend" who consistently betrays our trust, because she is, after all, our friend.

We hold on to unrealistic assessments of our lives because we are afraid of seeing ourselves and our relationships more honestly. Recognizing that a parent genuinely was or is abusive is known to be one of the most difficult assessments a child can make. If a child cannot trust even her parent, then whom *can* she trust in the world? Similarly, recognizing shortcomings and failures in our life means we must surrender comfortable illusions about ourselves. And running like an underground current beneath these rationalizations and oversights is our deep fear of the *consequences* of recognition, which would mean change in our relationships with others as well as in our own self-understanding. In this way our decorations serve our own weaknesses and inabilities, primarily our unwillingness to embrace reality and to make decisions accordingly.

Intellectualization

Wait a minute. So you know what your problems are? You understand why you have a drug habit that's killing you? You know why you act out of anger, why you keep getting into relationships that don't work, why you act compulsively, why you sabotage your future? You've been to therapy, to AA, to Co-Dependents Anonymous, to Adult Children of Dysfunctional Families, to Gamblers Anonymous, to Narcotics Anonymous? You've done the self-help route? Well then, how come problems are so hard to fix? If it's so easy to know what our problems are, then why is it so hard for us to settle them, leave them behind, and get on with our life?

This defense is called *intellectualization*. Beware, armchair psychologists, this technique may make you uncomfortable. What happens in intellectualization is we come a good way through the psychoanalytic process, we become able to identify the causes for certain behaviors in our life, but when it comes to taking responsibility for our life and making the changes we must make to harmonize our real life with our ideals, we're unable to follow through on what we've learned. So we intellectualize about the process, about our feelings. But do we allow ourselves to *feel* them?

This is where many people experience difficulty in the psychoanalytic process. Intellectual abilities are essential to the success of the therapeutic process—it is very important to be able to accurately identify the sources and causes for certain behaviors and feelings within ourselves, but intellectual skills, alas, can take us only so far. Certain aspects of the therapeutic process are intellectual, others are emotional and cathartic. And for the therapeutic process to be successful, we must allow ourselves to *feel our feelings*. But most of us experience a tremendous amount of difficulty with this assignment.

If you're an intellectual person, you can protect yourself against feelings for an entire lifetime. Intellectualize it, rationalize it, talk about it over coffee—just don't *feel* anything, for heaven's sake. Intellectualization is one of our most powerful and valuable self-management skills, but we need to recognize its limitations. Above all, we must be careful not to allow intellectual ability to become another defense against feelings and awarenesses—unless, of course, we genuinely do need to put some distance between our self and certain feelings. But eventually we want to experience our feelings with as few buffers as possible erected against them.

Intellectualization is a slippery and seductive defense. We can talk and act informed about all of the new ideas we are learning in psychology, but the truth is that psychology either allows us access to our feelings and teaches us to become conscious managers of them in our everyday life, or it's all just talk.

A Curious Friend

Repression's function genuinely is to protect us. The day we are diagnosed with cancer, the day a friend or family member dies suddenly, the day a lover betrays us, our ability to avoid reality for a while, to not deal with our feelings for a couple of days or so, can be a welcome buffer against the emotional storms provoked by such experiences. Our ability to avoid difficult feelings and awarenesses provides us with a margin of clearance above them. In this light, repression is like a stalling tactic. It is an opportunity to buy some time until the day comes when we must excavate the repressed material and work to integrate it into conscious awareness.

In the pages that follow, it is not my intention to diminish in any way the benefit that such a protective mechanism affords us. Anyone who has been through an especially traumatic situation knows the occasional need for numbness that repression so effectively fulfills. What I do wish to discuss, however, are two common misuses of repression, for it is its misuse that causes undesirable side effects. And the fact is that rather than consciously managing it, we tend to use this defense mechanism inappropriately.

Our first problem with repression is that instead of using it as a *temporary* buffer against disturbing feelings and awarenesses, we can fall into the trap of using it to permanently avoid difficult material. This is not a realistic navigation of our environment. Furthermore, avoidance is hardly a winning strategy for problem solving. Here we arrive at our first negative consequence of repression: *It never solves anything.* Repression is never more than a Band-Aid on a wound that will require further medical attention if it is going to heal properly.

Another problem with repression is our tendency to use it to manage problems that are not genuinely life threatening. Instead of doing the work needed for integration of difficult feelings and awarenesses, we can choose instead to adopt a lazy approach to self-management. We can choose not to see ourselves and our relationships as honestly as we are able. We can decline to accept and assert responsibility for events that fall within our realm of control. We can deny feelings and awarenesses that a more sympathetic response would hear and validate.

The fact that repression is an unconscious defense presents us with a familiar paradox. How can we be responsible for a defense over which we possess no control? Fair enough. Indeed, as long as we remain uneducated about repression, then there genuinely is very little we can do about its unconscious direction of our lives. Accordingly, our task now is to redress this state of affairs and return to conscious management those arenas of our lives that have been ceded to unconscious control.

UNIFYING FEELINGS AND AWARENESSES

Repression Is Optional

When all is said and done, we must recognize that repression is a strategy for managing feelings and awarenesses, not an inherent or inexorable component of our personalities. Repression is an *option.* Either we can repress feelings and awarenesses or we can resolve to manage this material consciously. It's our decision.

The remainder of this chapter is dedicated to enabling ourselves to achieve ever greater conscious control of our life. Our goal, stated simply, is to move areas of feeling and awareness that currently are managed unconsciously, through techniques of avoidance, into the realm of conscious awareness and decision making. The formidable challenge that lies before us is this: Dare we mix our conscious and unconscious knowledge? Can we live our intellectual and emotional lives without resorting to the lens-distorting defense of repression? Are we prepared to welcome the repressed material of our life? All of these tasks are necessary to achieve a unified personality.

As enticement toward this goal, I offer that our reward for the hard work of eliminating repression is psychological power. As we proceed, we will learn that an empowered ego does *not* need repression to manage feelings and awarenesses. The ego that has learned conscious management skills has learned to control repression, rather than repression controlling the ego. Which side of this coin we are on will create a world of difference in our lives.

If we choose to pursue this goal, then what we need as we begin along the path are tools—tools that will help us to help ourselves. The topic of mental health skills consumes the rest of our attention in this chapter.

The Therapeutic Path

The goal of psychoanalysis, in a broad sense, is to teach its clients the art of psychological and emotional healing. In the discussion that follows, I do not intend to introduce anything new, or different, even, from the healing process that psychotherapy instructs. The reason for this is that psychotherapy, when practiced properly, works. The therapeutic path of integration has been discovered and is successfully pursued each day by the countless thousands who have learned its course. What I do believe is helpful, however, is to divide the therapeutic process into its three essential stages: the *identification* of repressed feelings and awarenesses; the *acceptance* of these feelings and awarenesses, once we have made ourselves aware of them; and finally, our *resolution* toward these feelings and awarenesses, that is, a process of conscious decision making undertaken with regard to the new material.

Knowing the stages of the therapeutic process helps us locate our position on the "therapeutic path." The integration process, we may infer, will not always be an easy transition to effect. Put another way, there is a reason why repressed material is repressed. The integration of avoided feelings and awarenesses into conscious understanding will invariably be accompanied by some measure of pain. Accordingly, when we are in the midst of the integration process, knowledge of the process itself is very valuable. When our emotional moorings are cast adrift by some difficult experience, our confidence in the therapeutic process occasionally is our only support. Dividing the process also is useful because it serves to remind us that all stages are necessary for successful assimilations of repressed material. For example, it is not enough merely to be able to *identify* problem areas in our lives. For integration to be successful, both the cathartic experience of acceptance and the empowering experience of resolution must be fulfilled.

STEP ONE: IDENTIFICATION

Dreams and Identification

If you visit a therapist with a problem in your life, sooner or later you will be asked about your dreams. "Any nightmares?" the therapist will encourage. "Dreams of being out of control? Dreams where you can't find the brake on your car?"

If you answer yes, your therapist will want to know more. "Whose car were you driving? Was it your car or was it the family car?" If you tell your therapist it was a *new* car, his or her eyes will light up. "Ah! A new car! That you were taking out for a test drive? That reminds you of a new relationship you are in?"

For all players in the mental health game, dreams are highly valued shortcuts in what often are laborious, resistance-laden meanderings toward identification. Dreams enable us to accurately identify avoided feelings and awarenesses in a very short period of time, so that we can then proceed to the work of integrating this material into conscious awareness. Dreams are able to identify with precision the location of past events that hurt us or significantly affected our development to the point where we still, at some level, are recoiling from the impact. And dreams consistently pinpoint the origin of current unresolved feelings. Dreams offer a steady stream of access to material that, for practical purposes, simply would be otherwise unavailable. For all of these reasons, dream work is an invaluable tool for identifying unconscious feelings and awarenesses.

In chapter nine we explored dream construction and saw how dreams metamorphose from transparent to disguised representations when repressed material is included in their content. Accordingly, the occasion of diguised dreams should serve as an alert that we may be avoiding certain feelings and awarenesses. This is not to say that all disguised dreams contain repressed material. Indeed, as we improve in our dream interpretation skills, we likely will find that many dreams that we thought were disguised simply eluded our free-associative ability at first.

Dreams are an unparalleled tool for identification of repressed feelings and awarenesses. They should be included in all of our unification efforts. But because we have already explored this relationship, let us move on to the identification of repression in waking experience. Paying attention to the unconscious while we are awake may seem like a peculiar idea, but soon we will find that waking experience is abundantly rich with clues to the nature of unconscious feelings and awarenesses. The key is to learn to *look* for these clues.

Behaviors of Avoidance

Repression, as we said earlier, is a response to anxiety. The anxiety that accompanies repression is a result of the fact that the ego feels threatened by the material it is avoiding. When repression becomes active, keeping us distracted, confused, compulsive, single-minded, nervous, tense, and so forth, all of this activity inside us can be felt. Repression can be felt by a trained ego.

The paradox of this shift in our being, however, which is dramatic, is that it can be so difficult to recognize. When repression begins to operate, it immediately causes us to become off our center. We move from being conscious, present, and sensitive in our actions and in our experience of ourselves to being reactive, single-minded, forgetful, flighty, and compulsive. Despite the telltale clues, the transition still can be extremely difficult to identify. Why? Because when repression begins to operate, our ability for consciousness, as a rule, *vanishes.* Remember, repression does not want us to recognize our avoidance.

Single-mindedness, automaticity, being lost in thought, in fantasy, carrying on conversations with ourselves—what feature do all avoidance behaviors share? When we fall into them, we tend to perform them automatically. We can become consistently unreflective for extended periods of time.

In chapter eight, when we discussed consciousness in waking experience, we arrived at an unusual conclusion. We said that consciousness actually is only an intermittent characteristic of waking experience—that periods of consciousness alternate with periods of single-mindedness. We also said that one of the great illusions of consciousness is its seeming continuity. That is, we assume we are always conscious when we are awake, when in truth we are conscious only occasionally.

If we wish to learn where repression "hides" in waking experience, the place to begin looking is in behaviors we perform unconsciously. *The absence of consciousness in waking experience is our biggest clue to the presence of repression.* We also want to be educated about symptomologies of repression. Accordingly, when we notice tension; when we notice ourselves becoming anxious, disturbed, uneasy, unable to concentrate, distracted, single-minded; when we realize that we are operating in some reactive fog, that consciousness has been absent from our experience for an extended period of time; when we feel confusion of our emotions; when we feel the urge for compulsive behavior; when we see ourselves tighten physically and mentally when we enter some emotionally charged situation—when we notice ourselves move off our center—then we must stop. We simply must stop, and we must recognize our emotional disturbance. If we can do this, we are halfway through the identification process.

Free-Associating on Symptomologies of Repression

When we detect behaviors of avoidance operating within us, we are faced with the task of identifying their motivation. Given our knowledge of avoidance so far, we might phrase the riddle as follows: "What feeling or awareness is it that is already inside me, that I'm already feeling and that I'm already aware of, but that I do not wish to recognize?" Conceptually it's so easy. The feelings and awarenesses are already inside us. It should be a snap to figure out what's bothering us. Practically, though, it's so much more difficult. In short, this is the phenomenon of *resistance*. Even when we are aware of repression, it can be exceedingly difficult to coax the specific, repressed material to light.

To illustrate the process of free-associating on the symptomology of repression, I wish to offer the reader three examples. The first identification will be easy and will be accomplished without the use of any dreams to help us to identify our feelings. The latter two examples, on the other hand, both will require dream work to uncover the repressed material. In the last two examples, see if you can't figure out what's bothering me— before I do.

An Easy Identification

We've all had terribly busy weeks at work, where we constantly seem to be running behind schedule, where twenty tasks demand our attention all at once, where we race from appointment to appointment. They're stressful weeks. At the end of our day, we're exhausted. We eat dinner, we try to relax and unwind, but we are also aware that tomorrow the process will begin again.

Let's say you are having one of these weeks. Then, all of a sudden, in midweek, a friend calls and says he wants to go out. You haven't seen your friend for a while, and after all, he is one of your best friends. Before you know it, and without checking in on your feelings (these are the feelings that are avoided, performed out of attachment to an ideal of friendship), you agree to go out. Right after you get off the phone, a curious thing happens. You notice a dragging tension. "What is it?" you ask yourself. You take a moment to think. The feeling began just after you got off the phone with your friend. Soon enough you realize what you did. You just made plans to go out, when what you really want to do, in fact need to do, is to stay home and have some quiet time to yourself. Your week has been so busy that going out tonight just feels like more work.

A simple slip of the mind, or a subtle action of repression? Perhaps a little of both. But if you really don't want to go out tonight, and you conveniently forgot about this while your friend was on the telephone, then it may be that you felt obliged to fulfill your own, and your friend's, expectation of friendship. Which isn't necessarily a bad thing. The curious thing, though, is that you made the decision without considering your feelings and without taking the time to make a conscious decision that included acknowledgment of those feelings.

Perhaps you are thinking that my example is trite, that repression actually is more complicated than this and usually involves a great deal more analysis to successfully uncover.[45] Well, yes and no. Feelings and awarenesses that we are afraid of do not reveal themselves so easily to conscious awareness, as we are about to see. Nevertheless, my reason for including this example is to draw our attention in nearly the opposite direction. There is no doubt but that repression operates in relation to traumatic feelings and awareness. My point, however, is that repression operates in so many mundane situations as well. Indeed, the trained eye will see repression operate hundreds of times in the course

---

[45]Oedipal feelings, according to Freud and psychoanalytic schools, contain our most deeply repressed drives. The Oedipus complex concerns our infantile desire to have our mother sexually and, as a result, to murder our father, whom we perceive as a competitor for our mother's affection. (For women, the inverse dynamic is referred to as the Elektra complex.) As children (Oedipal and Elektra dynamics become emplaced between the ages of two and six), we are powerless to fulfill our desire. Our sexual advances toward our mother are rebuffed, and our father is clearly more powerful than we. As a compromise against losing our mother's affection, we learn to abandon or repress our desire for her by identifying with the values and behaviors that she wants us to learn. The same compromise occurs with our father, though for a different reason. We are afraid, in an immature sense, that our father will genitally mutilate us (castration complex) as punishment for our desire for our mother and as retaliation against our wish to kill him. So we repress our murderous feelings and begin a similar compromise of trying to please him.

of a normal day. It really is that common, and it really pervades that broad a spectrum of human behavior. It is important to learn the subtle operations of repression in addition to its more obvious manifestations.

This having been clarified, let us deal with some more difficult feelings.

The Riddle of the Shadow

Not long ago a good friend of mine, a contemporary, called me on the phone and delivered some very sad news: He had just been diagnosed with cancer. There was no doubt about it, either. The cancer showed up plainly on the X rays and they had already performed a biopsy. He was scheduled for surgery in a week.

Needless to say, I was devastated. After I got off the phone, I recall thinking that this was the first time a major disease had struck so close to home. We all grow up hearing about disease, about kidney and liver failure, dialysis, and triple heart bypasses, but for myself, this was the first time it was someone my own age. I sighed and thought about how my parents must have endured this many times, watching contemporaries stricken with disease. It was a sad time for me.

I was attentive to my feelings in the aftermath of this news. I thought of my friend often, said many prayers for him, and watched myself navigate my own feelings. "It's impossible," I often said to myself. "He's so *young.*" But damned if it wasn't true.

A few days after receiving this news, a curious process began. I remember I awoke one morning feeling tense and distracted. At first it was just an annoyance—an inability to concentrate, a wandering off of my mind during breakfast. I noticed it, dismissed it, then noticed it again. I worked to identify its source. It wasn't too hard to figure. "Hell, yes," I said to myself,

"I'm disturbed. My friend's in a lot of pain right now. *I'm* in a lot of pain."

For some reason, though, unlike other times when I identify sources of stress in my life, this disturbance didn't go away. I went about my day, but the nagging feeling stayed with me. I had the distinct sensation that a shadow was following me. What in heck was bothering me?

The next morning, when the feeling was still with me, I decided to do some serious identification work. I couldn't remember any dreams from the night before, so I did the next best thing. I made a mental list of all possible sources of tension and stress in my life, and then I held each source up in my mind's eye and allowed myself to feel my feelings. All of the usual concerns—money, relationships, family, career—and now my friend's new illness. I free-associated on each source, watching my thoughts, waiting for fantasies, listening for a ring of resonance with this new feeling. I felt nothing.

The next two days were unlike anything I have ever experienced. The uncomfortable feeling simply would *not* leave me. My analytic skills were exhausted, and as a result I was growing increasingly alienated from myself. I could not figure out what was disturbing me. By now the shadow was a full-blown externalized presence. "What?" I asked it. No reply. An occasional smoker, I was now chain-smoking. My apartment was growing increasingly claustrophobic.

At the time I was living in an isolated part of the country, but I knew some friends who lived a three-hour drive away. At a certain point the tension became unbearable. I got in my car and drove. When I arrived, I didn't tell my friends of my temporary insanity. I told them I'd gotten cabin fever and needed to unwind. I drank some beers and finally fell asleep, still a bundle of tension but relieved to be in the company of friends. That morning I had the following dream:

In the dream, I was sitting with someone, having a conversation. After awhile, I realized I didn't know whom I was speaking with. I looked up and immediately recognized that I was talking to Death. It was the grim reaper, just like in the movies. I turned to get a better look at his face. Death was wearing a black hood, but when I looked at him, I saw he had only one eye. His left eye was gone, the skin drawn tight over the empty socket. Underneath a gnarled nose was a broad stretch of white, pigmentless skin. Death was decidedly unattractive. Then, much to my dismay, Death reached out his hand and, with his finger, touched my shoulder.

When Death touched me, I understood the symbology. Or did I? I was vaguely lucid at this point in the dream and suddenly realized that I *had* to know. If my "number was up," then I wanted to know, because I figured I would have to face Death and prepare my last bit of time accordingly. If Death was just dropping by to say hello, on the other hand, I also wanted to know that, for any uncertainty in my present condition would confuse me terribly. I had a quick talk with my spirit guide, a spark of the divine that I believe lives inside me—inside us all. "I want to know," I said. I listened with all my being. Deep inside, I heard an answer. No, this was just a visit.

Did you solve the riddle of the Shadow before I did? My friend's illness made me aware of my *own* mortality. As it turns out, my concerns were much more selfish than I'd dared imagine.

The other story I want to tell doesn't deal with such deep themes.

Clearing My Windshield

Over the course of my life, like anyone, I have been involved in a number of relationships. Most have been pleasant and rewarding, but through the years, I never felt that I had found the right partner for myself. Then of course that day comes when you meet someone and you think, "This is it! I've found the one!" And you get carried away on the wings of angels and you are very happy and live in a world only lovers know, and you get married and have children and everything's wonderful. Unless, of course, you made the wrong choice.

Not too long ago, I made the wrong choice. Not too big a deal. It hurts and you get over it, you have to deal with the debris that's left in its wake, and hopefully you learn some valuable lessons from it. My problem was that after an appropriate period of mourning and healing and resolutions not to make the wrong choice again, I promptly went out and did just that. Ouch!

Survivors of unrequited love know the meaning of the saying, "Once bitten, twice shy." My situation now, however, was that I was twice bitten and, accordingly, four times shy. But the funny thing was, I didn't know it!

Don't misunderstand. In the aftermath of this second debacle, I was very pensive and sober about my feelings. I relived a lot of both relationships in my mind, worked to understand what had happened, and actually came out feeling pretty good about most of my participation in each. What I didn't anticipate, however, was how these two relationships, cumulatively, would impact my future relationships. It wasn't until I had the following dream that I began to piece it all together.

In the dream, I was in my car with my mother, who was driving. It had been raining out, and consequently the car windows were a little fogged. As the dream began, I reached over and turned on the fan to blow some cool air on the windshield. No problem. The windshield started to clear.

My mother drove up the street, driving my car skillfully, I noted. She said she knew a shortcut, a path we could take that would lead us where we wanted to go. We were in one part of a city and wanted to get to a different part. At this point in the dream, she stopped the car and asked me to look to my right. I opened the car door and saw a long set of stairs that climbed a tall embankment. The stairs, I recognized, would take us to a different part of the city. "Will your car make it?" my mother asked. I looked at the stairs and considered it. My car's been a lot of places. I thought it would make it. Still, it *is* a flight of stairs. "Um . . . yeah . . . well, maybe . . . But it's *stairs,* you know."

Then my mother saw the road she was looking for. It was in front of us, it was blacktop, and it wound around to our right. The problem, however, from my point of view, was that we were now standing amid hundreds of snakes. Big snakes, huge snakes, and medium and little snakes. In the dream, I stayed on the road a safe distance from them. I was intrigued by the snakes, but they also made me nervous.

As I was contemplating my fear of the snakes, I looked over and saw my mother leaning down to pull a huge boa constrictor onto the roadway behind us. She was using the snake to mark our path so that other travelers would also be able to find it. The snake she lifted was an old snake, a female snake that I sensed had had lots of babies. The snake didn't seem to mind or notice much as my mother moved it, and it soon settled down to sleep again. As I watched my mother, I was completely envious of her absence of fear. I was fascinated by the snakes and wanted to hold them, but I also knew I was deeply afraid of them. I decided to leave well enough alone.

At this point in the dream, my mother disappeared. I continued up the roadway alone. "So many snakes," I kept thinking. A medium-size snake caught my eye and I stopped to take a better look at it. It occurred to me that I was dreaming. I paused and looked at the hundreds of snakes strewn about the lawn. Definitely dreaming, I decided. Knowing I was dreaming, I looked back at the snake that had caught my eye. I wanted to touch it, to pick it up and handle it, but my fear was simply too great. I reminded myself that I was dreaming and that the snake was just a representation. "That may be," I answered myself, "but I am not going over there and touching that snake." I was afraid I'd get bitten.

When I woke from this dream, the symbology of the snake still eluded me. I was upset that I hadn't engaged the representation—asked it to metamorphose or struck up a conversation with it so that it would have revealed itself more. On the other hand, I had to acknowledge that I was really frightened of whatever the snake represented.

Awareness of repression is an odd feeling. Part of me wanted to know what the snake represented, but another part of me really didn't want to know. With a sigh, I turned to face my fears. I free-associated on the symbology of the snake: life force, energy, transformation, metamorphosis, death. I watched myself search for intellectual explanations. None of them rang true. I was still avoiding. The answer was close; all I had to do was allow myself to *feel* it. I closed my eyes and in my mind went back into the dream. I could see the snake and could still feel my fear. I asked the symbol to metamorphose. All of a sudden, like a genie from a bottle, the snake transformed into a curvaceous woman. Sexual energy? I was skeptical. But the more I thought about it, the more I realized that the metamorphosis was right on. I was afraid of getting hurt again. I had just recently resumed dating, and it was bringing back some difficult memories. More difficult, I realized, than I cared to acknowledge.

STEP TWO: ACCEPTANCE

The first step of the integration process, as we have said, is largely an intellectual step. When we work to make unconscious feelings conscious, we use our intellectual and analytic abilities as best we can to identify the feelings—to pull them up out of the depths of unconscious management and obfuscation. Our ability to free-associate, not only on the contents of our dreams but also on the feelings and behaviors of our waking life, is an essential component of this intellectual identification process.

Once we have identified feelings and awarenesses we have been avoiding, the second step is cathartic. Acceptance is a period during which we work to grow accustomed to new feelings. We lower our resistive strength and body armor and work to accept our feelings. If there is an area of our life that is causing us pain—a loss we have experienced, or an event whose remembrance causes pangs of regret, even several years later—then now is the time to explore it. When we encounter sensitive areas within us, we want to recognize these areas and acknowledge their difficulty. We can say it to ourselves: "I have a difficult time with this area." Not only can we say it, but for the time being we need to hold on to our difficult feelings, turn them over in our hearts, and learn their nature as best we can.

Why is feeling feelings so important? Why must *all* feelings be honored, even ones that hurt or that cause us pain to acknowledge? The answer is simple: because not feeling feelings—seriously—is just another way of avoiding them.

Earlier we said that a lesson we should take away from our exploration of repression is that nothing in the human mind simply "goes away." Because of this, we said, repression is an inherently unenlightened strategy for managing feelings. We can avoid feelings and awarenesses within us, but the truth is that we never can escape them.

The goal of acceptance is to learn to give voice to all feelings and awarenesses inside us, to not be *afraid* of feelings and awarenesses. The difference in management that we achieve is the removal of a primary level of self-censorship. Instead of regulating the feelings and awarenesses we allow ourselves to feel, regulation is moved to how we choose to respond to this material.

If you experiment with this transition in feelings management, you will immediately discover one of its most important benefits. Acknowledging feelings and awarenesses, whether the feelings are happy or sad, is always a self-affirming process. When we take time to inventory and acquaint ourselves with our feelings, we are deeming them legitimate, valid, and worthy of our attention. We are listening to ourselves—to our whole selves—with respect and sensitivity. In the same light, we quickly learn that not listening to our feelings is a genuinely unhealthful process. Not listening, in truth, is a very destructive form of self-censorship. It is a denial of ourselves, which in turn damages our sense of self-worth.

To effect this trick of self-management, we need fulfill only one criteria: We must adopt the policy that *all* of our feelings and awarenesses will be given voice, no matter what they are, no matter how much hurt attends the process, and no matter how much illusion we must surrender to bring the material into consciousness. If we wish to unify our conscious and unconscious awarenesses, we must allow this process to begin.

The process of validating all feelings and awarenesses is harder than it sounds. Unconscious feelings and awarenesses are able to frighten and confuse us, and the pain of acknowledgment occasionally may seem to outweigh the reward of integration. Nevertheless, a simple wisdom to remember about feelings is this: There is no such thing as a "bad" feeling. Feelings are just feelings. How we choose to *respond* to our feelings is where we can leave room for self-judgment.

STEP THREE: RESOLUTION

Do you like yourself? Play around with this exercise for a moment. Do it sometime when you are alone and have some quiet time. Ask yourself, "Do I like myself?" It's an important question, because whether or not we like ourselves (at this deeper, inner, self-evaluative level) is what self-esteem is all about. If our answer to this question is yes, we do like ourselves, then it is said that we possess healthy self-esteem, and our life choices should reflect this affirmation. If the answer is no—we find we don't like ourselves, or we don't like certain parts of ourselves very well—then our self-esteem is low, and this valuation will be reflected in our decision making.

Healthy self-esteem is cultivated by an individual's commitment to living her life in accordance with the values and goals she holds for herself. In *The Power of Self-Esteem,* Dr. Nathaniel Branden writes that healthy self-esteem is characterized by an individual's attempt to live consciously, responsibly, and with integrity; by the creation within oneself of a commitment to awareness, which Branden also calls "the will to understand"; by an individual developing the will to persevere in the face of adversity or temporary setbacks; by the ability for "strategic detachment"—"knowing that you are more than your problems"; by thinking independently when it comes to relationships, values, and goals; by independence versus conformity, self-expression versus self-repudiation, self-assertion versus self-surrender; by a willingness to tolerate aloneness; by honesty of intention; and by consistency of behavior with values.

Of this last characteristic, consistency of behavior with values, Branden observes, "When we behave in ways that conflict with our judgements of what is appropriate, we lose face in our own eyes. We respect ourselves less. If the policy becomes habitual, we trust ourselves less—or cease to trust ourselves at all."[46] Not surprisingly, self-esteem is also characterized by a well-developed sense of acceptance. Branden writes:

[46]Nathaniel Branden, *The Power of Self-Esteem* (Deerfield Beach, Fla.: Health Communications, Inc., 1992), 65.

To be self-accepting does not mean to be without a wish to change, improve or evolve. It means not to be at war with ourselves—not to deny the reality of what is true of us right now, at this moment of our existence. We deal here with the issue of respect for and acceptance of the facts—in this case, the facts of our own being. . . . Accepting what I am requires that I approach the contemplation of my experience with an attitude that makes the concept of approval or disapproval irrelevant: *the desire to be aware.*[47]

Having a healthy self-esteem is important because it reverberates through every single aspect of our life. When we strive to live in accordance with the values and standards we hold for ourselves, we feel good about ourselves. When we feel good about ourselves, it is easier for us to respect ourselves. If we respect ourselves, we expend the effort required to take good care of ourselves. When we possess a commitment to awareness and honesty, we endeavor to use all our ability to know, to see, and to understand relationships in our life—especially our relationship with our self.

When self-esteem is healthy, our sense of confidence is high; we like ourselves—why shouldn't others? We are not afraid of intimacy; we know and understand ourselves and have learned, usually through difficult experience, not to participate in behaviors that cause us *not* to like ourselves, that lower our self-esteem. When we fail to achieve our goals, our powers of recovery are swift. We are not afraid to acknowledge failure. To the contrary, we seek to learn where we failed, why we failed, what we overlooked, and what forces were at work that caused us to perform the behavior we do not like. When self-esteem is high, problems

[47]Ibid., 67–68.

are faced, not avoided. We feel confident in our ability to manage our future. We help ourselves to understand and resist the urge for self-destructive behaviors. There is a sense of continuity, stability, trust, and consistency to our personality. We like ourselves. We can rely on ourselves. We are good to ourselves.

When self-esteem is low, on the other hand, we do not feel this sense of consistency and trust in our personality. We are confused by our personality. There are conflicts in our lives that are not being faced and resolved. Our tolerance of unresolved feelings works to undermine our sense of power and control. Soon we grow accustomed to inconsistency, to irresolution, to the failure and sabotage of the goals we set for ourselves. We learn—again, usually through difficult experience—not to trust ourselves. We begin to think that we do not deserve to be happy, strong, able people with healthy relationships. In a curious twist of logic, we begin to seek out lifestyles and relationships that confirm our low self-opinions. We avoid healthy people because we feel different from them. We don't like ourselves, so we engage in self-destructive behaviors. We don't take good care of ourselves, even at the basic levels of nutrition, health, and personal hygiene. Possessing a low sense of self-esteem, possessing an awareness of the goals we might like for ourselves but feel forever exiled from attaining, is a condition of chronic disempowerment.

When self-esteem is low, there is only one healthy course of action to take: to begin the work of *repairing our self-esteem*. We do so, generally speaking, in two ways. First, we work to understand the causes of low self-esteem and to change the behaviors responsible for it. Second, we repair our self-esteem by learning to harmonize—through honest self-assessment, discipline, and perseverance—our real life with our ideals.

Sources of Low Self-Esteem

Unconscious behaviors have an inherently damaging effect on our sense of self-esteem. No matter how we try to rationalize our actions, each time we participate in an unconscious behavior of avoidance, it as an admission of personal powerlessness. We are unable to manage our feelings and awarenesses consciously. We are unable to identify, accept, and make conscious decisions about our responses to difficult psychic material. And so, in a nanosecond, and hoping we will not see what we are about to do, we make the handoff: Simultaneously we surrender the difficult feelings and awarenesses to unconscious management and begin the game of pretending that we did not do what we know we just did.

As an admission of powerlessness, I think we can understand why repression damages self-esteem. Another reason why it damages self-esteem is because repression is intrinsically dishonest. Recall the fundamental paradox of repression, discussed earlier: In every instance of repression, we already know what material it is we are avoiding recognizing at the conscious level. The same is true for feelings. We're already feeling, unconsciously, the feelings we are consciously avoiding. The unfortunate truth is that each and every time we play the game, repression is an illusion—a lie that we tell to ourselves. But the one person we can never successfully lie to is ourself.

The fact that repression is an unconscious defense makes its influence on self-esteem all the more insidious. The truth is that it is easy for us to blunder into using repression as a self-management skill without having any appreciation for its negative consequences. What is alarming, however, is that low self-esteem is one of the most vicious psychological dynamics we can enter. Indeed, a self-esteem that is untended is like a ship at sea adrift without a pilot. And the cold fact is that a man or woman who does not respect the psychological ocean will soon be brought down.

Self-Esteem and Decision Making

We are focusing on self-esteem in this section of our discussion because it has such an enormous impact on our ability to make healthy decisions. When self-esteem is high, it is easy for us to make healthy decisions. They make sense to us; they agree with our inner sense of what is proper and appropriate for us. When self-esteem is low, however, the curious truth is that we don't feel that we *deserve* healthy choices. What is more painful is that in keeping with this low self-assessment, we simply do not make healthy choices. It's a powerful law of self-esteem and a genuine catch-22: In order to feel good about ourselves, we need to make healthy and self-affirming decisions, but if we don't feel good about ourselves, it is almost impossible for us to make healthy decisions.

Healthy Self-Esteem Is Created Through Decisions and Actions

Self-esteem is not a fixed quality; rather, it is a constantly changing and growing experience of ourselves. If we live well today and meet our goals and ideals, we will carry this sense of satisfaction and well-being into tomorrow. But if we participate in behaviors today that we will later regret or find humiliating, then tomorrow our sense of self-esteem will be damaged. We are not living up to our own ideals. There is a contradiction between what we would like to believe about ourselves and the truth we know. Self-esteem is a self-valuation process that is constantly in motion. Self-esteem is earned, each and every day, by our daily decisions and actions.

Because self-esteem plays such an important role in our psychological power (our ability to make and maintain decisions), psychological wisdom suggests that we learn to care for it. A fundamental goal of resolution, accordingly, is to maintain our self-esteem. We do this in two ways: by making a commitment to honest self-assessment, and by consistently embracing decisions that enhance self-esteem. Despite the simplicity of our goal, resolution is often the most challenging of all therapeutic traverses. This is because in resolution, we are attempting to actually change our life; to become strong enough in ourselves to replace unhealthy methods of coping with feelings and awarenesses (unconscious skills) with healthy and constructive ones (conscious skills). In resolution we are working to achieve a genuine metamorphosis of self, where healthy and self-affirming decisions are embraced, and where unsuccessful coping strategies are consciously identified and, increasingly, left behind for good.

Assessing Self-Esteem

Individuals seeking to care for their self-esteem must learn to assess their self-esteem honestly. Honest self-assessment is characterized by one's commitment to truth and objectivity when assessing feelings about oneself. Honest self-assessment requires a willingness to acknowledge unpleasant feelings and awarenesses as well as pleasant and pleasing ones. For this reason, honest self-assessment invariably is more difficult than is false self-assessment. False self-assessment, on the other hand, is not committed to truth and objectivity in the self-evaluation process. False self-assessment willingly tolerates illusions about the self and employs defense mechanisms of repression to maintain these illusions.

The process of self-assessment is similar to the acceptance

stage of integration. We ask ourselves many of the same questions: How are we feeling about ourselves? How are we feeling about certain relationships and activities? Are we happy? Are we satisfied? Why or why not? What could we do to make our lives more consistent with our ideals? What behaviors do we see in ourselves that we wish we could lay aside? What behaviors do we wish we could cultivate? It can be a delicate inventory, and many of us will find it difficult to acknowledge feelings and awarenesses that conflict with our ideals. But learning to listen to *all* voices that express inner needs, feelings, and awarenesses is what honest self-assessment is all about. It's not how you *think* you should feel, it's how you *do* feel.

If you can figure this out, the next question is: What are you going to do about it?

Resolving Sources of Low Self-Esteem

Like anyone, as you lead yourself through the self-assessment process, you will find some areas of your life you are unhappy with. Your discontents may be large or small: Your work is not fulfilling. Some of your relationships are unsatisfying. You wish you could devote more time to your hobbies and avocation. Occasionally you feel depressed. Sometimes you are lazy. You wish you took better care of your health. You wish you were more assertive, less angry, happier, and so forth.

Why is your life like this? Who has told you that this is the lifestyle you deserve? Why is your work not fulfilling, why don't you embrace your hobbies more enthusiastically, and why are you in relationships that are unsatisfying? Why are you depressed? Why are you lazy? Why don't you take better care of your health? Who wrote this script you are acting out?

The answer, of course, is that we write our own scripts. But the curious part of this answer is that we write our scripts according to our sense of self-esteem. And while it is appropriate and correct for us to trace our sources of low self-esteem back to other people (family, friends, lovers, coworkers, social status, acquaintances, and so on), and to certain defining events in our life (betrayal, abuse, neglect, violation of personal boundaries), and fact is that we are the only ones who can give this low valuation to ourselves. Put another way, other people can tell us that we are undeserving of basic civil dignities; whether or not we believe them is a very different story.

One of the difficult distinctions to make in assessing self-esteem involves power. A sad fact of life on this planet (if the reader will excuse a generalization) is that enormous numbers of people are simply no damn good. People who have the smallest amounts of power abuse that power in impossibly tiresome ways. From the neighborhood bully who picks on eight- and ten-year-olds to the older child who mercilessly humiliates his younger siblings, from the blue-collar worker who beats his spouse to the high-powered executive who emotionally abuses hers, people with power take advantage of people without power. When you are on the short end of this equation, there is only one word to describe your condition: *powerlessness.* And we all know that a dog that is kicked too many times soon learns to carry its tail between its legs.

It is difficult to recover from acts of abuse that were committed when we were powerless. Abuse that occurs very early, from birth to three years, is known to be profoundly damaging, and the prognosis for recovery is not good. We are more likely to survive abuse that occurs in later years; the foundation was set before the abuser began to tinker. When we look in our life for sources of low self-esteem, we frequently will find that low self-opinions were implanted when we were quite young—and all of our teenage years are included in this category. The point is that if we were subjected to acts of abuse in our life, and there are very few of us who were not, it is important to recognize that we were taken advantage of when in a position of powerlessness. A fact of human development is that we are relatively powerless for an extended period of time (at least until we reach the age of majority).

The reason why power is such an important factor in assessing self-esteem involves the issue of responsibility. Even when we clearly are powerless over abusive, damaging, or painful events in our lives, it is an uncanny characteristic of human response that we tend to take responsibility for these events. If we are turned down for a job position, we immediately begin to doubt ourselves, even if we are eminently qualified for the spot. Someone treats us badly or abusively in a relationship and we soon wonder what we did to cause it. The child who is beaten soon learns that she is a bad child who deserves to be beaten. All of these are serious errors of attribution, of which all have the severely damaging effect that we begin to think less of ourselves. We begin to think we deserve less in our life. That we don't deserve to be in healthy relationships. That we don't deserve to be treated with decency and respect. That we don't deserve jobs or positions commensurate with our skills. And if we believe these self-valuations, the unfortunate consequence is that we will get what we think we deserve.

Another confounding factor in the assessment of self-esteem is that our responses to difficult feelings and awarenesses, because they are usually unconscious, become sources of low self-esteem in themselves. For example, the woman who drinks compulsively to avoid feelings of shame that stem from some earlier emotional abuse has added a new layer of confusion on top of the old one. What is particularly confusing is that the link between the feelings of shame and the compulsive behavior typically is lost. The result is that the woman knows she drinks compulsively (and she is ashamed about this); what she does not know is *why* she drinks.

In the resolution stage of the therapeutic process, we are unable to change our histories and miraculously grant ourselves a new sense of self-esteem. We are unable to change the fact that we were abused—that we were taken advantage of when we were in a position of powerlessness. Nor can we rewrite our history so that painful experiences, and the inadequate responses we made to manage them, are erased. Nevertheless, two important things can be done. The first is that we can learn to change our responses to those painful feelings and awarenesses; indeed, this is the primary task of resolution. We can make a conscious commitment to manage feelings and awarenesses in a way that does not damage our self-esteem. Because of the negative effect that unconscious skills have on self-esteem, this means that we must resolve ourselves, at every opportunity, to resist unconscious management skills in favor of conscious skills. Which means that every time we observe behaviors of avoidance, we must subject them to the therapeutic process of identification, acceptance, and resolution. The reason why we will be successful now, as opposed to earlier times, when we were confused by our behaviors, is because we are now armed with a very powerful set of psychological skills. If we are able to identify unconscious behaviors of avoidance, we will know to stop and begin the work of figuring out what feelings and awarenesses the behavior is serving to hide or obscure from our awareness. We use our emotional, intuitive, and free-associative skills to identify the feelings. Because we know avoidance is not a healthy way to manage feelings, we send ourselves down to the next step on the path. In acceptance, we hold on to these feelings because we know they are difficult for us to manage and because we recognize our tendency to avoid them. We make ourselves acquainted and comfortable with these new feelings. We remind ourselves that listening to feelings is always healthy, always self-affirming. Once we traverse this stage of the process, we send the feelings over to resolution. We want to make a decision about our feelings. We want to walk away from the resolution stage of managing feelings and awarenesses with a concrete, specific decision about our feelings. And the decision we want to make is *to not manage the feelings unconsciously anymore.*

The second goal of resolution is to liberate ourselves from errors of attribution that falsely burden our self-esteem. We need to recognize that we are not responsible for abuse committed when we were in a position of powerlessness. To the contrary, the perpetrator was responsible, and it is the perpetrator who carries the burden of low self-esteem. Our power today, and our responsibility, is to prevent further abuse. An integral task of claiming our own self-esteem is that we remove ourselves from positions where abuse is present or even possible. This type of preventive protectiveness does not mean that we cannot trust other people, but it does mean that we learn to be careful who we trust.

Effective self-management is informed about the therapeutic process. The individual who is successful in the process helps himself or herself to traverse its course at every step. When we uncover difficult feelings and awarenesses in our life, we need to know what steps we must take to integrate these feelings and awarenesses into our conscious awareness. We need to know what steps are required so that we do not slip back into managing the problem unconsciously. We want to make progress against repression within us, and we want to help ourselves achieve the resolutions we set for ourselves so that we are able to truly change our lives.

The road to self-mastery is long, and we should not expect to become expert at it very quickly. Self-knowledge and self-mastery are the gradually acquired fruits of the psychological education process. The goal of integrating difficult feelings and awarenesses is not to become perfect in managing our lives; it is simply to become better at managing our feelings and awarenesses. We must make the process of self-management continually more conscious, and to replace unhealthy coping skills with healthy coping skills. We will fail hundreds and even thousands of times in our attempts to manage ourselves. But each instance of failure is also an opportunity for learning, and we will find, as we persevere in our efforts for conscious control of our behavior, that we will also make great improvement.

If I can leave the reader with a final thought from this chapter, there is no question in my mind what it should be: Learn to pay attention to your sense of self-esteem. Care for it, nurture it, learn even to be selfish with it. Guard it like your most valuable possession. Self-esteem is one of the most warmly discussed topics in mental health today, for one simple, compelling reason: The relationship you maintain with yourself will be the most determining relationship of your life.

11

Searching for Consciousness

What, indeed, does man know of himself! Can he even once perceive himself completely, laid out as if in an illumined glass case? Does not nature keep much the most from him, even about his body, to spellbind and confine him in a proud, deceptive consciousness, far from the coils of the intestines, the quick current of the blood stream, and the involved tremors of the fibers? She threw away the key; and woe to the calamitous curiosity which might peer just once through a crack in the chamber of consciousness and sense that man rests upon the merciless, the greedy, the insatiable, the murderous, in the indifference of his ignorance—hanging in dreams, as it were, upon the back of a tiger. In view of this, whence in all the world comes the urge for truth?

FRIEDRICH NIETZCHE,
ON TRUTH AND LIE IN AN EXTRA-MORAL SENSE

It is the parable of the house that is being prepared by the servants for the arrival of the absent master. The house is in a state of chaos and instead of the cook being in the kitchen, she is in the garden, the gardener works in the kitchen, the groom in the pantry, and everybody is in the wrong place. Whenever a caller rings the front door bell a different servant opens the door and in answer to inquiries declares that he is the master of the house. At last some of the more discerning of the servants realize how disastrous is the state of affairs and they agree to try to work together to remedy it. These more responsible servants or "I"s decide to elect a deputy-steward who will put everybody in his place and give orders. In time the deputy-steward is replaced by a real steward and eventually, when the house has been brought into a satisfactory state, the master himself arrives.

—PETER OUSPENSKY,
VENTURE WITH IDEAS

Of all the minds who have attempted the great question of consciousness in human experience, perhaps no one is more intriguing to read than is the Russian philosopher Georgi Ivanovitch Gurdjieff. His writings are not widely known, but his discussions of consciousness invariably hold a ring of truth for lucid dreamers. Indeed, anyone who has worked diligently with the experiential development of the ability for consciousness within himself or herself will find an immediate friend in Gurdjieff.

Gurdjieff is perhaps most distinguished from other philosophers in that he was confident that he had identified and understood precisely the meaning of consciousness, which he described as self-remembering. As we saw in chapter eight, this concept of self-remembering coincides precisely with the understanding of consciousness we arrived at through our examination of lucid dreaming.

Gurdjieff believed that the development of consciousness was the foundation for all true psychological growth. Gurdjieff measured psychological development not only by a person's intellectual abilities but also by his or her experiential abilities— that is, a person's abilities "to be" and "to do." Both abilities, said Gurdjieff, require fluency and mastery, experientially, with the ability for consciousness.

The goal of developing consciousness, according to Gurdjieff, was to create a new "center" within oneself, from which one could self-observe honestly and objectively. It was through continual work at self-observation, from the "perch" of consciousness created within oneself, that one eventually could learn how one's "machine" works. Consciousness afforded its happy possessor self-unification, ever-increasing effectiveness in all pursuits, and freedom from illusion. Without consciousness, Gurdjieff said, humans were doomed to "mechanical," "accidental," and "automatic" living. Life will happen to us instead of our being able to control and create the events of our life.

I am including in this chapter a lengthy excerpt of Gurdjieff's writing to introduce lucid dreamers to his work and because his discussion touches upon some relevant themes. In the second half of the excerpt, Gurdjieff admonishes his audience to be wary of "charlatans and hucksters" in the field of self-development—those who promise simple paths to enlightenment. Even though the excerpt is a transcription of a talk given in 1914, Gurdjieff's words of admonition seem as applicable today as they were some eighty years ago. Today our popular culture swarms with "vendors of enlightenment," individuals who confidently assure us that "the enlightenment you seek is just a phone call away" on the Psychic Network Hotline or that by eating special candy bars and "brain" foods and by adding doses of potassium to our diets, we will veritably transform ourselves into enlightened beings by tomorrow morning. No warranty is offered for these techniques, of course. The psychic hotline, we read in small print at the bottom of the television screen, is "for entertainment purposes only," and all miracle foods are ingested entirely at the consumer's own risk.

Sensitives and psychics surely exist, and there is no question but that informed diets are a foundation of good health. Gurdjieff's admonition, however, really is directed against the miraculous nature of these "solutions" to everyday problems. Consciousness and empowerment, says Gurdjieff, are known processes, but they require *work*—long work, hard work, and consistent work. Work on developing one's ability for consciousness, developing one's ability for discrimination, and uncovering and gaining control over areas of automaticity within one's being. Woe indeed to the individual who thinks he or she will eat a candy bar and tomorrow "be" anything—except, perhaps, a bit more deluded. This, said Gurdjieff, is not the way.

Reader be warned: Gurdjieff intends the following excerpt to be provocative.[48] This passage will lead us to our final chapter.

Very often in conversation with people, one hears the direct or implied view that man as we meet with him in ordinary life could be regarded as almost the center of the universe, the "crown of creation," or at any rate that he is a large and important entity; that his possibilities are almost unlimited, his powers almost infinite. But even with such views there are a number of reservations: they say that, for this, exceptional conditions are necessary, special circumstances, inspiration, revelation and so on.

However, if we examine this conception of "man," we see at once that it is made up of features which belong not to one man but to a number of known or supposed separate individuals. We never meet such a man in real life, neither in the present nor as a historical personage in the past. For every man has his own weaknesses and if you look closely the mirage of greatness and power disintegrates.

But the most interesting thing is not that people clothe others in this mirage but that, owing to a peculiar feature of their own psyche, they transfer it to themselves, if not in its entirety, at least in part as a reflection. And so, although they are almost nonentities, they imag-

[48]G. I. Gurdjieff, *Views From the Real World* (New York: Arkana Press, 1973), 42–59.

ine themselves to be that collective type or not far removed from it.

But if a man knows how to be sincere with himself—not sincere as the word is usually understood, but
mercilessly sincere—then, to the question "What are
you?" he will not expect a comforting reply. So now,
without waiting for you to come nearer to experiencing
for yourselves what I am speaking about, I suggest that,
in order to understand better what I mean, each of you
should now ask himself the question "What am I?" I am
certain that 95 percent of you will be puzzled by this
question and will answer with another one: "What do
you mean?"

And this will prove that a man has lived all his life
without asking himself this question, has taken for
granted, as axiomatic, that he is "something," even something very valuable, something he has never questioned.
At the same time he is unable to explain to another what
this something is, unable to convey even any idea of it,
for he himself does not know what it is. Is the reason he
does not know because, in fact, this "something" does
not exist but is merely assumed to exist? Is it not strange
that people pay so little attention to themselves in the
sense of self-knowledge? Is it not strange with what dull
complacency they shut their eyes to what they really are
and spend their lives in the pleasant conviction that they
represent something valuable? They fail to see the
galling emptiness hidden behind the highly painted
facade created by their self-delusion and do not realize
that its value is purely conventional.

True, this is not always so. Not everyone looks at
himself so superficially. There do exist enquiring minds,
which long for the truth of the heart, seek it, strive to

solve the problems set by life, try to penetrate to the essence of things and phenomena and to penetrate into themselves. If a man reasons and thinks soundly, no matter what path he follows in solving these problems, he must inevitably arrive back at himself, and begin with the solution of the problem of what he is himself and what his place is in the world around him. For without this knowledge, he will have no focal point in his search. Socrates' words "Know thyself" remain for all those who seek true knowledge and being.

I have just used a new word—"being." To make sure that we all understand the same thing by it, I shall have to say a few words in explanation.

We have just been questioning whether what a man thinks about himself corresponds to what he is in reality, and you have asked yourselves what you are. Here is a doctor, there an engineer, there an artist. Are they in reality what we think they are? Can we treat the personality of each one as identical with his profession, with the experience which that profession, or the preparation for it, has given him?

Every man comes into the world like a clean sheet of paper; and then the people and circumstances around him begin vying with each other to dirty this sheet and to cover it with writing. Education, the formation of morals, information we call knowledge—all feelings of duty, honor, conscience and so on—enter here. And they all claim that the methods adopted for grafting these shoots known as man's "personality" to the trunk are immutable and infallible. Gradually the sheet is dirtied, and the dirtier with so-called "knowledge" the sheet becomes, the cleverer the man is considered to be. The more writing there is in the place called "duty," the more honest the possessor is said to be; and so it is with everything. And the dirty sheet itself, seeing that people consider its "dirt" as merit, considers it valuable. This is an example of what we call "man," to which we often even add such words as talent and genius. Yet our "genius" will have his mood spoiled for the whole day if he does not find his slippers beside his bed when he wakes up in the morning.

A man is not free either in his manifestations or in his life. He cannot be what he wishes to be and what he thinks he is. He is not like his picture of himself, and the words "man, the crown of creation" do not apply to him.

"Man"—this is a proud term, but we must ask ourselves what kind of man? Not the man, surely, who is irritated at trifles, who gives his attention to petty matters and gets involved in everything around him. To have the right to call himself a man, he must be a man; and this "being" comes only through self-knowledge and work on oneself in the directions that become clear through self-knowledge.

Have you ever tried to watch yourself mentally when your attention has not been set on some definite problem for concentration? I suppose most of you are familiar with this, although perhaps only a few have systematically watched it in themselves. You are no doubt aware of the way we think by chance association, when our thought strings disconnected scenes and memories together, when everything that falls within the field of our consciousness, or merely touches it lightly, calls up these chance associations in our thought. The string of thoughts seems to go on uninterruptedly, weaving together fragments of representations of former perceptions, taken from different recordings in our memories. And these recordings turn and unwind while our thinking apparatus deftly weaves its threads of thought continuously from this material. The records of our feelings revolve in the same way—pleasant and unpleasant, joy and sorrow, laughter and irritation, pleasure and pain, sympathy and antipathy. You hear yourself praised and you are pleased; someone reproves you and your mood is spoiled. Something new captures your interest and instantly makes you forget what interested you just as much the moment before. Gradually your interest attaches you to the new thing to such an extent that you sink into it from head to foot; suddenly you do not possess it any more, you have disappeared, you are bound to and dissolved in this thing; in fact it possesses you, it has captivated you, and this infatuation, this capacity for being captivated is, under many different guises, a property of each one of us. This binds us and prevents our being free. By the same token it takes away our strength and our time, leaving us no possibility of being objective and free—two essential qualities for anyone who decides to follow the way of self-knowledge.

We must strive for freedom if we strive for self-knowledge. The task of self-knowledge and of further self-development is of such importance and seriousness, it demands such intensity of effort, that to attempt it any old way and amongst other things is impossible. The person who undertakes this task must put it first in his life, which is not so long that he can afford to squander it on trifles.

What can allow a man to spend his time profitably in his search, if not freedom from every kind of attachment?

Freedom and seriousness. Not the kind of seriousness which looks out from under knitted brows with pursed lips, carefully restrained gestures and words filtered through the teeth, but the kind of seriousness that means determination and persistence in the search, intensity and constancy in it, so that a man, even when resting, continues with his main task.

Ask yourselves—are you free? Many are inclined to answer "yes," if they are relatively secure in a material sense and do not have to worry about the morrow, if they depend on no one for their livelihood or in the choice of their conditions of life. But is this freedom? Is it only a question of external conditions?

You have plenty of money, let us say. You live in luxury and enjoy general respect and esteem. The people who run your well-organized business are absolutely honest and devoted to you. In a word, you have a very good life. Perhaps you think so yourself and consider yourself wholly free, for after all your time is your own. You are a patron of the arts, you settle world problems over a cup of coffee and you may even be interested in the development of hidden spiritual powers. Problems of the spirit are not foreign to you and you are at home among philosophical ideas. You are educated and well read. Having some erudition in many fields, you are known as a clever man, for you find your way easily in all sorts of pursuits; you are an example of a cultured man. In short, you are to be envied.

In the morning you wake up under the influence of an unpleasant dream. The slightly depressed mood disappeared but has left its trace in a kind of lassitude and uncertainty of movement. You go to the mirror to brush your hair and by accident drop your hairbrush. You pick it up and just as you have dusted it off, you drop it again. This time you pick it up with a shade of impatience and because of that you drop it a third time. You try to grab it in midair but instead, it flies at the mirror. In vain you jump to catch it. Smash! . . . a star-shaped cluster of cracks appears in the antique mirror you were so proud of. Hell! The records of discontent begin to turn. You need to vent your annoyance on someone. Finding that your servant has forgotten to put the newspaper beside your morning coffee, your cup of patience overflows and you decide you can no longer stand the wretched man in the house.

Now it is time for you to go out. Taking advantage of the fine day, your destination not being far away, you decide to walk while your car follows slowly behind. The bright sun somewhat mollifies you. Your attention is attracted to a crowd that has gathered around a man lying unconscious on the pavement. With the help of the onlookers the porter puts him into a cab and he is driven off to the hospital. Notice how the strangely familiar face of the driver is connected in your associations and reminds you of the accident you had last year. You were returning home from a gay birthday party. What a delicious cake they had there! This servant of yours who forgot your morning paper ruined your breakfast. Why not make up for it now? After all, cake and coffee are extremely important! Here is the fashionable café you sometimes go to with your friends. But why have you remembered about the accident? You had surely almost forgotten about the morning's unpleasantness. . . . And now, do your cake and coffee really taste so good?

You see the two ladies at the next table. What a charming blonde! She glances at you and whispers to her companion, "That's the sort of man I like."

Surely none of your troubles are worth wasting time on or getting upset about. Need one point out how your mood changed from the moment you met the blonde and how it lasted while you were with her? You return home humming a gay tune and even the broken mirror only provokes a smile. But what about the business you went out for in the morning? You have only just re-membered it . . . that's clever! Still, it does not matter. You can telephone. You lift the receiver and the opera-tor gives you the wrong number. You ring again and get the same number. Some man says sharply that he is sick of you—you say it is not your fault, an altercation fol-lows and you are surprised to learn that you are a fool and an idiot, and that if you call again . . . The rumpled carpet under your foot irritates you, and you should hear the tone of voice in which you reprove the servant who is handing you a letter. The letter is from a man you re-spect and whose good opinion you value. The contents of the letter are so flattering to you that your irritation gradually dies down and is replaced by the pleasantly embarrassed feeling that flattery arouses. You finish reading it in a most amiable mood.

I could continue this picture of your day—you free man. Perhaps you think I have been exaggerating. No, this is a true scenario taken from life.

This was a day in the life of a man well known both at home and abroad, a day reconstructed and described by him that same evening as a vivid example of associa-tive thinking and feeling. Tell me where is the freedom when people and things possess a man to such an extent

that he forgets his mood, his business and himself? In a
man who is subject to such variation can there be any
serious attitude toward his search?

You understand better now that a man need not
necessarily be what he appears to be, that the question is
not one of external circumstances and facts but of the
inner structure of a man and of his attitude toward these
facts. But perhaps this is only true for his associations;
with regard to things he "knows" about, perhaps the situation is different.

But I ask you, if for some reason each of you was unable to put your knowledge to practical use for several
years, how much would remain? Would this not be like
having materials which in time dry up and evaporate?
Remember the comparison with a clean sheet of paper.
And indeed in the course of our life we are learning
something the whole time, and we call the results of this
learning "knowledge." And in spite of this knowledge,
do we not often prove to be ignorant, remote from real
life and therefore ill-adapted to it? We are half-educated
like tadpoles, or more often simply "educated" people
with a little information about many things but all of it
woolly and inadequate. Indeed it is merely information.
We cannot call it knowledge, since knowledge is an in-
alienable property of a man; it cannot be more and it
cannot be less. For a man "knows" only when he himself
"is" that knowledge. As for your convictions—have you
never known them to change? Are they not also subject
to fluctuation like everything else in us? Would it not be
more accurate to call them opinions rather than convictions, dependent as much on our mood as on our information or perhaps simply on the state of our digestion at
a given moment?

Every one of you is a rather uninteresting example of an animated automaton. You think that a "soul," and even a "spirit," is necessary to do what you do and live as you live. But perhaps it is enough to have a key for winding up the spring of your mechanism. Your daily portions of food help to wind you up and renew the purposeless antics of associations again and again. From this background separate thoughts are selected and you attempt to connect them into a whole and pass them off as valuable and as your own. We also pick out feelings and sensations, moods and experiences and out of all this we create the mirage of an inner life, call ourselves conscious and reasoning beings, talk about God, about eternity, about eternal life and other higher matters; we speak about everything imaginable, judge and discuss, define and evaluate, but we omit to speak about ourselves and about our own real objective value, for we are all convinced that if there is anything lacking in us, we can acquire it.

If in what I have said I have succeeded even to a small extent in making clear in what chaos is the being we call man, you will be able to answer for yourselves the question of what he lacks and what he can obtain if he remains as he is, what of value he can add to the value he himself represents.

I have already said that there are people who hunger and thirst for truth. If they examine the problems of life and are sincere with themselves, they soon become convinced that it is not possible to live as they have lived and to be what they have been until now; that a way out of this situation is essential and that a man can develop his hidden capacities and powers only by cleaning his machine of the dirt that has clogged it in the course of his life. But in order to undertake this cleaning in a rational way, he has to see what needs to be cleaned, where and how; but to see this for himself is almost impossible. In order to see anything of this one has to look from the outside; and for this mutual help is necessary.

If you remember the example I gave of identification, you will see how blind a man is when he identifies with his moods, feelings and thoughts. But is our dependence on things only limited to what can be observed at first glance? These things are so much in relief that they cannot help catching the eye. You remember how we spoke about people's characters, roughly dividing them into good and bad? As a man gets to know himself, he continually finds new areas of his mechanicalness—let us call it automatism—domains where his will, his "I wish," has no power, areas not subject to him, so confused and subtle that it is impossible to find his way about in them without the help and the authoritative guidance of someone who knows.

This briefly is the state of things in the realm of self-knowledge: in order to do you must know; but to know you must find out how to know. We cannot find this out by ourselves.

Besides self-knowledge, there is another aspect of the search—self-development. Let us see how things stand there. It is clear that a man left to his own devices cannot wring out of his little finger the knowledge of how to develop and, still less, exactly what to develop in himself.

Gradually, by meeting people who are searching, by talking to them and by reading relevant books, a man becomes drawn into the sphere of questions concerning self-development.

But what may he meet here? First of all an abyss of
the most unpardonable charlatanism, based entirely on
the greed for making money by hoaxing gullible people
who are seeking a way out of their spiritual impotence.
But before a man learns to divide the wheat from the
tares, a long time must elapse and perhaps the urge itself
to find the truth will flicker and go out in him, or will
become morbidly perverted and his blunted flair may
lead him into such a labyrinth that the path out of it, fig-
uratively speaking, will lead straight to the devil. If a man
succeeds in getting out of this first swamp, he may fall
into a new quagmire of pseudo-knowledge. In that case
truth will be served up in such an indigestible and vague
form that it produces the impression of a pathological
delirium. He will be shown ways and means of developing hidden powers and capacities which he is promised,
if he is persistent, will without much trouble give him
power and domain over everything, including animate
creatures, inert matter and the elements. All these sys-
tems, based on a variety of theories, are extraordinarily
alluring, no doubt precisely because of their vagueness.
They have a particular attraction for the half-educated,
those who are half-instructed in positivist knowledge.

In view of the fact that most questions studied from
the point of view of esoteric and occult theories often
go beyond the limits of data accessible to modern science, these theories often look down on it. Although on
the one hand they give positivist science its due, on the
other, they belittle its importance and leave the impression that science is not only a failure but even worse.

What is the use then of going to the university, of
studying and straining over official textbooks, if theories

of this kind enable one to look down on all other learning and to pass judgment on scientific questions?

But there is one important thing the study of such theories does not give; it does not engender objectivity in questions of knowledge, less so even than science. Indeed it tends to blur a man's brain and to diminish his capacity for reasoning and thinking soundly, and leads him toward psychopathy. This is the effect of such theories on the half-educated who take them for authentic revelation. But their effect is not very different on scientists themselves, who may have been affected, however slightly, by the poison of discontent with existing things. Our thinking machine possesses the capacity to be convinced of anything you like, provided it is repeatedly and persistently influenced in the required direction. A thing that may appear absurd to start with will in the end become rationalized, provided it is repeated sufficiently often and with sufficient conviction. And, just as one type will repeat ready-made words which have stuck in his mind, so a second type will find intricate proofs and paradoxes to explain what he says. But both are equally to be pitied. All these theories offer assertions which, like dogmas, usually cannot be verified. Or in any case they cannot be verified by the means available to us.

Then methods and ways of self-development are suggested which are said to lead to a state in which their assertions can be verified. There can be no objection to this in principle. But the consistent practice of these methods may lead the overzealous seeker to highly undesirable results. A man who accepts occult theories and believes himself knowledgeable in this sphere will not be able to resist the temptation to put into practice the knowledge of the methods he has gained in his research, that is, he will pass from knowledge to action. Perhaps he will act with circumspection, avoiding methods which from his point of view are risky, and applying the more reliable and authentic ways; perhaps he will observe with the greatest of care. All the same, the temptation to apply them and the insistence on the necessity for doing so, as well as the emphasis laid on the miraculous nature of the results and the concealment of their dark sides, will lead a man to try them.

Perhaps, in trying them, a man will find methods which are harmless for him. Perhaps, in applying them, he will even get something from them. In general, all the methods for self-development which are offered, whether for verification, as a means, or as an end, are often contradictory and incomprehensible. Dealing as they do with such an intricate, little-known machine as the human organism and with that side of our life closely connected with it which we call our psyche, the least mistake in carrying them out, the smallest error or excess of pressure can lead to irreparable damage to the machine.

It is indeed lucky if a man escapes from this morass more or less intact. Unfortunately very many of those who are engaged in the development of spiritual powers and capacities end their career in a lunatic asylum or ruin their health and psyche to such a degree, that they become complete invalids, unable to adapt to life. Their ranks are swelled by those who are attracted to pseudo-occultism out of a longing for anything miraculous and mysterious. There are also those exceptionally weak-willed individuals who are failures in life and who, out of considerations of personal gain, dream of developing in themselves the power and the ability to subjugate others. And finally there are people who are simply looking for variety in life, for ways of forgetting their sorrows, of finding distraction from the boredom of the daily round and of escaping its conflicts.

As their hopes of attaining the qualities they counted on begin to dwindle, it is easy for them to fall into intentional charlatanism. I remember a classic example. A certain seeker after psychic power, a man who was well off, well read, who had traveled widely in his search for anything miraculous, ended by going bankrupt and became at the same time disillusioned in all his researches.

Looking for another means of livelihood, he hit on the idea of making use of the pseudo-knowledge on which he had spent so much money and energy. No sooner said than done. He wrote a book, bearing one of those titles that adorn the covers of occult books, something like *A Course in Development of the Hidden Forces in Man.*

This course was written in seven lectures and represented a short encyclopedia of secret methods for developing magnetism, hypnotism, telepathy, clairvoyance, clairaudience, escape into the astral realm, levitation and other alluring capacities. The course was well advertised, put on sale at an exceedingly high price, although in the end an appreciable discount (up to 95 percent) was offered to the more persistent or parsimonious customers on condition that they recommend it to their friends.

Owing to the general interest in such matters, the success of the course exceeded all the expectations of its compiler. Soon he began to receive letters from purchasers in enthusiastic, reverent and deferential tones, addressing him as "dear teacher" and "wise mentor" and expressing deepest gratitude for the wonderful exposition and most valuable instruction which gave them the possibility of developing various occult capacities remarkably quickly.

These letters made a considerable collection and each of them surprised him until there at last came a letter informing him that with the help of his course someone had, in about a month, become able to levitate. This indeed overran the cup of his astonishment.

Here are his actual words: "I am astonished at the absurdity of things that happen. I, who wrote the course, have no very clear idea of the nature of the phenomena I am teaching. Yet these idiots not only find their way about in this gibberish but even learn something from it and now some superidiot has even learned to fly. It is, of course, all nonsense. He can go to hell. . . . Soon they will put him into a straitjacket. It will serve him right. We are much better off without such fools."

Occultists, do you appreciate the argument of this author of one of the textbooks on psychodevelopment? In this case, it is possible that somebody might accidentally learn something, for often a man, though ignorant himself, can speak with curious correctness about various things, without knowing how he does it. At the same time, of course, he also talks such nonsense that any truths he may have expressed are completely buried and it is utterly impossible to dig the pearl of truth out of the muckheap of every kind of nonsense.

"Why this strange capacity?" you may ask. The reason is very simple. As I have already said, we have no knowledge of our own, that is, knowledge given by life itself, knowledge that cannot be taken away from us. All our knowledge, which is merely information, may be valuable or worthless. In absorbing it like a sponge, we can easily repeat and talk about it logically and convincingly, while understanding nothing about it. It is equally easy for us to lose it, for it is not ours but has been poured into us like some liquid poured into a vessel. Crumbs of truth are scattered everywhere; and those who know and understand can see and marvel how close people live to the truth, yet how blind they are and powerless to penetrate it. But in searching for it, it is far better not to venture at all into the dark labyrinths of human stupidity and ignorance than to go there alone. For without the guidance and explanations of someone who knows, a man at every step, without noticing it, may suffer a strain, a dislocation of his machine, after which he would have to spend a great deal more on its repair than he spent damaging it.

What can you think of a solid individual who says of himself that "he is a man of perfect meekness and that his behavior is not under the jurisdiction of those around him, since he lives on a mental plane to which standards of physical life cannot be applied"? Actually, his behavior should long ago have been the subject of study by a psychiatrist. This is a man who conscientiously and persistently "works" on himself for hours daily, that is, he applies all his efforts to deepening and strengthening further the psychological twist, which is already so serious that I am convinced that he will soon be in an insane asylum.

I could quote hundreds of examples of wrongly directed search and where it leads. I could tell you the names of well-known people in public life who have become deranged through occultism and who live in our midst and astonish us by their eccentricities. I could tell you the exact method that deranged them, in what realm they "worked" and "developed" themselves and how these affected their psychological makeup and why.

But this question could form the subject of a long and separate conversation so, for lack of time, I will not permit myself to dwell on it now.

The more a man studies the obstacles and deceptions which lie in wait for him at every step in this realm, the more convinced he becomes that it is impossible to travel the path of self-development on the chance instructions of chance people, or the kind of information culled from reading and casual talk.

At the same time he gradually sees more clearly— first a feeble glimmer, then the clear light of truth which has illumined mankind throughout the ages. The beginnings of initiation are lost in the darkness of time, where the long chain of epochs unfolds. Great cultures and civilizations loom up, dimly arising from cults and mysteries, ever changing, disappearing and reappearing.

The Great Knowledge is handed on in succession from age to age, from people to people, from race to race. The great centers of initiation in India, Assyria, Egypt, Greece, illumine the world with a bright light. The revered names of the great initiates, the living bearers of the truth, are handed on reverently from generation to generation. Truth is fixed by means of symbolical writings and legends and is transmitted to the mass of people for preservation in the form of customs and ceremonies, in oral traditions, in memorials, in sacred art through the invisible quality in dance, music, sculpture and various rituals. It is communicated openly after a definite trial to those who seek it and is preserved by oral transmission in the chain of those who know. After a certain time has elapsed, the centers of initiation die out one after another, and the ancient knowledge departs through underground channels into the deep, hiding from the eyes of the seekers.

The bearers of this knowledge also hide, becoming unknown to those around them, but they do not cease to exist. From time to time separate streams break through to the surface, showing that somewhere deep down in the interior, even in our day, there flows the powerful ancient stream of true knowledge of being.

To break through to this stream, to find it—this is the task and the aim of the search; for, having found it, a man can entrust himself boldly to the way by which he intends to go; then there only remains "to know" in order "to be" and "to do." On this way a man will not be entirely alone; at difficult moments he will receive support and guidance, for all who follow this way are connected by an uninterrupted chain.

Perhaps the only positive result of all wanderings in the winding paths and tracks of occult research will be that, if a man preserves the capacity for sound judgment and thought, he will evolve that special faculty of discrimination which can be called flair. He will discard the ways of psychopathy and error and will persistently search for true ways. And here, as in self-knowledge, the principle which I have already quoted holds good: "In order to do, it is necessary to know; but in order to know, it is necessary to find out how to know."

To a man who is searching with all his being, with all his inner self, comes the unfailing conviction that to find out how to know in order to do is possible only by finding a guide with experience and knowledge, who will take on his spiritual guidance and become his teacher. And it is here that a man's flair is more important than anywhere else. He chooses a guide for himself. It is of course an indispensable condition that he choose as a guide a man who knows, or else all meaning of choice is lost. Who can tell where a guide who does not know may lead a man?

Every seeker dreams of a guide who knows, dreams about him but seldom asks himself objectively and sincerely—is he worthy of being guided? Is he ready to follow the way?

Go out one clear starlit night to some open space and look up at the sky, at those millions of worlds over your head. Remember that perhaps on each of them swarm billions of beings, similar to you or perhaps superior to you in their organization. Look at the Milky Way. The earth cannot even be called a grain of sand in this infinity. It dissolves and vanishes, and with it, you. Where are you? And is what you want simply madness?

Before all these worlds ask yourself what are your aims and hopes, your intentions and means of fulfilling them, the demands that may be made upon you and your preparedness to meet them.

A long and difficult journey is before you; you are preparing for a strange and unknown land. The way is infinitely long. You do not know if rest will be possible on the way nor where it will be possible. You should be prepared for the worst. Take all the necessities for the journey with you.

Try to forget nothing, for afterwards it will be too late and there will be no time to go back for what has been forgotten, to rectify the mistake. Weigh up your strength. Is it sufficient for the whole journey? How soon can you start?

Remember that if you spend longer on the way you will need to carry proportionately more supplies, and this will delay you further both on the way and in your preparations for it. Yet every minute is precious. Once having decided to go, there is no use wasting time.

Do not reckon on trying to come back. This experiment may cost you very dear. The guide undertakes only to take you there and, if you wish to turn back, he is not obliged to return with you. You will be left to yourself, and woe to you if you weaken or forget the way—you will never get back. And even if you remember the way, the question still remains—will you return safe and sound? For many unpleasantnesses await the lonely traveler who is not familiar with the way and the customs which prevail there. Bear in mind that your sight has the property of presenting distant objects as though they were near. Beguiled by the nearness of the aim toward which you strive, blinded by its beauty and ignorant of the measure of your own strength, you will not notice the obstacles on the way; you will not see the numerous ditches across the path. In a green meadow covered with luxuriant flowers, in the thick grass, a deep precipice is hidden. It is very easy to stumble and fall over it if your eyes are not concentrated on the step you are taking.

Do not forget to concentrate all your attention on the nearest sector of the way—do not concern yourself about far aims if you do not wish to fall over the precipice.

Yet do not forget your aim. Remember it the whole time and keep up in yourself an active endeavor toward it, so as not to lose the right direction. And once you have started, be observant; what you have passed through remains behind and will not appear again; so if you fail to notice it at the time, you never will notice it.

Do not be overcurious nor waste time on things that attract your attention but are not worth it. Time is precious and should not be wasted on things which have no direct relation to your aim.

Remember where you are and why you are here.

Do not protect yourselves and remember that no effort is made in vain.

And now you can set out on the way.

12

Mental Health

It is customary for other medical specialists to accuse psychiatrists of practicing an inexact and unscientific discipline. The fact of the matter, however, is that more is known about the cause of neurosis than is known about the vast majority of other human disorders. Through psychoanalysis it is possible to trace the etiology and development of a neurosis in an individual patient with an exactitude and precision which is seldom matched elsewhere in medicine. It is possible to come to know exactly and precisely how, when, where and why an individual develops a particular neurotic symptom or behavior pattern. It is also possible to know with equal exactitude and precision just how, when, where and why a particular neurosis can be cured or has been healed.

—M. Scott Peck,
The Road Less Traveled

My science was the only way I had of extricating myself from that chaos. Otherwise the material would have trapped me in its thicket, strangled me like jungle creepers. I took great care to try to understand every single image, every item of my psychic inventory, and to classify them scientifically—so far as this was possible—and, above all, to realize them in actual life. That is what we usually neglect to do. We allow the images to rise up, and maybe we wonder about them, but that is all. We do not take the trouble to understand them, let alone draw ethical conclusions from them. This stopping-short conjures up the negative effects of the unconscious.

—Jung,
The Undiscovered Self

When we awaken in the morning, do our dreams take us by surprise? Do we ask ourselves, "Dear Lord, where did that dream come from?" or are our dreams more mundane? The reason I ask is not to detract from the mystery and spontaneity of our dream life but rather to assess the quality of communication between our conscious and unconscious levels of awareness.

In chapter nine I suggested that as we routinely monitor our dreams, we must ask ourselves whether or not we were aware yet of the feelings and awarenesses being represented. Is the material in our dreams familiar to us, at least partially, or does it arrive each morning unannounced? When communication between conscious and unconscious abilities is good—when we have trained ourselves through dream work and the practice of consciousness in waking experience to *listen* to our mind and body and to *integrate* feelings and awarenesses into conscious awareness—then our dreams increasingly represent concerns with which we already are familiar. As a consequence of our familiarity with this material, our dreams also become more *transparent*.

NIGHTMARES

Nightmares, which we have not yet discussed specifically, are dramatic examples of transparency and obscurity. Nightmares are perhaps best defined as representations of feelings and awarenesses that cause dreamers a great deal of anxiety.[49] Within this typology of anxiety-producing dreams, however, we soon learn

---

[49]Nightmares, which occur in dream sleep, are distinguished from night terrors, which occur in the early part of the night in non–dream sleep. Sufferers of night terrors awaken abruptly from slow-wave sleep with an urgent sense of panic and fear, and usually report only one pervasive type of feeling or sensation: "I felt like someone was sitting on me, suffocating me, and there was nothing I could do about it. I thought I was going to die." By contrast, nightmares contain all of the familiar elements of dreams: involved plot

that there are two distinct types of nightmares. In transparent nightmares, dreamers understand the origin of their dreams; in obscured nightmares, they don't.

For example, Vietnam War veterans, as a sociological group, suffer from an extremely high rate of what is known as post-traumatic stress syndrome.[50] A common symptom of PTSS is nightmares. But these nightmare sufferers, in contrast to many, know what their dreams are about. In their dreams the veterans are once again in Vietnam, they are on patrol, and they are under attack and being ambushed. What is important to note, however, is that these dreams, as a rule, are transparent representations of previously experienced traumas. The war scenes, the atrocities, the fears and confusion—all are concretely represented. When the vets dream of these events, they relive the original trauma.

When dreamers do not understand their nightmares, on the other hand, when feelings and awarenesses are disguised, camouflaged, projected, and displaced, this is evidence that certain feelings and awarenesses are being avoided through repression. To illustrate, one is immediately led to consider the dreams of men and women who suffered sexual abuse as children but repressed it at such an early age that no conscious memory of it exists. These individuals also report an abnormally high incidence of nightmares, but unlike sufferers of PTSS, the origin of their dreams is obscured. In extremely disguised dreams, victims of sexual abuse experience nightmares that include feelings of

---

lines, various dream characters, and representations in a three-dimensional sensory environment. Also, sufferers of night terrors, as a rule, do not recall their nocturnal "panic attacks." Their occasion are reported by friends, family, and lovers the following day. Nightmares, on the other hand, are almost always recalled because we awaken directly from them.

[50]Almost anyone exposed to severe trauma—a natural disaster, a car accident, having a close friend die—will experience anxiety dreams in the days and weeks following the trauma.

being attacked, persecuted, suffocated, or being chased and un-able to escape. In these dreams, the perpetrator of the abuse is not clearly identified. In more transparent dreams, clues of sex-ual violation are included. Men and women dream of being raped, of being physically attacked, of having chronic difficulty in relationships with members of the same sex or the opposite sex. Despite such clues, the source of the abuse may remain unidentified.

If these dreamers are attuned to their dreams, they will rec-ognize that some sort of trauma is indicated. But the identifica-tion process typically remains shrouded in confusion, for there is no conscious memory of abuse. What is one to make of dreams, anyway? Aren't nightmares relatively normal? If a parent was in-volved or complicit in the abuse (which often is the case) then the odds of the victim receiving support or illumination from his or her parents are poor. The child grows up, but the night-mares and the questions remain. "Was I raped? Was I abused? How old was I? What will happen if I begin asking questions? Can I endure the shame of acknowledgment of abuse? Can I tolerate the awareness that my parents may not be who I wish they were?" The memory lingers, but it is too painful to be ex-perienced directly. What is interesting to observe, however, in keeping with our original line of inquiry, is that the dreams of abuse victims become progressively transparent as they are guided through the therapeutic process. As the pain is absorbed into conscious management, the nightmares also eventually stop. This is the uniform experience of nightmare sufferers who suc-cessfully traverse the healing process.

Most of us are fortunate not to have to deal with nightmares and the difficult feelings they represent. Nevertheless, we should still recognize the significance of obscurity of dream content. The rule of thumb is the more obscured our dreams are, the more likely it is that avoided material is included in them. Accordingly, dream workers should keep a continual eye open to the level of obscurity in their dreams. Eventually dream workers should be able to identify, through the process of free association, all of the thoughts, feelings, and awarenesses included in their dreams. While this goal may seem impossibly distant to the nascent dream worker, it is in fact an entirely reasonable goal. All dreams should be understood by the dreamer who creates them.

The achievement of transparency in one's dream life is a great accomplishment. The transparent reflection of feelings and awarenesses indicates that the dreamer is succeeding in his or her efforts to remove the distorting filters of repression, which previously were erected to buffer him or her from experiencing difficult feelings and awarenesses directly. When a dreamer experiences concrete representations of difficult feelings and awarenesses—feelings of confusion or of the need for corrective action in his or her own life, contradictory feelings with regard to lovers, close friends, and family members—he actually should take great encouragement from these dreams. The dream worker is growing increasingly able to manage difficult feelings and awarenesses consciously. The reduction and elimination of disguise from one's waking life, and, accordingly, from one's dream life, is a hard-won accomplishment that all dream workers should experience warm satisfaction in achieving.

THE CHALLENGE OF UNIFICATION

For a book on dreams to concentrate as much as this one does on repression is unusual. Most dream books sketch the operation of repression briefly and then hastily refer the reader to Freud for elaboration, as if repression were merely a bit player in relation to more important psychological dynamics. Anyone who studies psychoanalysis or is engaged in therapy with an analyst, however, will soon recognize that repression lies at the root of essentially all neuroses. As a result, while we can sympathize that repression is perhaps not the most engaging or entertaining of subjects for inclusion in a book on dreams, in the same breath one is forced to conclude that any discussion of dreams that fails to include such an investigation is hopelessly inadequate and in fact omits perhaps the single most relevant aspect of dreaming that dream workers need to learn. For dream workers to make genuine progress in self-understanding and to benefit in their everyday life from their study of dreams, they *must* become able to identify and observe the operation of repression within themselves and others. And they must become intimately acquainted with the experiential skills that allow them to untangle and resist the operation of repression when they observe it operating within themselves. Mastery of the defense mechanism of repression is an essential element of the psychological education process. To this end, I wholeheartedly encourage readers to embrace the thoughtful and long-term exploration of repression within themselves, which any informed understanding of dreams, and of the human mind, requires.

In chapter eleven I alluded to the possibility that the exploration of repression might be an arena of self-discovery so challenging that we should not venture in without the assistance of a trained guide. Repression is a challenging subject, and while it is possible to frame the mechanism within relatively simple models of avoidance, the experience of uncovering repressed feelings and awarenesses and then navigating our way through this unknown territory into a healthy state of integration and resolution is a difficult path to traverse. The truth is that it can be an especially difficult path to walk without help, support, and guidance from individuals familiar with the terrain.

Dream work must be recognized as an extremely active attempt to bring previously unconscious material into the realm of active awareness. And while it is true, fabulously true, that conscious exploration of the unconscious opens us to extraordinary new vistas of the mind and of psychodynamics, it is also true that not all discoveries dream work yields us about ourselves and others will be pleasant. We all have personal habits and records of behavior that we are not overly proud of, or at least that we are not anxious to place under a bright light of scrutiny. But both dream work and the practice of consciousness in waking experience are spotlights, and if we follow through on the evidence presented before us by these tools of illumination, they will force us to confront aspects of our own and others' behavior that may be displeasing to us, which, in short, may contradict some of the illusions we like to believe. The first time we begin to get glimmerings that our relationships with others, and with ourselves, are not as ideal as we may have believed; the first time we recognize consistent patterns of avoiding responsibility for behaviors we have performed in the past and may still perform in the present; the first time we allow ourselves to experience feelings, emotions, and memories we have not allowed ourselves to experience previously—all of these are potentially unsettling discoveries that dream work routinely makes available to a listening ear. And in this unfamiliar terrain, it is easy for us to lose our balance and orientation.

To this end, I wish to make some final observations and suggestions for the practicing dream worker. As the reader pursues dream work and gradually becomes confronted with the reality of repression in his or her waking experience—indeed, with the persistence and pervasiveness of repression in his or her life—he or she will occasionally become uncomfortable. The process of uncovering repressed feelings and awarenesses is difficult precisely because it is emotionally disturbing, because we are uncovering layers of illusion that allowed us to perceive our world as we wanted to see it, rather than as we actually, subconsciously, were experiencing it. Invariably we can feel disappointed, and even ashamed, that we have so willingly employed this mechanism in the construction of our waking world. My answer to this problem is twofold.

As we work to integrate repressed feelings and awarenesses into our conscious personality—indeed, as we work to make *all* feelings and awarenesses accessible to consciousness[51]—it is helpful to remember that in our past we used repression as a strategy to manage these feelings and awarenesses when other coping skills eluded us. My point is that no one is born with the skills needed to manage difficult experiences consciously. To the contrary, conscious management skills are *learned* skills.

When we understand repression as a basic coping skill—indeed, as an instinctual survival skill—it is possible for us to view our choices and actions in a kinder light than we may have been inclined previously. When we chose to repress certain feelings and awarenesses, chances are we did so because we did not possess any other skills at the time with which to manage these experiences. And we survived. As such (and I really wish to emphasize this point), when we discover repression in ourselves or we see it operating in others, there should be no shame or embarrassment about having discovered it there. Repression serves a purpose. What we do need is understanding.

My second answer to this problem of repression concerns the actions we are able to take now, in light of our psychological education.

PSYCHIC DETERMINISM

As we become more familiar with the patterns of psychological dynamics, eventually we learn that the mind is not a mechanism

---

[51]Freud's synopsis of the therapeutic process was, "Where id was, there shall ego be."

governed by random events and chance occurrences but rather is a regular and predictable system. One of the first laws of psychoanalysis, as elaborated by Charles Brenner in his seminal work *An Elementary Textbook of Psychoanalysis*, is the principle of "psychic determinism." Brenner writes,

The sense of this principle is that in the mind, as in physical nature about us, nothing happens by chance, or in a random way. Each psychic event is determined by the ones which preceded it. Events in our mental lives that may seem to be random and unrelated to what went on before are only apparently so. In fact, mental phenomena are no more capable of such a lack of causal connection with what preceded them than are physical ones. Discontinuity in this sense does not exist in mental life.[52]

This principle has been embraced by nearly all segments of the professional psychoanalytic community. In the passage above, Brenner is summarizing Freud, and both of the excerpts at the head of this chapter—one from Jung and the other from a more contemporary psychiatrist, M. Scott Peck—continue to reflect this view. I propose that as we make progress in our psychological sophistication, we too will grow to appreciate this principle. The important consequence of this appreciation, however, is that gradually we will become able to discern order and structure in what previously appeared to be random and disconnected psychological events. We will also begin to grasp the idea that concepts such as "mental health" and "personal effectiveness" are not elusive personality characteristics of mysterious origin but rather are qualities of mind that correspond, with

[52]Charles Brenner, *An Elementary Textbook of Psychoanalysis* (New York: Anchor Books, 1974), 2.

astonishing precision, to the quality of the relationship we maintain between conscious and unconscious aspects of our personality. "Unification of the personality," similarly, will move from
being a theoretical construct to being a recognizable (and
demonstrable, through dream work) consequence of psychological integration. In the same way, qualities such as personal happiness, the absence of self-destructive behaviors, and strong
powers of emotional recovery will all be recognized as consistent manifestations of healthy self-esteem. As both Jung and
Peck hinted at, the mind, when it is free of organic damage, is a
consistent and predictable machine. The happy news at the end
of the psychological journey is that mental health, happiness,
personal effectiveness, and healthy self-esteem, are all attainable
qualities of personality if we are willing to walk the path required to achieve these goals.

PSYCHOANALYTIC TOOLS

In this book we have consistently emphasized the role of mental
health skills—consciousness in waking experience and the practice of identification, acceptance, and resolution skills—as tools
for unifying conscious and unconscious feelings and awarenesses.
Paying attention, in waking experience, to our hearts, minds, and
bodies, and practicing the mental health skills of identification, acceptance, and resolve, speed the growth of self-awareness and
self-understanding. The everyday practice of mental health skills
is essential to maintaining transparency of communication between one's conscious and unconscious abilities.

Before we begin our discussion of why dream work is an especially instructional forum in which to develop mental health
skills, I first wish to examine the resistance that so many people
exhibit toward psychological education. Generally speaking,
many people seem to possess the attitude that mental health is

something that either you have or you don't. Enveloped within this assertion is the implied opinion that mental health is a given from birth. That is, you come from a good family, you grow up right, and somehow you are one of those magical, successful people who rarely has an off day. While there is an element of truth to this observation—the family *is* the arena in which most of us learn our basic responses to life—the characterization nevertheless fails to take into account the factors that are necessary for anyone's mental health, whether from a "good" family or not. It also implies that therapy—that is, diligent practice of learning mental health skills—is something of a lost cause. Either you have it or you don't, right?

Despite the meteoric rise of analytic therapy in the past century, a powerful social stigma remains attached to anyone who seeks out psychological help or endeavors to maintain a relationship with a therapist or psychiatrist. Reading books on psychology is considered acceptable in most circles, but if one wishes to see a therapist, which is really only a more formalized process of psychological education, one immediately is subjected to stigmas of being "weak," "unable to take it," and of course "crazy."

As we pursue our psychological education, it is important to understand these types of stigma; the sooner we learn the forces that motivate these beliefs, the sooner we can dispense with their attempted influence on us. First, it would be ignorant for us not to recognize that resistance to psychological knowledge, as a rule, is based overwhelmingly on fear of uncovering repressed aspects of the personality. That is, typically it is the person who wants least to learn about psychodynamics who has the most to hide from it. This is easy enough to understand. But to place the misguidedness of this stigma in larger perspective, let us consider an analogy.

If we were working in our kitchen, doing some household

repair, and inadvertently cut ourselves on the back of the hand, what would our response be? Would we ignore the wound? Would we try to pretend that we were not injured, despite the blood flowing from it? Of course not. To the contrary, most of us would stop what we were doing immediately and investigate the situation. We would inspect the wound and ask ourselves a series of questions: Is it a flesh wound or did we cut ourselves more deeply? Did we damage any nerves or tendons? Do we need professional care or is a Band-Aid sufficient? In the days following the injury, we would monitor its status. We would change its bandage, expose it to sunlight and fresh air to speed its healing, and take care not to get the area infected. Within a few weeks, the wound would be healed. There would be no guilt or shame about having received the wound, though we might determine to be more careful next time working with tools. But as for taking care of the injury, we did what was obvious.

Why, then, is mental health care so much more complicated? Why do the preservation skills that are automatic when we are confronted with a physical injury suddenly vanish when we receive an emotional wound? In fact, if we cared for our emotional injuries half as well as we care for our physical injuries, we would be markedly more healthy as a society. But the fact is that we do not. We are embarrassed by our emotional wounds. We do think others will think we are crazy, stupid, or somehow less of a person for being emotionally hurt. So instead of doing the obvious, we often do just the opposite. We hide our wounds, and we even try to pretend that we have never received *any* injuries in our long lives. The fact that emotional wounds are to a considerable degree "invisible" facilitates this process of concealment. What is the result of this lack of care for emotional injuries? What else could it be? Our wounds do not heal properly. A further outcome of this neglect, however, with infinitely more far-reaching consequences, is that we never really learn *how* to heal emotional wounds. There is a world of difference between surviving and living with an abundance of emotional health. The former is a state of chronic disempowerment, the latter a state of chronic empowerment. On which side of this equation do we wish to live?

The truth is that it is crazy *not* to think that an instrument as sensitive and delicate as the human mind could be injured and damaged. It happens all the time. What we need to do is take care of our emotional health on a regular basis by learning the same skills that professional healers have at their disposal. Above all, we need to get over our inhibitions about seeking help and about using the skills we acquire to take care of our mental health.

DREAM WORK WILL EDUCATE YOU

In chapter eight I suggested that dream work is distinguished from other types of psychological education in that it is an experiential acquaintanceship with one's personal psychodynamics. Unlike other approaches to psychological understanding, dream workers do not study repression and defense mechanisms dispassionately and from a distance. Dream workers do not watch psychological mechanisms operate only in *other* people or merely read about their operation in books. They also undertake the task of observing psychodynamics operate within themselves. Dream work is *applied* psychology, if you will. When dreams cause us to recognize feelings and awarenesses we have been avoiding in waking experience, it is an experiential confrontation with the operation of repression. Similarly, when dreams reflect resolution of formerly unconscious conflicts (for example, the cessation of anxiety dreams regarding certain experiences or relationships in our lives), it is confirmation of the effectiveness of conscious integration and resolution of the feelings and awarenesses that surround the event. Because of its experiential nature, dream work is a vital counterbalance to the tendency of the ego to intellectualize, or adorn in some other way, the realities of psychological experience. Dream work is a consistent reminder to the ego of the presence and reality of the unconscious mind.

Not only does dream work assist our goal of making psychological knowledge experiential (the task Jung alludes to in the passage at the head of this chapter), but by forcing us to confront psychological defense mechanisms, it also intiates the process of gaining conscious control over these mechanisms. There is no way to overstate the significance of these skills. If we do not learn to actively resist the operation of repression within us, if we do not learn to replace unconscious management skills with conscious ones, then all of our efforts toward psychological education, alas, have truly been for naught. Put another way, it is one thing to talk about mental health; it is quite another to enjoy it.

To effect this transition in "management style," we must achieve a working knowledge of the skills of identification, acceptance, and resolution. Dream work is an excellent forum in which to develop these skills. Are our dreams becoming more transparent? Are we improving in our ability to identify and address unconscious conflict within us? Are we learning to lower our resistance to unconscious knowledge and awarenesses? Have we improved in our ability to feel our feelings? Are we becoming more experienced with the pattern of identification, acceptance, and resolution? Are we able to observe our feelings resolving, our sense of self-esteem rising, and our dream content changing when we succeed in resolving difficult issues and emotions? Have we become alert to the symptomologies of low self-esteem? Are we able to use our dreams to help us understand its causes? Are we able to identify concrete steps that we need to take in our lives to repair our self-esteem? Are we growing more confident with the *system* of mental health?

Feelings and awarenesses, as we have stressed repeatedly in this book, are far more difficult to identify and accurately recognize than any of us might anticipate. No one is a natural master at identifying the sources for unconsciously motivated behaviors, and even people trained in the field are still challenged by the game of identification. It is because of this difficulty that we all experience in identifying feelings and awarenesses that dreams, in all therapeutic settings, continue to be so highly valued.

Acceptance, similarly, poses its own share of difficulties. In acceptance we are challenged to maintain contact with difficult feelings and awarenesses and to avoid repressing their significance to us yet again. But this task, we find, is also more difficult than it first appears. For example, it is not an uncommon occurrence, even when we are actively attentive to our feelings, to think we are long over some pain from our past. Our unconscious, however, as a rule is a far more accurate chronicler of our life than is our ego. If it is evident through our dreams that we are still wrestling with some difficult experience from our past—we dream repeatedly of an old relationship or trauma— then these dreams are clear evidence that the area we thought we resolved almost certainly is not. There is still work to be done. We must go back and reexplore the area, work to feel our feelings, and work to resolve the issues.

While acceptance is a period of active self-confrontation, resolution, as alluded to in chapter ten, really is only a fancy name for decision making. Now that we have confronted our feelings and awarenesses, what are we going to do about them? If we realize that certain relationships we maintain in our life are unhealthy or damaging to our sense of self-esteem, if we encounter undesired aspects of our behavior, then it is through the active practice of decision making that we set out to make these changes. Resolution is the deliberate and conscious process of setting goals for ourselves, and of monitoring our progress toward these goals. And our dreams, at every step of the way, will reflect the success, or inadequacy, of our daytime determinations.

PSYCHOLOGICAL EMPOWERMENT

The consistent practice of dream work, because of the psychological sophistication and experience that accrues, ultimately enables us to direct and create change in our life where previously we lacked the skills and knowledge to effect these changes. Psychological education enables us to cease having to cope with large segments of our personality controlled by unconscious responses to unconscious feelings and awarenesses, and allows us instead to understand the motivations for these feelings and awarenesses and be able to make conscious decisions about our responses. For the first time for many of us, we will be growing strong enough to choose how we wish to build and construct our life, rather than being at the mercy of unconscious reactions to events. And this is where we do, indeed, begin to take charge, command, and ever-increasing response-ability for our life.

While it is natural for us to be excited at this prospect of psychological empowerment—this, after all, is the grail we are pursuing—we need to be aware that empowerment does not come without its costs. At the end of his life, in his memoirs, Carl Jung addressed this cost succinctly:

> The images of the unconscious place a great responsibility upon a man. It is . . . a grave mistake to think that it is enough to gain some understanding of the images and that knowledge can here make a halt. Insight into them

must be converted into an ethical obligation. . . . Failure
to understand them, or a shirking of ethical responsibility, deprives [a man] of his wholeness and imposes a
painful fragmentariness on his life.[53]

As we progress in our study of psychodynamics, we invariably will encounter a curious consequence of our education: It
will become increasingly difficult for us to avoid feelings and
awarenesses *unknowingly*. Specifically, tactics of defense and eva-
sion that yesterday were palatable are not digested so smoothly
today. Not only will we recognize repression when it is manifest
in dreams, we will also grow increasingly sensitive to the uneasy
feeling that attends the presence of repression in waking experience; in short, we will learn when we are kidding ourselves.

Accordingly, psychological education places a decision before us: Do we wish to be honest in our understanding of ourselves, or are we willing (pardon my obscurity) to settle for
something "less"? If we decide to settle for something less, if we
arrive at this juncture of knowledge only to turn around and
deny and abnegate the potentiality of our unified self, then the
painful awareness that attends such a decision is that we do so
knowingly. Committing ourselves to personal honesty, on the
other hand, means we also commit to harmonizing our real life
with our ideals for ourselves and to the difficult and lifelong
work that such an orientation entails. For better or worse, psychological education places an intractable dilemma on us, and as
Jung observed, there really is no going back. Like Adam and Eve
in the tale of Genesis, we have left the innocence of unconscious
living and moved into the responsibility of knowledge and
awareness.

While both paths can appear intimidating, one course is

---

[53]Carl Jung, *Memories, Dreams, Reflections* (New York: Vintage Books, 1989), 192–193.

much easier to follow. It is natural that we are frightened at this latter course—of beginning an open and honest relationship with ourselves—but to this end I suggest that we move forward with the confidence that there is nothing that we cannot handle within ourselves. We must go forward confident in our increasing self-mastery and in our ability, if we confront disturbing or intitially horrifying feelings, memories, and awarenesses, that we will get over our distress and manage these feelings and awarenesses consciously.

We draw our confidence on this path toward psychological unification from two sources. The first is our knowledge of psychodynamics. Repression, we should know by now, is never a successful, long-term technique for managing feelings and awarenesses. The reason why it never succeeds and is a dishonest technique for managing feelings and awarenesses is because we always know, unconsciously, whatever it is that we are attempting to avoid knowing consciously. Likewise, we are always feeling, unconsciously, whatever it is that we are attempting to avoid feeling consciously. These are facts of the repressive dynamic. As a result, when we see repression operating within us, we should recognize it for the simple defense that it is. We should also know exactly what to do with it: Do our best to understand why it is there and then work to remove it, as quickly as possible, from our psychological repertoire. We must commit to replacing unconscious management skills with conscious management skills.

The second source of confidence we tap is drawn from our experience with the therapeutic process. And it is here, perhaps, that it is appropriate to broach the topic of psychological maturity.

Released from their cage of enforced unconsciousness, repressed feelings and awarenesses can strike at the unprepared ego with staggering ferocity. Indeed, allowing illusions to pass, be they about ourselves or others, may be the most difficult of all psychological hurdles. Nevertheless, while it is true that bringing unconscious feelings and awarenesses into conscious awareness can be emotionally distressing, it is also true that after awhile we grow accustomed even to this process. The feelings come, they rise up like a wave, and we stand with a great sense of foreboding in their dark shadow. If we hold fast to our principle of unification, however, and invite the waves to crash down upon us, soon we find that even the largest waves roll back to sea, and we remain standing on the seashore. A bit wet, perhaps, a little disheveled and with a braid of seaweed hanging about our shoulders, but still standing. *Success.* We unleashed the feeling or awareness. Now we can sit with it. Whatever the feeling or awareness is. We have been betrayed. We have lived with an illusion for an awfully long time. We perceive qualities in ourselves that we do not like. *It's okay.* Next we set out on the path of figuring out what to do with our newfound feelings and awarenesses: "I will work to change my ways. I will set limits to certain relationships. I resolve to take better care of myself." We fail and succeed in our resolutions. We fail and succeed again. We fail and succeed a third, fourth, fifth, and sixth time, but as we continue to learn from our successes and failures, eventually we succeed. The feelings and awarenesses lose their power to operate on us unconsciously. We integrate. And when we look back on our experience of integration, we see that we succeeded by standing by our commitment to unify our conscious and unconscious awarenesses and by having the resolution to follow through on the knowledge we opened ourselves to. We took the right path.

The battle between what we don't want to know and what we do know, between what we don't want to feel and what we do feel, is a drama enacted within a labyrinth of paradox. Tremendous defenses swelling with pride, virtue, and righteous indignation are erected against feelings and awarenesses we vow will never share the same house with us. But when the war is over, these same feelings and awarenesses are recognized as some of our truer friends. Cherished illusions whose undoing we are sure will be the death of us are pierced, but before we have time to mourn their passing, we realize they never were trustworthy allies—they gave only the illusion of support, until we were strong enough to stand by ourselves.

The goal of unification, always, is to *unify*! The sooner we learn this pattern of integrating feelings and awarenesses as opposed to staying frozen in resistance to them, the sooner we will wrest the grail of psychological victory for ourselves. But to begin this process, we must first deem ourselves worthy of being kings in our own castles and grant ourselves the psychic liberation to rule. We must adopt the principle that there are no feelings or awarenesses we do not want to know, no territory in our self where we are not allowed, no hiding place that will not be uncovered. This is psychological maturity, and it is the source of psychological power. All feelings and awarenesses are received, explored, allowed.

Psychological education requires growth, decision, and change. And there is no question but that our first steps into this realm of responsibility and accountability can be terrifying. We can be plagued by self-doubt, fearful at our lack of confidence, and certain of imminent failure. This process more than any other needs the benefit that perspective lends us. If we step back from our life, we may as well ask ourselves what the heck *else* we're on this planet for. So we will fail. So we will make mistakes. Our job, tomorrow, is to get a little bit *better* at the process. And when we are trapped in the mire of some struggle that appears all-encompassing, we similarly must remember the wisdom of seeing the forest amid the trees. We must be able to see our long-term growth curve for ourselves. It's never too late to begin the process of learning, and to begin the process of learning how to get *better* with learning. We will have to admit things about ourselves and others that are potentially horrifying, disturbing, and painful, but directly alongside this fear and intimidation, a voice from our future calls to us to get on with the process, to get over our initial fears, and to get into the ring. The time to begin the process of psychological unification—and to start it up again if we have stopped—is now.

The past, it is said, has the ability to suck blood out of the future like a vampire. When psychological growth is viewed through the lens of the analytic eye, the carnage of defeated human lives is ample evidence that this is so. But another truth is that we each can reconcile ourselves with our pasts, as long as we are able to learn from them. Some lessons in life are harder to learn from than others. Some lessons require repeated visits to the troughs of disillusionment and despair. But no pain is greater than that which attends the knowing abandonment of the self. Innocence is innocence, and exists unto a world of its own. Knowledge, however, carries with it a powerful—and tempting—responsibility.

Index

Acceptance, 176, 187–89, 195–96, 199, 236, 241
Active awareness, 153, 154, 155, 233
  and repression, 159
Active sleep, 26
Advanced technology devices, 118–19
Anxiety, 239–40
  defined, 228n
  and nightmares, 228–31
  and repression, 163–64, 178, 179
Architecture of sleep
  and Freudian theory, 19–21
  and mental health, 11n
Aristotle, 68
Aserinsky, Eugene, 4–5, 17, 24
Astral projection, 77
"Automatic" living, 203–4, 213–14, 215
Avoidance, 170
  and identification, 178–79
  and low self-esteem, 193–94
  overcoming, 199–200
Awakening and returning to sleep trick, 117–18
Awareness, 33–34
  avoiding, 169–70

commitment to, 191
conscious, vs. unconscious, 161–62
five stages of, in dream, 85–90
and repression, 162–65
two-tiered, 153–57

"Being," 207–8
Bergman, Ingmar, 17n
Biorhythm, 102n
Black-and-white, dreams in, 71–72
Body
  inhibition of, and sleep, 57–61
  temperature, 49, 103n
"Borderline" personalities, 21–22
Brain
  EEG sleep studies, 4–7
  and thermoregulatory process, 26n, 47
Brandon, Dr. Nathaniel, 190–91
Breathing, 49
Brenner, Charles, 235

Calloway, Hugh, 122
Camouflage, 170–71
Castenada, Carlos, 127
Cat experiment, 28

Center, creating new, 203
Charlatans, 204, 215–16
Christian Gnostic gospels, 65*n*
Circadian rhythm, 103*n*
Cleaning, 214–15
Clerc, Oliver, 91, 95
Clues, about dreaming, 109–11
Color, in dreams, 71–72
"Completion" of consciousness, 122
Compulsive behavior, 170, 178, 179
Condensation and association, 136–37
Confidence, 191, 244
Confusion, 165–66, 168–70, 178, 179
Conscious management skills, 234
Consciousness
    absence of, in waking, 179
    attenuation of, 57–58, 60–61
    difficulty of defining, 2, 30–39
    dreaming, vs. awake, 29, 35–39
    as duality, 40–41
    evolution of, 43–45
    Gurdjieff on search for, 203–26
    learning mechanism of, 89–90
    loss of, and sleep, 2–3, 5
    maintaining, in dreamscape, 126–27, 129
    and memory, 44–45
    and neural activity, 9
    not essential to dream sleep, 47
    research on, while dreaming, 62–70
    during sleep, 34–35
    stabilizing, in dreamscape, 121–26, 127
    techniques for awakening, while dreaming, 91–121
    and unconscious, 160–62
    See also Active awareness; Awareness
Coping skills, 168

"Critical faculty," 122–23
Curiosity, 114–17

Decision making, 241–42
    and self-esteem, 194–95
Deconstructing dreams, 138–42
Deep sleep, defined, 12
Defense mechanisms, 245–46
Delage, Yves, 128–29
DELTA or slow-wave sleep
    EEG, 10
Denial, 148
Depression, 11*n*, 12, 20
    and dream deprivation, 22–23
Desynchronized activity
    biology of, 49
    defined, 7–9
    and dreams, 12, 27–28
    and wake state, 27
Desynchronized sleep (D-sleep), 26
Disguised dreams, 134–35, 142–53, 157
    and identification, 177–78
    and repression, 143–45
Distortions, 144–45, 152–53
Distraction, 165–66, 168, 178, 179, 182–83
Dream analysis, 135–57, 138*n*
    and external stimuli, 54–57
    Freudian, 21
Dream deprivation, 119–20
Dreaming
    attenuation of consciousness and body during, 57–61
    biological function of, 46–49
    lessons of, and duality, 159–62
    techniques to awaken consciousness while, 91–131
Dream journal, 105–7, 109–11
Dream Psychology and the New Biology of Dreaming (West), 47

Dreams
   "awakeness" during, 27–28, 31
   consciousness during, and reflec-
      tivity, 41
   deciphering meanings of, 135–57
   and desynchronized activity, 7–8
   as disturbers of sleep, 49–50
   and early EEG studies, 4, 19–20
   elusiveness of memory of, 2–3, 14,
      16, 44
   five stages of awareness during, 85–
      90
   Freudian theory of, 15–24, 48
   as guardians of sleep, 51–53
   and identification, 176–78
   misconceptions about, 71–77
   monitoring, 228–47
   and neurobiological function of
      body, 20–21
   physiology, 119–20
   questions to ask while monitoring,
      228–47
   rebound phenomena, 47
   reports, accuracy of, 65–67
   as representations of thought, 133–
      35
   as self-contained, misconception,
      76–77
   and self-interactive process, 133–
      35
   sexual arousal during, 78–82
   time spent in, 15–16
   true nature of, 82–85
Dreamscape, construction of, 135–53
Dreamscape (film), 69
Dream sleep
   amount of, 12–13
   body response to, 59–61
   and circadian rhythm, 103*n*
   consciousness during, 30–39
   cycle, manipulating, 120–21
   deepness and lightness of, 50–51
   defined, 12
   density, 120*n*
   deprivation experiments, by
      Freudians, 21–22
   function of, 25–26
   names for, 26
   regularity of, and Freudian theory,
      19–21, 23–24
   universality of, 25–26, 46–47
   waking and, 13–14
Dream work, 233–51
   psychological education through,
      239–42
Duality
   and repression, 158–74
   and self-remembering, 97–98
   unifying, 174–201
Dual-sense modality device, 118–19

Ego, 17, 23, 68, 234*n*, 241
   and dream work, 240
   overcoming repression, 175
   and repressed feelings, 160, 244–45
   resistance of, to unconscious, 161
   and unconscious, in lucid dream-
      ing, 88–89, 133–35
Electroencephalograph (EEG), 62–63
   defined, 6
   and Freudian theory, 21–24
   limits of, 66
   and paradoxical sleep, 26–27
   and stages of sleep, 10–13
   and study of sleep, 4–14
   and time spent dreaming, 16
Elektra complex, 181*n*
*Elementary Textbook of Psychoanalysis,
   An* (Brenner), 235
Emotional disturbance, 179
Empowerment, 239
Erection, 78, 79

Evolution, 43–45, 57–59
External stimuli, 73–74
  and dream analysis, 54–57
  incorporation of, 52–54
Eye movements
  and lucid dreams, 63
  reason for, 28
Eyeshades, to detect REM, 118

Failure, 191
False awakenings, 124–26
Fears, 113
Feelings
  acknowledging, 188–89
  feeling, vs. intellectualizing, 172–73
  integrating repressed, 244–46
  through memory, 141–42
  unconscious management of, 199–201
Fellini, Federico, 17*n*
Female impotence, 80–81
Feynmann, Richard, 114, 115–16
Fleisher, S., 100, 101
Foulkes, D., 100, 101
Fox, Oliver (Hugh Calloway), 122–23
Free association, 18, 138–42
  and nightmares, 231
  on symptomologies of repression, 179–87
Freedom, 209–10, 212–13
Freud, Sigmund, 19*n*, 25, 48, 52, 62, 68, 71, 77, 108, 132, 158, 161, 234*n*, 235
  and accelerated time, 72–75
  and dreams and meaning, 136
  and free association, 138–39
  and pleasure-unpleasure principle, 160
  psychodynamic model, 15–24
  and repression, 163, 231–32

  and sex, 81–82
  and two-tiered awareness, 153–54
  Freudian psychoanalysts, 16–17, 48, 56

Gilmore, Edith, 114, 117
Goals, setting, 242
Good sleep, EEG patterns of, 7
"Guillotine dream," 73–75
Gurdjieff, G. I., 96, 96*n*, 203–26

Happiness, 236
Harmonizing, 192
Hearne, Michael "Keith," 62–63, 67
Heart rate, 49
Hervey de Saint Denys, Marquis d', 114–15
Hormonal balance, 26*n*
Hypermnesic, 84
Hypnagogic imagery, 11
Hypnagogic states, 56

Id, 17, 81, 234*n*
  defined, 18
Identification, 176–87, 199, 215, 231, 236, 241
Immune system, 58*n*
Inactive awareness, 153–57, 159
Incongruity, 107–11
Independence, 190
In Search of the Miraculous (Ouspensky), 96
Insomnia, 12
Integration, 196, 245
  and listening to dreams, 228
  and repression, 174
  as therapeutic path, 175–76, 201
Intellectualization, 171–73
Interaction during dreams, and choice, 85

Interpretation of Dreams, The (Freud), 15–16, 52, 73

Jaynes, Julian, 30, 94–95
Jouvet, Michael, 28
Jung, Carl, 72, 89, 158, 161, 227, 236, 240, 242–43
Kleitmann, Nathaniel, 4–5, 17, 24
Knowledge, 207–8, 213, 220–23, 242–43, 247

LaBerge, Stephen P., 64, 67–68
Language of dreams, 132–57
Latent content, 108, 109
Libido, 23
Light dream, 11
Lucid dreamer(s)
    becoming sophisticated, 126–27
    famous, 114
    sophisticated, 127–31
Lucid dreams (lucidity), 60
    and beginnings and endings, 76–77
    curiosity leads to, 114–17
    as "gift," 69–70
    and nightmares, 111–13
    Ouspensky and, 55–56
    and real time vs. dream time, 75
    recall of, vs. ordinary dreams, 44
    research on, 63–70
    and sex, 77–78, 81–82
    techniques for developing, 102–31
    and true nature of dreams, 82–83
    and unconscious mind, 85–90
Lucidity Letter, 95, 112

Male impotence, 79–80
Manifest content, 108–9
Maury, 73–75

Mechanical living, 203–4. *See also* "Automatic" living
Memory or recall of dreams, 2–3
    and consciousness, 44–45
    during dream sleep, 84–85
    and Freudian theory, 16, 19n, 20, 25
    improving, 103–7
Mendelson, Dr. Wallace, 40
"Mental Activity in Relaxed Wakefulness" (Foulkes and Fleisher), 101
Mental health
    defined, 235–36
    and dream deprivation, 21–23, 26n
    and Freudian view of dreams, 18–19
    as given, 237
    skills development, 175–201, 236
    therapy as path to, 237–38
    and unification, 236
Mental illness
    and discovery of dream sleep, 24
    neurobiological underpinnings of, 24–26
Microawakenings, 13
Motor neurons, 59–60
Muscular atonia, 28–29

Narayana, Dr. Ram, 129–30
Neurobiology, 47, 48
    birth of, 24
    of consciousness, 44–45
    and mental illness, 24–26
Neuroendocrine system, 26n
Neurons, 5–9
Nietzsche, Friedrich, 202
Nightmares, 111–13, 176–77
    defined, 228–229n
    listening to, 228–31

Ninety-minute sleep cycle, 13–14
Nocturnal penile tumescence study, 79
Nonreflective waking state, 101

Oedipal feelings, 181*n*
On Dreams (Freud), 138–39
Orgasm, 79–81
Ouspensky, Peter, 54–57, 96–100, 101, 127, 202

Paradoxical sleep, 26
Paralysis, in dreams, 54
Partial lucidity, stages of, 121–23
Peck, M. Scott, 227, 235, 236
Personal effectiveness, 235–36
Physiological tricks, 117–21
"Pleasure-unpleasure" principle, 160
Post-traumatic stress syndrome (PTSS), 229
Powerlessness, overcoming, 197–99
Power of Self-Esteem, The (Branden), 190–91
Procrastination, 165–66
Pseudo-occultism, 218–20
Psychiatry, 24–26
Psychic determinism, 234–36
Psychoanalysis, 231–32
   dream theory overturned, 14–24
   goals of, 175–76
   vs. neurobiology, 25
   and psychic determinism, 235
   tools of, 236–39
Psychodynamic model, 19, 20, 22, 25, 244
Psychological education, 246–47
   dilemma of, 243–44
   and dreamwork, 239–42
Psychological empowerment, 242–47
Psychological isomorphism, 25
Psychological maturity, 244–46
Psychotherapy, 231–32

   goals of, 175–76
   resistance to, 237–39
Pyramidal tract, 28

Rapid eye movement (REM) sleep, 26
   and EEG, 10
   pressure, 119–21
Reactivity, 169–70
Rechtschaffen, Dr. Allan, 37–39, 40, 41, 58, 100–101, 122–23
Recurring dreams, 55, 56
Reflective stream (reflectivity), 39, 40
   absence of, in dreams, 41–42, 60, 100–101
   and consciousness while waking, 92–93
   and lucid dreams, 122–23
Regression, 168–69
Reid, Thomas, 111–12, 117
Religion, and lucid dreams, 65*n*
Repression, 81, 143–44, 158–59
   and anxiety, 163–64
   difficulty of seeing, 162–63
   and disguised dreams, 144–53
   feelings and awareness avoided through, 165–74
   free-associating on symptomologies of, 179–87
   getting help with identifying, 232–34
   and limiting of awareness and ego, 160
   and low self-esteem, 193–94
   as optional, 174–75
   and psychological education, 243, 244–46
   recognizing, 178–79
   and single-mindedness, 166–67
   as temporary buffer, 173–74
   and tensions, 167–68

as two-edged sword, 161
Resistance
  to awareness, 148, 160–61
  overcoming, 180
  to psychological education, 236–37
Resolution, 176, 189–201, 236, 241–42
Reticular formation, 29

Saint Augustine, 65*n*, 68
Schizophrenia, 11*n*
Self
  true, and dreams, 132–35
  unconscious as part of, 160–61
Self-affirmation, 200
  and acceptance, 189
Self-assessment, 195–96
Self-awareness, 236
Self-destructive behavior, 192
Self-development, Gurdjieff on, 215–26
Self-esteem
  assessing, 195–96
  attaining healthy, 236, 240–42
  and decision making, 194–95
  high, 191–92
  low, 192
  repairing, 192
  and resolution stage, 189–201
  resolving sources of low, 196–201
  sources of low, 193–94
Self-expression, 190
Self-identification, 132–33
  and unconscious, 160
Self-interactive process, 133–35
Self-knowledge, 207–9, 215, 223
Self-management, making conscious, 200–201
Self-remembering, 203
  defined, 97–102

finding, 127
Self-unification, as goal, 162
Sense environment, 8, 9
Sensory cortex, 29
Sensory environment, 83–85, 87
Seriousness, 209–10
Sex, 77–82
  Freud and, 81–82
  in lucid dreamscape, 77
Sexual abuse victims, 229–30
Sexual fantasies, 77–78, 82
"Simplex" identification process, 161
"Single-locus" recording, 6–7
Single-mindedness, 100
  alternations between consciousness and, 101–2
  and dream experience, 41
  and identification, 178–79
  and repression, 166–67
"Single-Mindedness and Isolation of Dreams, The" (Rechtschaffen), 37–39
Sleep
  amount needed, 1, 57–59
  consciousness during, 34–39
  cycles, knowing, 102–3
  deprivation, 58, 59*n*
  mysteries of, 1–3
  normal pattern of, 11–13
  orderliness of, 9–12, 11*n*
  research on brain during, 3–14
  types, 7–8
"Spacing out," 100
Sparrow, G. Scott, 121, 124, 127
Stage 1 sleep, 9, 10, 11
Stage 2 sleep, 10, 11–12
Stage 3 sleep, 10, 11, 12
Stage 4 sleep, 9, 10, 12, 27, 51
Stages of sleep
  defined, 9–13
  dreaming as deepest, 50–51
  and EEG, 7, 10, 11

Stages of sleep (*cont.*)
knowing your own, 102–3
and synchronous activity, 9
Strategic detachment, 190
Superawareness, 160
Superconscious, 160
Superego, 17, 18, 19
Surely You're Joking, Mr. Feynmann (Feynmann), 115
Synchronized activity, 7, 8
and deep sleep, 12
degrees of, during sleep, 9
Synthesis, 137–38

Tension, 167–68, 179–83
Therapeutic path, 175–76, 244
three stages of, 176, 188, 199
Thermoregulatory processes, 26*n*, 47
Tholey, Peter K., 68
Tibetan Book of the Dead, 65*n*
Time
accelerated, 72–75
nature of, in dreams, 15–16, 75, 76
spent dreaming, 16
spent sleeping, 59
Transparent dreams, 134–35, 177
as goal, 228, 231
Trauma, 229*n*

Unconscious, 68
acceptance of, in lucid dream, 85–90
and awareness, 153–57
awareness of, 159–60
behaviors, and low self-esteem, 193–94

and conscious, 160–62
and defense mechanisms, 163–64
and defenses, 143–44
defined, 40–41
dreams as representation of, 135–36
and ego, 88–89
feelings, pain of bringing into awareness, 245
Freudian view of, 17, 18
and management of feelings, 199–200
management skills, changing, 240–42
and self, 160
Unification
defined, 236
as challenge, 231–32
of feelings and awarenesses, 174–201
as goal, 244, 245–47

Values, and behavior, 190
Vietnam War veterans, 229
Visualization, 134
Voluntary stream of consciousness, 39, 40, 93

Wake-up time, 13–14
Waking state
and consciousness, 92–102
and desynchronized activity, 8
EEG, 10
Warm-blooded animals, 48–49
West, Lewis J., 47–48